Modern Poets of France

Books by Louis Simpson

Poetry

The Arrivistes: Poems 1940–49
Good News of Death and Other Poems
A Dream of Governors
At the End of the Open Road
Selected Poems
Adventures of the Letter I
Searching for the Ox
Caviare at the Funeral
The Best Hour of the Night
People Live Here: Selected Poems 1949–83
Collected Poems
In the Room We Share
Jamaica Poems
There You Are
Nombres et poussière

Literary Criticism

James Hogg: A Critical Study
*Three on the Tower: The Lives and Works of Ezra Pound, T. S. Eliot
and William Carlos Williams*
*A Revolution in Taste: Studies of Dylan Thomas, Allen Ginsberg,
Sylvia Plath and Robert Lowell*
A Company of Poets
The Character of the Poet
Ships Going into the Blue

Other

Riverside Drive (novel)
An Introduction to Poetry
North of Jamaica (autobiography)
Selected Prose
The King My Father's Wreck (memoirs)
Modern Poets of France: A Bilingual Anthology

Modern Poets of France

A BILINGUAL ANTHOLOGY

Louis Simpson

Story Line Press
1997

Published by Story Line Press, Inc.,
Three Oaks Farm, Brownsville, OR 97327

This publication was made possible thanks in part to the generous support
of the Nicholas Roerich Museum, the Andrew W. Mellon Foundation, the
Charles Schwab Corporation Foundation and our individual contributors.

Indices by Miriam Simpson
Cover photograph by Louis Simpson
Book design by Chiquita Babb

Library of Congress Cataloging-in-Publication Data
Modern poets of France : a bilingual anthology / Louis Simpson.
    p. cm.
    Poems in English and French on facing pages.
    Includes index.
    ISBN 1-885266-44-8 (pbk.)
    1. French poetry—20th century—Translations into English.
    2. French poetry—19th century—Translations into English.
    3. French poetry—20th century. 4. French poetry—19th century.
    I. Simpson, Louis Aston Marantz. 1923– .
PQ1170.E6M576 1997
841'.91208—dc21   97-16001
                                           CIP

Acknowledgments

Translations were published in these anthologies and periodicals:

APR (The American Poetry Review): STÉPHANE MALLARMÉ, "Sea Breeze," "The Tomb of Poe," "Virginal, vivid, beautiful, will this be," "The Afternoon of a Faun." ROBERT DESNOS, "Almonymous," "Cold Throats," "Dream, the Night of May 27-28, 1923, " "The Spaces of Sleep," "Identity of Images," "Fantomas, A Complaint," "Halfway."

Black Moon: PHILIPPE SOUPAULT, "Palace Cinema," "Sporting Goods."

Five Points: PAUL VERLAINE, "Autumn Song," "The Young Fools," "Tears Fall in My Heart," "I've had no luck with women," "My Apology."

The Formalist: VICTOR HUGO, "Words in the Shadow." THÉOPHILE GAUTIER, "Art," "Carmen." CHARLES BAUDELAIRE, "Hymn to Beauty." ARTHUR RIMBAUD, "The Drunken Boat."

The Harvard Review: CATHERINE POZZI, "Nyx." ANDRÉ BRETON, "Free Union." PAUL ELUARD, "The Lover."

The Hudson Review: VALERY LARBAUD, "Ode," "Night in the Port," "Indian Ocean," "The Old Cahors Station," "Yaravi," "The Gift of Himself," "Images."

Image: GÉRARD DE NERVAL, "El Desdichado" (there titled "Disinherited"), "Lines in Gold."

Modern French Theatre: The Avant-Garde, Dada, and Surrealism ed. George Wellwarth and Michael Benedikt: GUILLAUME APOLLINAIRE, "Prologue, *The Breasts of Tiresias.*"

The New Criterion: MARCELINE DESBORDES-VALMORE, "Apart," "In the Street," "The Roses of Saadi," "Withered Laurel." CHARLES BAUDELAIRE, "Correspondences," "The Swan." JULES LAFORGUE, "Another Complaint of Lord Pierrot," "Legend."

The Poetry of Surrealism: An Anthology, ed. Michael Benedikt: GUILLAUME APOLLINAIRE, "Zone."

The Southern Review: JULES LAFORGUE, "Complaint of the Pianos," "Solo by Moonlight."

The Virginia Quarterly Review: ARTHUR RIMBAUD, "Evil," "At the Green Cabaret," "Vowels."

It is necessary to be absolutely modern.

RIMBAUD

Contents

Preface

John Dryden had a clear idea of what translation should be. Samuel Johnson in his life of Dryden explains it briefly: "Where correspondence cannot be obtained, it is necessary to be content with something equivalent. . . . A translator is to be like his author; it is not his business to excel him." This is how I have made these translations, always keeping the original in sight, not altering the author's meaning, form, or style in any important way.

But poems are written with imagination, and translations have to be too. The translator will have to add words and leave words out, may even have to change an image, in order to obtain "something equivalent." In the fourth line of "Le Bateau ivre" Rimbaud says that Redskins have nailed the men hauling his boat "aux poteaux de couleur," "to colored poles." How did the poles come to be colored? Perhaps they were painted, or were they striped with blood? An image of poles with spiraling, colored stripes came to mind, the kind most readers would have seen, and I wrote "barbershop poles." Would Rimbaud have objected? I do not think so—he took images from everyday life as well as his reading about whales and waterspouts.

Desnos in his poem about Fantomas says that Hélène saved Fandor's life:

> . . . elle sauva Fandor
> Qu'était condamné à mort.

That is,

> . . . she saved Fandor
> Who was condemned to death.

This doesn't do much for a poem that is usually dramatic and lively. The situation brought Pocahontas to mind, so I wrote:

> When Fandor's number was up,
> Like Pocahontas she shouted "Stop!"

Someone may object, "A translator is to be like his author; it is not his business to excel him." Yes, but provided that the form, style and meaning of the original are not distorted, surely the translator is permitted to use his imagination when this will make the poem more understandable to the audience of his own time and place. This, after all, is the whole point of translation.

If the poem is in rhyme, the translation should rhyme. To translate rhyming lines into blank verse or free verse gives a false impression of the original. When I was unable to follow a pattern of rhyme or meter and make a line that sounded right in English I would alter the pattern. The alexandrine, the line with twelve syllables used by Corneille and Racine, was standard in French poetry. It was what the "moderns" broke away from. Poets writing in English have not liked the alexandrine—they have preferred Shakespeare's line of ten syllables, the pentameter. I have usually translated alexandrines into pentameters.

Before translating "L'Après-midi d'un faune" I glanced at some of the available translations. Mallarmé's poem is in rhyme and meter but the translators had put it into unrhymed, unmetered English. As for meaning, frequently they could not make one out and the reader was left to puzzle over a row of words taken from a dictionary. These ridiculous translations were in books that would be used in universities.

A friend says that I must make it clear that this is a personal selection, for some well known names have not been represented—Paul Valéry for example. Very well, this is a personal selection. I hope that readers will judge the collection by what I have included, not by what I have left out.

Another friend, a French poet and critic, has said that I must explain why, in a collection that traces the line of "the modern," I have included José-Maria de Heredia. Heredia and the poets of the Parnassian "school" took one tenet of "modernity," the autonomy of art, and carried it to an extreme. Gautier said that the work of art had a reality of its own, it was not just a comment on life. Fine! I think that most artists and writers would agree. But the Parnassians interpreted this to mean that art would exclude elements taken from life. (Gautier himself did not hold such a narrow view—his poems deal with a variety of subjects and express a range of attitudes).

The Parnassians wrote about antiquity and mythical characters. Their poems were set among exotic scenes. Leconte de Lisle in *Poèmes antiques* and *Poèmes barbares,* and Heredia in *Les Trophées,* used language as though it were paint or marble, for purely sensory effects. They aimed to make their writing last by excluding the contemporary. They wrote in a "classical" style and eschewed expressions of feeling. As Baudelaire said, such writing falls into "an abstract and indefinable beauty" ("La Modernité"). It is lacking in ideas and monotonous. Splendid as Heredia's descriptions may be, they are like the decorations in opera houses, merely picturesque.

But I have included three sonnets by Heredia. I have done so in order to show, by contrast, in what "the modern" consists. Fortunately the sonnets are entertaining. I can read a Parnassian poet . . . for a while. But the moderns make you feel and think.

Modern artists, in Baudelaire's phrase, looked for "the eternal in the transitory." The struggle to make poetry out of the contemporary imbued their poetry with feeling and makes it live today.

I see that in explaining the inclusion of Heredia I have explained my decision not to include Paul Valéry. There are ideas in Valéry but it is only with difficulty that one can discover what they are: the writing is abstract and vague. Above all, there is nothing of the life of his time — consequently nothing of the life of ours.

The reputations of authors rise and fall. The spirit of the time makes what they say seem urgent. They have influential friends. When what they write no longer seems "relevant," and the guard changes, they disappear as quickly as they came. One cannot account for the success of Anna de Noailles except by her being a Countess. André Gide wrote her flattering letters. When she was dead he left her out of his anthology of French poetry.

On the other hand, there are poets who are unjustly neglected. New ones are coming into view, and it is a lucky poet indeed who is not forgotten within a few years. One of the pleasures I had in making this anthology was to discover the poetry of Marceline Desbordes-Valmore. At first glance the clarity of her writing and the pastoral scenes she describes evoke eighteenth century neoclassicism, but a little more acquaintance with her work shows why Baudelaire and Verlaine thought her a kindred spirit, and why Yves Bonnefoy has said that she is "the first authentic voice of feminine poetry in modern times in our language."

Throughout the span of time I have measured there were very few women in France whose poetry even approaches the excellence of the poetry of Desbordes-Valmore. I have applied the same standards in reading female poets that I use in reading male poets: I have included a poet if his or her poetry is excellent and also innovative. But the poetry women wrote in France in the nineteenth century and early decades of the twentieth is unadventurous in form and style. It is sentimental. In short, there is nothing modern about it. The women of France must have received very little encouragement to be poets. The situation has been changing in recent years, and today there are female poets in France who are knowledgeable, adventurous, interesting. But the poetry being written today is outside the scope of this book.

The partisans of "modernity" were in revolt against mainstream, bourgeois values. They also broke with the attitudes of a previous generation of writers and artists, the Romantics. The moderns aimed to create new forms and styles of art as the expression of new modes of thought and feeling—and they succeeded. Writings by Baudelaire, Rimbaud, and Mallarmé that were said to be obscene or incomprehensible, paintings by Manet and Cézanne that had been rejected by "the guardians of art," became the classics of following generations. The ideas of the Symbolists and Surrealists influenced art and literature throughout the world. There is no longer a need to defend "modern art"—as Fredric Jameson says, "its once scandalous productions are in the university, in the museum, in the street."

I have begun the anthology with poems by Desbordes-Valmore. Victor Hugo follows. Hugo looms above the nineteenth century. He was a magnificent poet who wrote on a variety of subjects in a wide range of forms. But he is not in "the tradition of the new" that I have aimed to represent—he is the embodiment of Romanticism. Gautier, Baudelaire, and Flaubert were making a deliberate break with the attitudes Hugo expressed.

The two poems by Hugo I have included suggest his range. "Words from the Shadow" reveals a side he is not usually credited with having . . . a charming, tender, humorous poem of man-and-woman love, from the woman's point of view. The other poem, "Expiation," is by the Victor Hugo most people know, the poet of large effects and resonant phrases. "Expiation" is the first in a sequence of poems that describe the downfall of Napoleon The retreat from Moscow gives Hugo an opportunity to display all his powers of imagination . . . and hyperbole. Like other men throughout the nineteenth century, Hugo is fascinated by Napoleon—he thinks him incomparably grand. He will therefore show the great man's fall on a mythic scale. It is possible that during the retreat of the French army a bugler was frozen in the saddle on a frozen horse. But many frozen buglers on frozen horses? This is what Hugo would have us believe.

There is a lack of reality about such writing. It may provide sensations, but the reader who is not naive wants literature to convey truth as well as pleasure. Moving pictures with a sound track can give more of the sensations that "colorful writing" provides. But poetry that is written with total intelligence, the kind we find in Dante and Baudelaire, makes a music of ideas and language that is not evoked by any other form of art.

Baudelaire in the essay I have mentioned says that the artist who has been gifted with an active imagination is looking for something that he, Baudelaire, may be permitted to call "modernity," for there is no better word to express the idea in question. "It is a matter of disengaging from the fashion of the moment what it may contain of poetry . . . extracting the eternal from the transitory."

It is no doubt excellent, Baudelaire says, to study the ancient masters, but that can only be a superfluous exercise if your aim is to understand the character of present beauty. You do not have the right to hold the transitory and fugitive in contempt—in suppressing that element you fall into "an abstract and indefinable beauty." The mysterious beauty that human life expresses involuntarily as it passes must be extracted. "Nearly all our originality comes from the stamp that the present impresses on our sensations."

*

I wish to thank three people. My wife Miriam's liking for a few translations I had done encouraged me to continue. A friend, Jon Manchip White, also liked what he saw, but he asked why I had translated these poets and not others who were well known. This made me find the reason: these were the poets I liked, and I liked them because they were "modern." The selection would make clear what the word meant.

It was fun walking with Serge Fauchereau through the Verdeau and Jouffroy "passages" once frequented by the Surrealists. And Serge's high opinion of Fargue and Reverdy made me read their poems with close attention. I think that I shall always be reading them.

L. S.

Modern Poets of France

Marceline Desbordes-Valmore

Souvenir

Quand il pâlit un soir, et que sa voix tremblante
S'éteignit tout à coup dans un mot commencé;
Quand ses yeux, soulevant leur paupière brûlante,
Me blessèrent d'un mal dont je le crus blessé;
Quand ses traits plus touchants, éclairés d'une flamme
    Qui ne s'éteint jamais,
S'imprimèrent vivants dans le fond de mon âme;
    Il n'aimait pas, j'aimais!

A Memory

When he grew pale, and his voice trembled,
And suddenly he could no longer speak;
When his eyes, burning beneath the lid,
Gave me a wound I thought he felt alike;
When all his charms, lighted by a fire
       That has never faded,
Were printed in the depth of my desire,
       He did not love. I did.

Les Séparés

N'écris pas. Je suis triste, et je voudrais m'éteindre.
Les beaux étés sans toi, c'est la nuit sans flambeau.
J'ai refermé mes bras qui ne peuvent t'atteindre,
Et frapper à mon coeur, c'est frapper au tombeau.
      N'écris pas!

N'écris pas. N'apprenons qu'à mourir à nous-mêmes.
Ne demande qu'à Dieu . . . qu'à toi, si je t'aimais!
Au fond de ton absence écouter que tu m'aimes,
C'est entendre le ciel sans y monter jamais.
      N'écris pas!

N'écris pas. Je te crains; j'ai peur de ma mémoire;
Elle a gardé ta voix qui m'appelle souvent.
Ne montre pas l'eau vive à qui ne peut la boire.
Une chère écriture est un portrait vivant.
      N'écris pas!

N'écris pas ces doux mots que je n'ose plus lire:
Il semble que ta voix les répand sur mon coeur;
Que je les vois brûler à travers ton sourire;
Il semble qu'un baiser les empreint sur mon coeur.
      N'écris pas!

Apart

Do not write. I am sad, and want my light put out.
Summers in your absence are as dark as a room.
I have closed my arms again. They must do without.
To knock at my heart is like knocking at a tomb.
                    Do not write!

Do not write. Let us learn to die, as best we may.
Did I love you? Ask God. Ask yourself. Do you know?
To hear that you love me, when you are far away,
Is like hearing from heaven and never to go.
                    Do not write!

Do not write. I fear you. I fear to remember,
For memory holds the voice I have often heard.
To the one who cannot drink, do not show water,
The beloved one's picture in the handwritten word.
                    Do not write!

Do not write those gentle words that I dare not see,
It seems that your voice is spreading them on my heart,
Across your smile, on fire, they appear to me,
It seems that a kiss is printing them on my heart.
                    Do not write!

Le Mal du pays

Je veux aller mourir aux lieux où je suis née;
Le tombeau d'Albertine est près de mon berceau;
Je veux aller trouver son ombre abandonnée;
Je veux un même lit près du même ruisseau.

Je veux dormir. J'ai soif de sommeil, d'innocence,
D'amour! d'un long silence écouté sans effroi,
De l'air pur qui soufflait au jour de ma naissance,
Doux pour l'enfant du pauvre et pour l'enfant du roi.

J'ai soif d'un frais oubli, d'une voix qui pardonne.
Qu'on me rende Albetine! elle avait cette voix
Qu'un souvenir du ciel à quelques femmes donne;
Elle a béni mon nom . . . autre part . . . autrefois!

Autrefois! . . . qu'il est loin le jour de son baptême!
Nous entrâmes au monde un jour qu'il était beau:
Le sel qui l'ondoya fut dissous sur moi-même,
Et le prêtre pour nous alluma qu'un flambeau.

D'où vient-on quand on frappe aux portes de la terre?
Sans clarté dans la vie, où s'adressent nos pas?
Inconnus aux mortels qui nous tendent les bras,
Pleurants, comme effrayés d'un sort involontaire.

Où va-t-on quand, lassé d'un chemin sans bonheur,
On tourne vers le ciel un regard chargé d'ombre?
Quand on ferme sur nous l'autre porte, si sombre!
Et qu'un ami n'a plus que nos traits dans son coeur?

Homesickness

I want to die where I was born. My cradle
And the tomb of Albertine are close together.
I want to go and find her abandoned shade,
Lie in the same bed near the same stream with her.

I long for sleep, and innocence, and love,
As when I lay with no fear listening
To the pure air that softly blew above
The children of the poor man and the king.

I thirst for forgetfulness, a voice that pardons.
Give me back Albertine! She had the voice
Granted to some women by the heavens.
She blessed my name, in other places, once.

How distant our baptism seems to be!
We came into the world in sunny weather.
The same salt melted on her as on me.
One candle flamed for both of us together.

Knocking at the gate, whence have we come?
Where do our footsteps turn? Unknown to those
Holding out their arms to us in welcome,
We weep before a fate we did not choose.

Where do we go when, at the journey's end,
We look to heaven, and the other gate
Is closed behind us, and only a friend
Recalls us as we were, some cherished trait?

Ah! quand je descendrai rapide, palpitante,
L'invisible sentier qu'on ne remonte pas,
Reconnaîtrai-je enfin la seule âme constante
Qui m'aimait imparfaite et me grondait si bas?

Te verrai-je, Albertine! Ombre jeune et craintive?
Jeune, tu t'envolas peureuse des autans:
Dénouant pour mourir ta robe de printemps,
Tu dis: "Semez ces fleurs sur ma cendre captive."

Oui! je reconnaîtrai tes traits pâles, charmants,
Miroir de la pitié qui marchait sur tes traces,
Qui pleurait dans ta voix, angélisait tes grâces,
Et qui s'enveloppait dans tes doux vêtements!

Oui, tu ne m'es qu'absente, et la mort n'est qu'un voile,
Albertine! et tu sais l'autre vie avant moi,
Un jour, j'ai vu ton âme aux feux blancs d'une étoile;
Elle a baisé mon front, et j'ai dit: C'est donc toi!

Viens encor, viens! j'ai tant de choses à te dire!
Ce qu'on t'a fait souffrir, je le sais! j'ai souffert.
O ma plus que soeur! viens: ce que je n'ose écrire,
Viens le voir palpiter dans mon coeur entr'ouvert!

Ah, when with fearful trembling, rapidly
I walk the steep path to the other world,
Shall I recognize the one who loved me,
Frail as I was, and would gently scold?

Albertine, shall I see you? As you fly
From southerly winds, youthful, fearful shade,
Unfastening your spring frock as you die,
You say, "Strew flowers on my ashen bed."

Yes, I shall know the pale and charming face
That mirrored all your pity, all the kindness
Weeping in your voice, that made your grace
Angelic, and was enveloped in your dress.

You are only absent, Death is only a veil,
Albertine. You have only walked ahead.
One evening in a star I saw your soul.
It kissed my brow and, "This is you!" I said.

Come again! I have so much to tell you,
My more than sister, that I dare not write.
What you have suffered, I have suffered too.
Come back and see it written in my heart!

Dans la rue

par un jour funèbre de Lyon

LA FEMME

Nous n'avons plus d'argent pour enterrer nos morts.
Le prêtre est là, marquant le prix des funérailles;
Et les corps étendus, troués par les mitrailles,
Attendent un linceul, une croix, un remords.

Le meurtre se fait roi. Le vainqueur siffle et passe.
Où va-t-il? Au Trèsor, toucher le prix du sang.
Il en a bien versé . . . mais sa main n'est pas lasse;
Elle a, sans le combattre, égorgé le passant.

Dieu l'a vu. Dieu cueillait comme des fleurs froissées
Les femmes, les enfants qui s'envolaient aux cieux.
Les hommes . . . les voilà dans le sang jusqu'aux yeux.
L'air n'a pu balayer tant d'âmes courroucées.

Elles ne veulent pas quitter leurs membres morts.
Le prêtre est là, marquant le prix des funérailles;
Et les corps étendus, troués par les mitrailles,
Attendent un linceul, une croix, un remords.

Les vivants n'osent plus se hasarder à vivre.
Sentinelle soldée, au milieu du chemin,
La mort est un soldat qui vise et qui délivre
Le témoin révolté qui parlerait demain . . .

In the Street

on a day of funerals at Lyon

THE WOMAN

We have run out of money to bury our dead.
The priest is there, figuring what the price will be,
And the corpses stretched out, holed by artillery,
Want a shroud, a cross, remorseful words to be said.

Murder is king. The victor whistles as he goes
To the Treasury, to be paid for blood he shed.
He has shed plenty, but his hand is not tired
From fighting. There was no fighting at all, God knows.

God picked up each soul like a perishing flower.
Women and children went flying up to the skies,
And men . . . there they are, in blood up to their eyes.
Angry souls, too many to be borne by the air.

They don't want to leave their members behind, the dead.
The priest is there, figuring what the price will be,
And the corpses stretched out, holed by artillery,
Want a shroud, a cross, remorseful words to be said.

Those who are still alive do not know where to go.
Stationed in every street and road for pay,
Death is a soldier who aims and they take away
The rebel who would bear witness tomorrow.

Prenons nos rubans noirs, pleurons toutes nos larmes;
On nous a défendu d'emporter nos meurtris.
Ils n'ont fait qu'un monceau de leurs pâles débris:
Dieu! bénissez-les tous; ils étaient tous sans armes!

Let us take our black ribbons, and wear one on the arm.
It has been forbidden to take the pale remains
Of our murdered. They have heaped them on the stones.
God bless them all! They were all of them unarmed.

Les Roses de Saadi

J'ai voulu ce matin te rapporter des roses;
Mais j'en avais tant pris dans mes ceintures closes
Que les noeuds trop serrés n'ont pu les contenir.

Les noeuds ont éclaté. Les roses envolées
Dans le vent, à la mer s'en sont toutes allées.
Elles ont suivi l'eau pour ne plus revenir.

La vague en a paru rouge et comme enflammée.
Ce soir, ma robe encore en est toute embaumée . . .
Respires-en sur moi l'odorant souvenir.

The Roses of Saadi

I wanted to bring you roses this morning.
There were so many I wanted to bring,
The knots at my waist could not hold so many.

The knots burst. All the roses took wing,
The air was filled with roses flying,
Carried by the wind, into the sea.

The waves were red, as though they were burning.
My dress still has the scent of the morning,
Remembering roses. Smell them on me.

Rêve intermittent d'une nuit triste

O champs paternels hérissés de charmilles
Où glissent le soir des flots de jeunes filles!

O frais pâturage où de limpides eaux
Fond bondir la chèvre et chanter les roseaux!

O terre natale! à votre nom que j'aime,
Mon âme s'en va toute hors d'elle-même;

Mon âme se prend à chanter sans effort;
A pleurer aussi, tant mon amour est fort!

J'ai vécu d'aimer, j'ai donc vécu de larmes;
Et voilà pourquoi mes pleurs eurent leurs charmes;

Voilà, mon pays, n'en ayant pu mourir,
Pourquoi j'aime encore au risque de souffrir;

Voilà, mon berceau, ma colline enchantée
Dont j'ai tant foulé la robe veloutée,

Pourquoi je m'envole à vos bleus horizons,
Rasant les flots d'or des pliantes moissons.

La vache mugit sur votre pente douce,
Tant elle a d'herbage et d'odorante mousse.

Et comme au repos appelant le passant,
Le suit d'un regard humide et caressant.

Intermittent Dream of a Sad Night

Land of our fathers where at eventide
Across the fields like waves young women glide!

Where fresh pasture and a limpid spring
Make the goat bound and the lake reeds sing!

O native land, my soul is greatly moved
To hear your name that I have always loved;

My soul without an effort turns to song,
And also weeping, for my love is strong!

Love was my life, so I was often sad,
But love was mingled with the grief I had;

That is why I have longed for death in vain,
And though it be suffering, I love again.

My cradle, enchanted hillside where I ranged,
Whose velvet dress I often disarranged,

That is why, toward your distant sky,
Skimming the golden waves of grain I fly.

The cow is lowing on the slope. She has
Fragrant moss to eat, and so much grass,

And follows with a moist, caressing eye,
Calling him to rest, the passerby.

Jamais les bergers pour leur brebis errantes
N'ont trouvé tant d'eau qu'à vos sources courantes.

J'y rampai débile en mes plus jeunes mois,
Et je devins rose au souffle de vos bois.

Les bruns laboureurs m'asseyaient dans la plaine
Où les blés nouveaux nourissaient mon haleine.

Albertine aussi, soeur des blancs papillons,
Poursuivait les fleurs dans les mêmes sillons;

Car la liberté toute riante et mûre
Est là, comme aux cieux, sans glaive, sans armure,

Sans peur, sans audace, et sans austérité,
Disant: "Aimez-moi, je suis la liberté!

Je suis le pardon qui dissout la colère,
Et je donne à l'homme une voix juste et claire.

Je suis le grand souffle exhalé sur la croix
Où j'ai dit: Mon père! on m'immole, et je crois!

Le bourreau m'étreint: je l'aime! et l'aime encore,
Car il est mon frère, ô père que j'adore!

Mon frère aveuglé qui s'est jeté sur moi,
Et que mon amour ramènera vers toi!"

O patrie absente! ô fécondes campagnes,
Où vinrent s'asseoir les ferventes Espagnes!

Antiques noyers, vrais maîtres de ces lieux,
Qui versez tant d'ombre où dorment nos aieux!

Shepherds whose sheep have wandered from the fold
Will nowhere find such springs as your fields hold.

An infant when I crawled there, pale and weak,
The air breathed from your woods reddened my cheek.

The sunburned laborers would set me down
Among the new corn that my breath fed on.

Albertine, sister of butterflies, also
Pursued the flowers that grew in the same row.

For liberty is laughing in the field
As in the sky, with neither sword nor shield,

Without fear, sternness or audacity,
Saying, "I am liberty, love me!

The pardon that makes anger disappear,
I give man a voice that is just and clear.

I am the cross exhaling a great breath:
'Father, they are slaying me. I have faith!

The hangman grasps me. I love him! And the more
For he is my brother, father whom I adore!

My blind brother, who throws himself on me,
Whom my love will bring back to your mercy.'"

O absent fatherland! My fertile country
Where the fervent Spaniards came to stay;

True masters of the land, old walnut trees
Shading so well our fathers' resting places;

Echos tout vibrants de la voix de mon père
Qui chantait pour tous: "Espère! espère! espère!"

Ce chant apporté par des soldats pieux
Ardents à planter tant de croix sous nos cieux,

Tants de hauts clochers remplis d'airain sonore
Dont les carillons les rapellent encore:

Je vous enverrai ma vive et blonde enfant
Qui rit quand elle a ses longs cheveux au vent.

Parmi les enfants nés à votre mamelle,
Vous n'en avez pas qui soit si charmant qu'elle!

Un veillard a dit en regardant ses yeux:
"Il faut que sa mère ait vu ce rêve aux cieux!"

En la soulevant par ses branches aisselles
J'ai cru bien souvent que j'y sentais des ailes!

Ce fruit de mon âme, à cultiver si doux,
S'il faut le céder, ce ne sera qu'à vous!

Du lait qui vous vient d'une source divine
Gonflez le coeur pur de cette frêle ondine.

Le lait jaillissant d'un sol vierge et fleuri
Lui paîra le mien qui fut triste et tari.

Pour voiler son front qu'une flamme environne
Ouvrez vos bluets en signe de couronne:

Des pieds si petits n'écrasent pas les fleurs,
Et son innocence a toutes leurs couleurs.

My father's voice that echoed when he sang:
"Hope" and "Hope" and "Hope" again it rang,

The song of men who burned with piety
And yearned to sow the cross beneath our sky,

And many steeples filled with resonant bronze
That still recalls them in its carillons . . .

I am sending you my child, the quick and fair
Who laughs when wind is playing in her hair.

Of all the children you have fed at breast
This one is more enchanting than the rest.

An old man said once, looking in her eyes,
"Her mother must have dreamed her in the skies!"

And often as I lifted her I thought,
My hands beneath her arms, I felt wings sprout!

This fruit of my soul that so gently grew
If I must yield her, it is only to you.

With your milk that comes from a holy fountain
Fill the pure heart of this frail undine.

Mine ran sad and dry, but your milk springs
From virgin soil and happy harvestings.

To veil her forehead that a flame rings round
Open your cornflowers, so gayly crowned:

Such little feet do not crush the flowers,
And her innocence has all their colors.

Un soir, près de l'eau, des femmes l'ont bénie,
Et mon coeur profond soupira d'harmonie.

Dans ce coeur penché vers son jeune avenir
Votre nom tinta, prophète souvenir,

Et j'ai répondu de ma voix toute pleine
Au souffle embaumé de votre errante haleine.

Vers vos nids chanteurs laissez-la donc aller;
L'enfant sait déjà qu'ils naissent pour voler.

Déjà son esprit, prenant goût au silence,
Monte où sans appui l'alouette s'élance,

Et s'isole et nage au fond du lac d'azur
Et puis redescend le gosier plein d'air pur.

Que de l'oiseau gris l'hymne haute et pieuse
Rende à tout jamais son âme harmonieuse! . . .

Que vos ruisseaux clairs, dont les bruits m'ont parlé,
Humectent sa voix d'un long rythme perlé!

Avant de gagner sa couche de fougère,
Laissez-la courir, curieuse et légère,

Au bois où la lune épanche ses lueurs
Dans l'arbre qui tremble inondé de ses pleurs,

Afin qu'en dormant sous vos images vertes
Ses grâces d'enfant en soient toutes couvertes.

Des rideaux mouvants la chaste profondeur
Maintiendra l'air pur alentour de son coeur,

One evening women blessed her, standing by
Water, and my heart gave a deep sigh.

In that young heart, bent upon things to be
Your name rang, prophetic memory,

And with all my voice I gave an answer
To the fragrance of your wandering air.

Then let her go where nests sing in the sky,
For children know that they are born to fly.

Already her spirit has a taste for silence
And rises up to where the skylarks dance,

And, isolated, swims beneath the azure,
And comes back down, her throat filled with pure air.

May the gray bird's hymn, so high and pious,
Forever make her soul harmonious!

May your clear streams whose music spoke to me
Moisten her throat with pearls of melody!

Before she goes to her bed of fern and night
Let her go running, curious and light,

To the wood where the moon shines on a tree
In a sheet of tears and trembling quietly,

So she may sleep beneath green images
And they will cover all her infant graces.

The depth of those chaste curtains as they stir
Will keep the air around her heart still pure,

Et, s'il n'est plus là, pour jouer avec elle,
De jeune Albertine à sa trace fidèle,

Vis-à-vis les fleurs qu'un rien fait tressaillir
Elle ira danser, sans jamais les cueillir,

Croyant que les fleurs ont aussi leurs familles
Et savent pleurer comme les jeunes filles.

Sans piquer son front, vos abeilles là-bas
L'instruiront, rêveuse, à mesurer ses pas;

Car l'insecte armé d'une sourde cymbale
Donne à la pensée une césure égale.

Ainsi s'en ira, calme et libre et content,
Ce filet d'eau vive au bonheur qui l'attend;

Et d'un chêne creux la Madone oubliée
La regardera dans l'herbe agenouillée.

Quand je la berçais, doux poids de mes genoux,
Mon chant, mes baisers, tout lui parlait de vous,

O champs paternels, hérissés de charmilles
Où glissent le soir des flots de jeunes filles.

Que ma fille monte à vos flancs ronds et verts,
Et soyez béni, doux point de l'Univers!

And if she does not have, to play with her,
An Albertine, her faithful follower,

She will face the flowers and dance with them,
But never take the flower from the stem,

Thinking that flowers have their mothers too
And know how to cry as children do.

Not stinging her forehead, your bees down there
Will teach her dreamy head to step with care,

For the insect has a muffled cymbal
That makes the caesura when one muses equal.

So she will go, calm, free, and at peace,
A thread of living water, to happiness,

And the Madonna in the hollow tree
Will see her on the grass with bended knee.

Her sweet weight on my lap, all I would do,
My songs, my kisses, everything spoke of you,

Land of our fathers where at eventide
Across the fields like waves young women glide.

May my daughter climb on your green breast,
Sweet spot in the Universe, and be blessed!

La Couronne effeuillée

J'irai, j'irai porter ma couronne effeuillée
Au jardin de mon père où revit toute fleur;
J'y répandrai longtemps mon âme agenouillée:
Mon père a des secrets pour vaincre la douleur.

J'irai, j'irai lui dire, au moins avec mes larmes:
"Regardez, j'ai souffert. . . ." il me regardera,
Et sous mes jours changés, sous mes pâleurs sans
      charmes,
Parce qu'il est mon père il me reconnaîtra.

Il dira: "C'est donc vous, chère âme désolée!
La terre manque-t-elle à vos pas égarés?
Chère âme, je suis Dieu: ne soyez plus troublée;
Voici votre maison, voici mon coeur, entrez!"

O clémence! ô douceur! ô saint refuge! ô père!
Votre enfant qui pleurait vous l'avez entendu!
Je vous obtiens déjà puisque je vous espère
Et que vous possédez tout ce que j'ai perdu.

Vous ne rejetez pas la fleur qui n'est plus belle,
Ce crime de la terre au ciel est pardonné.
Vous ne maudirez pas votre enfant infidèle,
Non d'avoir rien vendu, mais d'avoir tout donné.

Withered Laurel

I shall go, I shall bring my withered laurel
To his garden where the flower lives again.
I shall pour my soul out to him as I kneel:
My father has secret ways of healing pain.

I shall go, I shall tell him, at least with tears,
"Look, I have suffered." And he will see.
Under my changed days and the pallor of years,
Because he is my father he will know me.

He will say, "There you are at last, dear sadness!
Do you still yearn for the earth you used to roam?
Dear soul, I am your God. Now be at peace:
Here is my heart, come in! Here is your home!"

O mercy! Sweetness! Holy refuge! Father,
You listened to your daughter when she wept!
I hoped for you and so already have you,
And everything that I have lost you kept.

You will not reject what is not beautiful:
Heaven pardons what the world holds criminal.
You will not damn your child who was unfaithful,
Not for having nothing, but for giving all.

Victor Hugo

Paroles dans l'ombre

Elle disait: C'est vrai, j'ai tort de vouloir mieux;
Les heures sont ainsi très-doucement passées;
Vous êtes là; mes yeux ne quittent pas vos yeux,
Où je regarde aller et venir vos pensées.

Vous voir est un bonheur; je ne l'ai pas complet.
Sans doute, c'est encor bien charmant de la sorte!
Je veille, car je sais tout ce qui vous déplait,
A ce que nul fâcheux ne vienne ouvrir la porte;

Je me fais bien petite, en mon coin, près de vous;
Vous êtes mon lion, je suis votre colombe;
J'entends de vos papiers le bruit paisible et doux;
Je ramasse parfois votre plume qui tombe;

Sans doute, je vous ai; sans doute, je vous voi.
La pensée est un vin dont les rêveurs sont ivres,
Je le sais; mais, pourtant, je veux qu'on songe à moi.
Quand vous êtes ainsi tout un soir dans vos livres,

Sans relever la tête et sans me dire un mot,
Une ombre reste au fond de mon coeur qui vous aime;
Et, pour que je vous voie entièrement, il faut
Me regarder un peu, de temps en temps, vous-même.

Words in the Shadow

She said, "I am wrong to want something more, it's true.
The hours go by very quietly just so.
You are there. I never take my eyes from you.
In your eyes I see your thoughts as they come and go.

To watch you is a joy I have not yet got through.
No doubt it is still very charming of its kind!
I watch, for I know everything that annoys you,
So that nothing comes knocking when you're not inclined.

I make myself so small in my corner near you.
You are my great lion, I am your little dove.
I listen to your leaves, the peaceful froufrou.
Sometimes I pick up your pen when it falls off.

Without a doubt I have you. Surely I see you.
Thinking is a wine on which the dreamers are drunk,
I know. But sometimes I'd like to be dreamed of too.
When you are like that, in your books, all evening, sunk,

Not lifting your head or saying a word to me,
There is a shadow deep down in my loving heart.
For me to see you whole, it is necessary
To look at me a little, sometimes, on your part."

L'Expiation

Il neigeait. On était vaincu par sa conquête.
Pour la première fois l'aigle baissait la tête.
Sombres jours! l'empereur revenait lentement,
Laissant derrière lui brûler Moscou fumant.
Il neigeait. L'âpre hiver fondait en avalanche.
Après la plaine blanche une autre plaine blanche.
On ne connaissait plus les chefs ni le drapeau.
Hier la grande armée, et maintenant troupeau.
On ne distinguait plus les ailes ni le centre:
Il neigeait. Les blessés s'abritaient dans le ventre
Des chevaux morts; au seuil des bivouacs désolés
On voyait des clairons à leur poste gelés
Restés debout, en selle et muets, blancs de givre,
Collant leur bouche en pierre aux trompettes de cuivre.
Boulets, mitraille, obus, mêlés aux flocons blancs,
Pleuvaient; les grenadiers, surpris d'être tremblants,
Marchaient pensifs, la glace à leur moustache grise.
Il neigeait, il neigeait toujours! la froide bise
Sifflait; sur le verglas, dans des lieux inconnus,
On n'avait pas de pain et l'on allait pieds nus.
Ce n'étaient plus des coeurs vivants, des gens de guerre;
C'était un rêve errant dans la brume, un mystère,
Une procession d'ombres sous le ciel noir.
La solitude vaste, épouvantable à voir,
Partout apparaissait, muette vengeresse.
Le ciel faisait sans bruit avec la neige épaisse
Pour cette immense armée un immense linceul.
Et, chacun se sentant mourir, on était seul.
"Sortira-t-on jamais de ce funeste empire?
Deux ennemis! le Czar, le Nord. Le Nord est pire."

Expiation

It was snowing. For the first time, conquered
By his conquest, the eagle bowed his head.
Dark days! Slowly the emperor returned,
Leaving behind a Moscow that smoked and burned.
It was snowing. At the end of the white plain
Another stretched, as white and vast again.
The leaders and the flags were swept away . . .
An army yesterday, a herd today.
No longer could one see the wings and center.
It was snowing. Wounded men sought shelter
In the belly of dead horses. Where they camped
One saw buglers frozen, stone mouths clamped
To copper trumpets, silent, white with frost,
Still upright in the saddle at their post.
Ball, grape, and shell were falling with the snow.
The grenadiers, surprised that they shook so,
Marched pensively, ice on the gray moustache.
It was snowing, always snowing! The cold lash
Whistled. These warriors had no bread to eat,
They walked across the ice with naked feet.
No longer living hearts, they seemed to be
A dream lost in a fog, a mystery,
A march of shadows under a black sky.
Vast solitudes, appalling to the eye,
Stretched out, mute and revengeful, everywhere.
The sky was weaving silently, of air,
A shroud for the Grand Army. And each one
Could feel that he was dying, and alone.
"Shall we ever leave this empire of the Czar?
The Czar and the North . . . The North is worse by far."

On jetait les canons pour brûler les affûts.
Qui se couchait, mourait. Groupe morne et confus,
Ils fuyaient; le désert dévorait le cortège.
On pouvait, à des plis qui soulevaient la neige,
Voir que des régiments s'étaient endormis là.
O chutes d'Annibal! Lendemains d'Attila!
Fuyards, blessés, mourants, caissons, brancards, civières,
On s'écrasait aux ponts pour passer les rivières.
On s'endormait dix mille, on se réveillait cent.
Ney, que suivait naguère une armée, à présent
S'évadait, disputant sa montre à trois cosaques.
Toutes les nuits, qui vive! alerte, assauts! attaques!
Ces fantômes prenaient leur fusil, et sur eux
Ils voyaient se ruer, effrayants, ténébreux,
Avec des cris pareils aux voix des vautours chauves,
D'horribles escadrons, tourbillons, d'hommes fauves.
Toute une armée ainsi dans la nuit se perdait.
L'empereur était là, debout, qui regardait.
Il était comme un arbre en proie à la cognée.
Sur ce géant, grandeur jusqu'alors épargnée,
Le malheur, bûcheron sinistre, était monté;
Et lui, chêne vivant, par la hache insulté,
Tressaillant sous le spectre aux lugubres revanches,
Il regardait tomber autour de lui ses branches.
Chefs, soldats, tous mouraient. Chacun avait son tour.
Tandis qu'environnant sa tente avec amour,
Voyant son ombre aller et venir sur la toile,
Ceux qui restaient, croyant toujours à son étoile,
Accusaient le destin de lèse-majesté,
Lui se sentait soudain dans l'âme épouvanté.
Stupéfait du désastre et ne sachant que croire,
L'empereur se tourna vers Dieu; l'homme de gloire
Trembla; Napoléon comprit qu'il expiait
Quelque chose peut-être, et, livide, inquiet,

They jettisoned the guns to burn the wood.
To lie down was to die. Confused, they fled
And were devoured in the fields of snow.
One saw by mounds and ridges that below
Whole regiments were sleeping. Oh the falls
Of Hannibal! The days after Attila!
Fugitives, wounded, caissons, shafts, the mass
Crushed at the bridges as it strove to pass . . .
A hundred woke . . . ten thousand were left sleeping.
Ney, who had led an army, was escaping,
Fighting to save his watch from three cossacks.
Every night "Qui vive!" Alerts, alarms, attacks!
These phantoms grasped their rifles . . . terrifying
Shadows were rushing towards them, crying
Like vultures. Squadrons of savage men
Struck like a whirlwind and were gone again.
So a whole army would be lost by night.
The emperor was there, he watched, upright
As a tree that must endure the woodsman's blow.
On this giant, a greatness spared till now,
Misfortune the grim woodsman climbed. Each stroke
Of the axe insulted the man, the living oak.
He trembled at the vengeances, each blow
Saw a branch falling to the earth below.
Leaders and soldiers, each in his turn fell.
While love around his tent stood sentinel,
Watching his shadow on the canvas wall,
And those to his bright star remaining loyal
Accused the heavens of lèse-majesté,
Suddenly his inmost soul gave way.
Stunned by disaster, reft of all belief,
The emperor turned to God; the glorious chief
Trembled; he thought that he was expiating
Something perhaps, and contemplating

Devant ses légions sur la neige semées:
"Est-ce le châtiment," dit-il, "Dieu des armées?"
Alors il s'entendit appeler par son nom
Et quelqu'un qui parlait dans l'ombre lui dit, "Non."

His legions of the dying and the dead,
"God of the armies," Napoleon said,
"Is this my punishment?" And from the snow
And darkness all around, a voice said, "No."

Gérard de Nerval

El Desdichado

Je suis le ténébreux, le veuf, l'inconsolé,
Le prince d'Aquitaine à la tour abolie:
Ma seule *étoile* est morte, et mon luth constellé
Porte le *soleil noir* de la *Mélancolie.*

Dans la nuit du tombeau, toi qui m'as consolé,
Rends-moi le Pausilippe et la mer d'Italie,
La *fleur* qui plaisait tant à mon coeur désolé,
Et la treille où le pampre à la rose s'allie.

Suis-je Amour ou Phébus, Lusignan ou Biron?
Mon front est rouge encor du baiser de la reine;
J'ai rêvé dans la grotte où nage la sirène . . .

Et j'ai deux fois vainqueur traversé l'Achéron;
Modulant tour à tour sur la lyre d'Orphée
Les soupirs de la sainte et les cris de la fée.

El Desdichado

I am the dark, the widowed, disconsolate one,
The Prince of Aquitaine at the ruined tower.
My only star is dead; in my lute's constellation
Melancholy's black sun is the ruling power.

In the night of the tomb, if you have pity for me,
Give me Italy again, the sea and the flower
That was my sad heart's pleasure. Let me see
The vine branch with the rose entangled bower.

Am I Love or Phoebus, Lusignan or Biron?
On my brow the kiss of a queen is still not dim;
I have dreamed in the grotto where sirens swim . . .

And twice a conqueror I have crossed Acheron,
On the lyre of Orpheus exchanging sighs
Of a holy man with a wind-blown fairy's cries.

Vers dorés

Eh quoi! tout est sensible!

PYTHAGORE

Homme, libre penseur! te crois-tu seul pensant
Dans ce monde où la vie éclate en toute chose?
Des forces que tu tiens ta liberté dispose,
Mais de tous tes conseils l'univers est absent.

Respecte dans la bête un esprit agissant.
Chaque fleur est une âme à la Nature éclose;
Un mystère d'amour dans le métal repose;
"Tout est sensible!" Et tout sur ton être est puissant.

Crains, dans le mur aveugle, un regard qui t'épie;
A la matière même un verbe est attaché . . .
Ne la fais pas servir à quelque usage impie!

Souvent dans l'être obscur habite un Dieu caché;
Et comme un oeil naissant couvert par ses paupières,
Un pur esprit s'accroît sous l'écorce des pierres.

Lines in Gold

Why not! Everything feels!

PYTHAGORAS

Man, do you think yours is the only soul?
Look around you. Everything that you see
Quivers with being. Though your thoughts are free,
One thing you do not think about, the whole.

Beasts have a mind. Respect it. Flowers too.
Look at one. Nature brought forth each petal.
There is a mystery that sleeps in metal.
"Everything feels!" and has power over you.

Be careful! The blind wall is spying on us.
Even matter is connected to a word . . .
Do not make it serve some unholy purpose.

A god in darkness often walks obscured.
As eyelids of a newborn infant open
A spirit wakes and gazes in the stone.

Théophile Gautier

L'Art

Oui, l'oeuvre sort plus belle
D'une forme au travail
      Rebelle,
Vers, marbre, onyx, émail.

Point de contraintes fausses!
Mais que pour marcher droit
      Tu chausses,
Muse, un cothurne étroit.

Fi du rhythme commode,
Comme un soulier trop grand,
      Du mode
Que tout pied quitte et prend!

Statuaire, repousse
L'argile que pétrit
      Le pouce
Quand flotte ailleurs l'esprit;

Lutte avec le carrare,
Avec le paros dur
      Et rare,
Gardiens du contour pur;

Emprunte à Syracuse
Son bronze où fermement
      S'accuse
Le trait fier et charmant;

Art

Yes, artwork is better
When the means used rebel:
     Meter,
Marble, onyx, enamel.

Not for crippling fashion,
Muse, but a straighter walk,
     Put on
High heels, a "learned sock."

In rhythm I despise
The kind like an old shoe,
     The size
Every foot goes into!

Sculptor, do not succumb
To easiness, the clay
     The thumb
Works when the mind's away;

Struggle with Carrara's
Hardness, Paros's rare
     Quarries
Where the pure contours are;

From Syracuse you get
Bronze where a fugitive
     Proud trait
Solidly seems to live;

D'une main délicate
Poursuis dans un filon
    D'agate
Le profil d'Apollon.

Peintre, fuis l'aquarelle,
Et fixe la couleur
    Trop frêle
Au four de l'émailleur.

Fais les sirènes bleues,
Tordant de cent façons
    Leurs queues,
Les monstres des blasons;

Dans son nimbe trilobe
La Vierge et son Jésus,
    Le globe
Avec la croix dessus.

Tout passe. L'art robuste
Seul a l'éternité.
    Le buste
Survit à la cité.

Et la médaille austère
Que trouve un laboureur
    Sous terre
Révèle un empereur.

Les dieux eux-mêmes meurent,
Mais les vers souverains
    Demeurent
Plus forts que les airains.

With skill that's delicate
Unerringly follow
    The agate
Profile of Apollo.

Painter, shun aquarelle.
If you find your color
    Too frail,
See the enameller.

Show sirens with blue scales
Twisting a hundred ways
    The tails
A coat of arms portrays;

In her trefoil nimbus
The Virgin you emboss,
    Jesus,
The globe beneath the cross.

All passes. Art alone
Lasts till eternity.
    The stone
Bust survives the city.

The medal in the ground
Some sweating laborer
    Has found
Reveals an emperor.

The gods themselves have passed,
But poems fill their thrones.
    Words cast
In lines will outwear bronze.

Sculpte, lime, cisèle;
Que ton rêve flottant
Se scelle
Dans le bloc résistant!

Sculptor, file and chisel
Your dream till it exists,
Made real
In the block that resists.

Carmen

Carmen est maigre, un trait de bistre
Cerne son oeil de gitana.
Ses cheveux sont d'un noir sinistre,
Sa peau, le diable la tanna.

Les femmes disent qu'elle est laide,
Mais tous les hommes en sont fous,
Et l'archevêque de Tolède
Chante la messe à ses genoux;

Car sur sa nuque d'ambre fauve
Se tord un énorme chignon
Qui, dénoué, fait dans l'alcôve
Une mante à son corps mignon.

Et, parmi sa pâleur, éclate
Une bouche aux rires vainqueurs;
Piment rouge, fleur écarlate,
Qui prend sa pourpre au sang des coeurs.

Ainsi faite, la moricaude
Bat les plus altières beautés,
Et de ses yeux la lueur chaude
Rend la flamme aux satiétés.

Elle a, dans sa laideur piquante,
Un grain de sel de cette mer
D'où jaillit, nue et provocante,
L'âcre Vénus du gouffre amer.

Carmen

Carmen is thin, her gypsy eyes
Are shadowed on the underside.
Her hair is ominously black,
The Devil must have tanned her hide.

The women say she looks a mess
But men go crazy night and day,
And the Archbishop of Toledo
Is always kneeling down to pray.

For an enormous knot of hair
Is fastened to her yellow nape,
And this, untwisted in her bed,
Hangs down and cloaks her cunning shape.

And, from her pallor, suddenly
Laughter erupts on mocking lips;
Red pepper, or a scarlet flower
Dyed with the blood in which it dips.

Made as she is, this sallow girl
Beats all the duchesses in Spain.
The light that's burning in her eyes
Brings ashen men to life again.

In her seductive ugliness
There's salt, the fresh astringency
Of Venus in her nakedness
Leaping out of the bitter sea.

Charles Baudelaire

Correspondances

La Nature est un temple où de vivants piliers
Laissent parfois sortir de confuses paroles;
L'homme y passe à travers des forêts de symboles
Qui l'observent avec des regards familiers.

Comme de longs échos qui de loin se confondent
Dans une ténébreuse et profonde unité,
Vaste comme la nuit et comme la clarté,
Les parfums, les couleurs et les sons se répondent.

Il est des parfums frais comme des chairs d'enfants,
Doux comme les hautbois, verts comme les prairies,
Et d'autres, corrompus, riches et triomphants,

Ayant l'expansion des choses infinies,
Comme l'ambre, le musc, le benjoin et l'encens,
Qui chantent les transports de l'esprit et des sens.

Correspondences

Nature is a temple. The columns are
Alive and sometimes vaguely seem to talk;
There are symbols in the forests where we walk
That watch us, and they seem familiar.

As echoes in the distance come together
Mysteriously and merge and sound as one,
Vast as night and shining like the dawn,
Perfumes, colors, sounds speak to each other.

There are perfumes fresh as the flesh of an infant,
As soft as oboes, green as a prairie,
And others corrupt, rich, and triumphant,

Expanding as things do in infinity,
Like amber, musk, benjamin, and incense,
Singing the ecstasies of spirit and sense.

Hymne à la beauté

Viens-tu du ciel profond ou sors-tu de l'abîme,
O Beauté? ton regard, infernal et divin,
Verse confusément le bienfait et le crime,
Et l'on peut pour cela te comparer au vin.

Tu contiens dans ton oeil le couchant et l'aurore;
Tu répands des parfums comme un soir orageux;
Tes baisers sont un philtre et ta bouche une amphore
Qui font le héros lâche et l'enfant courageux.

Sors-tu du gouffre noir ou descends-tu des astres?
Le Destin charmé suit tes jupons comme un chien;
Tu sèmes au hasard la joie et les désastres,
Et tu gouvernes tout et ne réponds de rien.

Tu marches sur des morts, Beauté, dont tu te moques;
De tes bijoux l'Horreur n'est pas le moins charmant,
Et le Meurtre, parmi tes plus chères breloques,
Sur ton ventre orgueilleux danse amoureusement.

L'éphémère ébloui vole vers toi, chandelle,
Crépite, flambe et dit: Bénissons ce flambeau!
L'amoureux pantelant incliné sur sa belle
A l'air d'un moribund caressant son tombeau.

Que tu viennes du ciel ou de l'enfer, qu'importe,
O Beauté! monstre énorme, effrayant, ingénu!
Si ton oeil, ton souris, ton pied, m'ouvrent la porte
D'un Infini que j'aime et n'ai jamais connu?

Hymn to Beauty

Where do you come from, Beauty? From the skies
Or the abyss? Infernal and divine
We see both good and evil in your eyes,
And that is why you are compared to wine.

Your glance is sunset and the rising sun,
Your perfumes like a storm fill the night air.
Your kisses are magic. This love potion
Makes heroes tremble and boys bravely dare.

Do you rise out of the dark? Fall from the stars?
Destiny like a dog walks close behind you.
You sow your joys at random and disasters,
Govern and give no account of what you do.

You walk on the dead, Beauty, whom you scorn.
Horror is not your least prized jewelry,
And Murder dangles with the ornaments
In a love dance on your prideful belly.

The ephemeral, dazed, flies to you, candle,
Crackles, flames and "Bless this fire!" cries.
The one bent over his love is like a man who'll
Caress his gravestone, panting as he dies.

No matter where, Beauty, from hell or heaven,
Huge monster with appalling, innocent mien,
If only your eye, your smile, your foot would open
The Infinite I love and have never seen.

De Satan ou de Dieu, qu'importe? Ange ou Sirène,
Qu'importe, si tu rends, — fée aux yeux de velours,
Rythme, parfum, lueur, ô mon unique reine! —
L'univers moins hideux et les instants moins lourds?

From Satan or from God, angel or siren,
What does it matter, fairy with velvet eyes,
Rhythm, perfume, light, if only, O my queen,
You lighten my days in a universe I despise.

Le Cygne

I

Andromaque, je pense à vous! Ce petit fleuve,
Pauvre et triste miroir où jadis resplendit
L'immense majesté de vos douleurs de veuve,
Ce Simoïs menteur qui par vos pleurs grandit,

A fécondé soudain ma mémoire fertile,
Comme je traversais le nouveau Carrousel.
Le vieux Paris n'est plus (la forme d'une ville
Change plus vite, hélas! que le coeur d'un mortel);

Je ne vois qu'en esprit tout ce camp de baraques,
Ces tas de chapiteaux ébauchés et de fûts,
Les herbes, les gros blocs verdis par l'eau des flaques,
Et, brillant aux carreaux, le bric-à-brac confus.

Là s'étalait jadis une ménagerie;
Là je vis, un matin, à l'heure où sous les cieux
Froids et clairs le Travail s'éveille, où la voirie
Pousse un sombre ouragan dans l'air silencieux,

Un cygne qui s'était évadé de sa cage,
Et, de ses pieds palmés frottant le pavé sec,
Sur le sol raboteux traînait son blanc plumage.
Près d'un ruisseau sans eau la bête ouvrant le bec

Baignait nerveusement ses ailes dans la poudre,
Et disait, le coeur plein de son beau lac natal:
"Eau, quand donc pleuvras-tu? quand tonneras-tu, foudre?"
Je vois ce malheureux, mythe étrange et fatal,

The Swan

To Victor Hugo

I

Andromache, I think of you. The Simois,
Little river that once shone with reflections
Of the majesty of your widow's sorrow,
Great with your tears, that now sadly runs,

Brought back to life my fertile memory
As I was crossing the new Carrousel.
Old Paris is no more (the heart of a city
Changes sooner, alas, than the heart of a mortal);

In my mind's eye only, I see barracks,
Rough-hewn capitals and columns, grass,
Blocks turning green in puddles, bric-a-brac
Scattered in windows, shining behind the glass.

There was a display, a menagerie,
And once I saw there, at the time of day
When Labor wakes under a clear, cold sky
And a dust storm rises from the highway,

A swan that somehow had escaped its cage,
Scraping webbed feet on the stony walk,
Over rough ground dragging its white plumage,
Near a dry stream bed opening its beak,

Bathe its wings in the dust. And with a heart
Full of its beautiful native lake, it said,
"Water, when will you rain? Thunder, when will you start?"
I see the unhappy one, so strangely fated,

Vers le ciel quelquefois, comme l'homme d'Ovide,
Vers le ciel ironique et cruellement bleu,
Sur son cou convulsif tendant sa tête avide,
Comme s'il adressait des reproches à Dieu!

II

Paris change! mais rien dans ma mélancolie
N'a bougé! palais neufs, échafaudages, blocs,
Vieux faubourgs, tout pour moi devient allégorie,
Et mes chers souvenirs sont plus lourds que des rocs.

Aussi devant ce Louvre une image m'opprime:
Je pense à mon grand cygne, avec ses gestes fous,
Comme les exilés, ridicule et sublime,
Et rongé d'un désir sans trêve! et puis à vous,

Andromaque, des bras d'un grand époux tombée,
Vil bétail, sous la main du superbe Pyrrhus,
Auprès d'un tombeau vide en extase courbée;
Veuve d'Hector, hélas! et femme d'Hélénus!

Je pense à la négresse, amaigrie et phtisique,
Piétinant dans la boue, et cherchant, l'oeil hagard,
Les cocotiers absents de la superbe Afrique
Derrière la muraille immense du brouillard;

À quiconque a perdu ce qui ne se retrouve
Jamais, jamais! à ceux qui s'abreuvent de pleurs
Et tètent la Douleur comme une bonne louve!
Aux maigres orphelins séchant comme des fleurs!

Ainsi dans la forêt où mon esprit s'exile
Un vieux Souvenir sonne à plein souffle du cor!
Je pense aux matelots oubliés dans une île,
Aux captifs, aux vaincus! . . . à bien d'autres encor!

Toward the sky, like the man in Ovid,
Toward the cruelly blue, ironic sky,
On its convulsive neck stretch its avid head,
As though it were reproaching the Deity!

II

Paris changes! But none of my melancholy
Has budged. New palaces, scaffolds, blocks,
Old suburbs . . . all becomes an allegory.
My memories are heavier than the rocks.

Standing before the Louvre, I feel the weight
Of an image, my big swan, with his insane
Gestures, like exiles, ridiculous but great,
Gnawed by unappeasable desire. And then,

Andromache, you, from your hero's embrace
Torn like cattle, under the hand of Pyrrhus,
Kneeling by a tomb, praying to empty space;
Widow of Hector, wife of Helenus!

I think of the negress, gaunt, tubercular,
Trudging in the mud, and looking around her
With haggard eyes for the palms of Africa
Behind the huge wall of fog that surrounds her;

Of those who have lost what can never again
Be found. Never! Who water Grief with tears
And like a good she-wolf suckle their pain;
I think of orphans shriveling like flowers.

In the forest where my spirit lives in exile
Memory sounds again . . . *le son du Cor!*
I think of sailors deserted on an isle,
Of captives, the vanquished . . . and many more!

Les Aveugles

Contemple-les, mon âme; ils sont vraiment affreux!
Pareils aux mannequins; vaguement ridicules;
Terribles, singuliers comme les somnambules;
Dardant on ne sait où leurs globes ténébreux.

Leurs yeux, d'où la divine étincelle est partie,
Comme s'ils regardaient au loin, restent levés
Au ciel; on ne les voit jamais vers les pavés
Pencher rêveusement leur tête appesantie.

Ils traversent ainsi le noir illimité,
Ce frère du silence éternel. O cité!
Pendant qu'autour de nous tu chantes, ris et beugles,

Éprise du plaisir jusqu'à l'atrocité,
Vois! je me traîne aussi! mais, plus qu'eux hébété,
Je dis: Que cherchent-ils au Ciel, tous ces aveugles?

The Blind

Look at them, my soul! How frightful they are,
Like mannequins, yet somehow laughable . . .
Somnambulists, grotesque and terrible,
Darting their murky globes you don't know where.

Their eyes from which the holy spark has fled
Lifted as though looking into the distant
Heavens . . . Never toward the pavement
Do you see them turn their heavy, dreaming head.

So they traverse a black infinity,
Brother of eternal silence. O city!
While you sing, and laugh, and yell, your mind

Bent on pleasure, even atrocity,
I'm staggering too, but more dazed than they.
What are they searching for in the sky, the blind?

Le Crépuscule du soir

Voici le soir charmant, ami du criminel;
Il vient comme un complice, à pas de loup; le ciel
Se ferme lentement comme une grande alcôve,
Et l'homme impatient se change en bête fauve.

O soir, aimable soir, désiré par celui
Dont les bras, sans mentir, peuvent dire: Aujourd'hui
Nous avons travaillé! C'est le soir qui soulage
Les esprits que dévore une douleur sauvage,
Le savant obstiné dont le front s'alourdit,
Et l'ouvrier courbé qui regagne son lit.
Cependant des démons malsains dans l'atmosphère
S'éveillent lourdement, comme des gens d'affaire,
Et cognent en volant les volets et l'auvent.
À travers les lueurs que tourmente le vent
La Prostitution s'allume dans les rues;
Comme une fourmilière elle ouvre ses issues;
Partout elle se fraye un occulte chemin,
Ainsi que l'ennemi qui tente un coup de main;
Elle remue au sein de la cité de fange
Comme un ver qui dérobe à l'Homme ce qu'il mange.
On entend çà et là les cuisines siffler,
Les théâtres glapir, les orchestres ronfler;
Les tables d'hôte, dont le jeu fait les délices,
S'emplissent de catins et d'escrocs, leurs complices,
Et les voleurs, qui n'ont ni trêve ni merci,
Vont bientôt commencer leur travail, eux aussi,
Et forcer doucement les portes et les caisses
Pour vivre quelques jours et vêtir leurs maîtresses.

Nightfall

Night is at hand, the criminal's ally,
Entering with a wolfish step. The sky
Closes slowly like the door in a wall,
And man turns into a wild animal.

Night, lovely night, longed for by the one
Whose arms can say, without lying, "We have done
A day's work!" Night that will bring relief
To spirits devoured by some savage grief:
The scholar with his heavy, sinking head,
The stooped laborer homing to his bed.
But demons are getting up like businessmen,
Heavily, and going to work again,
Flapping canopies and banging shutters.
Among the lights the wind flares and gutters
Prostitution kindles in the streets
And like an ant hill opens all her exits;
Pushes her way, deciding where to go,
An enemy planning to strike a blow;
In the breast of the city stirs up mud,
A worm that steals from man to get its food.
Here a kitchen clatters, there a theater
Calls to you, and you hear an orchestra.
The rooms where gambling spreads its delicacies
Fill up with tarts, and their accomplices,
Crooks and thieves who grant no truce or pity,
They too will soon commence their industry,
Forcing doors gently open, and cash boxes,
To live a while and clothe their mistresses.

Recueille-toi, mon âme, en ce grave moment,
Et ferme ton oreille à ce rugissement.
C'est l'heure où les douleurs des malades s'aigrissent!
La sombre Nuit les prend à la gorge; ils finissent
Leur destinée et vont vers le gouffre commun;
L'hôpital se remplit de leurs soupirs. Plus d'un
Ne viendra plus chercher la soupe parfumée,
Au coin du feu, le soir, auprès d'une âme aimée.

Encore la plupart n'ont-ils jamais connu
La douceur du foyer et n'ont jamais vécu!

My soul, this is the moment to take thought,
Collect yourself, and shut that roaring out.
Those who are sick will suffer more. Dark night
And destiny now seize them by the throat.
They sink into the gulf all face in common.
Their sighs fill the hospital. More than one
Will not return to smell the soup together
With the beloved, sitting by the fire.

And yet the greater part have never known
How sweet home is, a life all of your own!

Enivrez-vous

Il faut être toujours ivre. Tout est là: c'est l'unique question. Pour ne pas sentir l'horrible fardeau du Temps qui brise vos épaules et vous penche vers la terre, il faut vous enivrer sans trêve.

Mais de quoi? De vin, de poésie ou de vertu, à votre guise. Mais enivrez-vous.

Et si quelquefois, sur les marches d'un palais, sur l'herbe verte d'un fossé, dans la solitude morne de votre chambre, vous vous réveillez, l'ivresse déjà diminuée ou disparue, demandez au vent, à la vague, à l'étoile, à l'oiseau, à l'horloge, à tout ce qui fuit, à tout ce qui gémit, à tout ce qui roule, à tout ce qui chante, à tout ce qui parle, demandez quelle heure il est; et le vent, la vague, l'étoile, l'oiseau, l'horloge, vous répondront: "Il est l'heure de s'enivrer! Pour n'être pas les esclaves martyrisés du Temps, enivrez-vous; enivrez-vous sans cesse! De vin, de poésie ou de vertu, à votre guise."

Be Drunk

You have to be always drunk. That's all there is to it — it's the only way. So as not to feel the horrible burden of time that breaks your back and bends you to the earth, you have to be continually drunk.

But on what? Wine, poetry or virtue, as you wish. But be drunk.

And if sometimes, on the steps of a palace or the green grass of a ditch, in the mournful solitude of your room, you wake again, drunkenness already diminishing or gone, ask the wind, the wave, the star, the bird, the clock, everything that is flying, everything that is groaning, everything that is rolling, everything that is singing, everything that is speaking . . . ask what time it is, and wind, wave, star, bird, clock will answer you: "It is time to be drunk! So as not to be the martyred slaves of time, be drunk, be continually drunk! On wine, on poetry, or on virtue, as you wish."

Les Fenêtres

Celui qui regarde du dehors à travers une fenêtre ouverte, ne voit jamais autant de choses que celui qui regarde une fenêtre fermée. Il n'est pas d'objet plus profond, plus mystérieux, plus fécond, plus ténébreux, plus éblouissant qu'une fenêtre éclairée d'une chandelle. Ce qu'on peut voir au soleil est toujours moins intéressant que ce qui se passe derrière une vitre. Dans ce trou noir ou lumineux vit la vie, rêve la vie, souffre la vie.

Par-delà des vagues de toits, j'aperçois une femme mûre, ridée déjà, pauvre, toujours penchée sur quelquechose, et qui ne sort jamais. Avec son visage, avec son vêtement, avec son geste, avec presque rien, j'ai refait l'histoire de cette femme, ou plutôt sa légende, et quelquefois je me la raconte à moi-même en pleurant.

Si c'eût été un pauvre vieux homme, j'aurais refait la sienne tout aussi aisément.

Et je me couche, fier d'avoir vécu et souffert dans d'autres que moi-même

Peut-être me direz-vous: "Es-tu sûr que cette légende soit la vraie?" Qu'importe ce que peut être la réalité placée hors de moi, si elle m'a aidé à vivre, à sentir que je suis et ce que je suis?

Windows

The one who looks in an open window from outside never sees as many things as the one who looks at a closed window. There is no deeper, more mysterious, more fertile, more shadowy, more dazzling object than a window lit by a candle. What one can see in sunlight is always less interesting than what is taking place behind a window. In that black or luminous hole life is being lived, life is dreaming, life is suffering.

Beyond waves of roofs I see a mature woman, already wrinkled, poor, always bending over something, and who never goes out. With her face, her dress, her gesture, with almost nothing, I have reconstructed the history of that woman, or rather her story, and sometimes I tell it to myself in tears.

If it had been a poor old man, I would have done the same just as easily.

And I go to bed, proud of having lived and suffered in others as for myself.

Perhaps you will say to me, "Are you sure that this story is the true one?" What does it matter what the reality outside myself may be, if it has helped me to live, to know that I am and what I am?

Anywhere out of the world
N'IMPORTE OÙ HORS DU MONDE

Cette vie est un hôpital où chaque malade est possédé du désir de changer de lit. Celui-ci voudrait souffrir en face du poêle, et celui-là croit qu'il guérirait à côté de la fenêtre.

Il me semble que je serais toujours bien là où je ne suis pas, et cette question de déménagement en est une que je discute sans cesse avec mon âme.

"Dis-moi, mon âme, pauvre âme refroidie, que penserais-tu d'habiter Lisbonne? Il doit y faire chaud, et tu t'y ragaillardirais comme un lézard. Cette ville est au bord de l'eau; on dit qu'elle est bâtie en marbre, et que le peuple y a une telle haine du végétal, qu'il arrache tous les arbres. Voilà un paysage selon ton goût; un paysage fait avec la lumière et le minéral, et le liquide pour les réfléchir!"

Mon âme ne répond pas.

"Puisque tu aimes tant le repos, avec le spectacle du mouvement, veux-tu venir habiter la Hollande, cette terre béatifiante? Peut-être te divertiras-tu dans cette contrée dont tu as souvent admiré l'image dans les musées. Que penserais-tu de Rotterdam, toi qui aimes les forêts de mâts, et les navires amarrés au pied des maisons?"

Mon âme reste muette.

"Batavia te sourirait peut-être davantage? Nous y trouverions d'ailleurs l'esprit de l'Europe marié à la beauté tropicale."

Pas un mot. — Mon âme serait-elle morte?

"En es-tu donc venue à ce point d'engourdissement que tu ne te plaises que dans ton mal? S'il en est ainsi, fuyons vers les pays qui sont les analogies de la Mort. — Je tiens notre affaire, pauvre âme! Nous ferons nos malles pour Tornéo. Allons plus loin encore, à l'extrême bout de la Baltique; encore plus loin de la vie, si c'est possible; installons-nous au pôle. Là le soleil ne frise qu'obliquement la terre, et les lentes alternatives de la lumière

Anywhere Out of the World

Life is a hospital where each patient is possessed by the desire to change beds. This one would like to suffer facing the stove, that one believes that he would be cured next to the window.

It seems to me that I would always be well where I am not, and this question of moving is one that I discuss endlessly with my soul.

"Tell me, my soul, poor chilly soul, what would you think of living in Lisbon? It must be warm there, and you would perk up like a lizard. The town is on the water; they say it is built of marble and that the people have such a hatred of vegetation that they tear up all the trees. There is a landscape to your taste; a landscape made of light and mineral and liquid to reflect them!"

My soul does not answer.

"Since you are so fond of repose, accompanied by the spectacle of movement, do you want to go and live in Holland, that blissful land? Perhaps you would find it diverting to live in the country whose image you have often admired in museums. What would you think of Rotterdam, you who like forests of masts, and ships moored at the foot of houses?"

My soul remains silent.

"Batavia perhaps would prove more attractive? Moreover, there we would find the spirit of Europe wedded to the beauty of the tropics."

Not a word. Could my soul be dead?

"Then have you arrived at such a degree of apathy that you take pleasure only in your disease? If that is the case, let us fly to countries that are the likenesses of Death. I know what to do, poor soul! We shall pack our trunks for Tornio. Let us go even farther, to the far end of the Baltic; even farther from life, if that is possible; let us take up residence at the pole. There the sun only skims the earth obliquely, and the slow alternations of light

et de la nuit suppriment la variété et augmentent la monotonie, cette moitié du néant. Là, nous pourrons prendre de longs bains de ténèbres, cependant que, pour nous divertir, les aurores boréales nous enverront de temps en temps leurs gerbes roses, comme des reflets d'un feu d'artifice de l'Enfer!"

Enfin, mon âme fait explosion, et sagement elle me crie: "N'importe où! n'importe où! pourvu que ce soit hors de ce monde!"

and darkness suppress variety and augment monotony, that half of oblivion. There we shall take long baths of shadows while, for our amusement, the aurora borealis will send us from time to time rosy sheaves, like the reflections of fireworks in Hell!"

Finally my soul explodes, and in her wisdom cries: "Anywhere! Anywhere! So long as it is out of this world!"

José-María de Heredia

Persée et Andromède

ANDROMÈDE AU MONSTRE

La Vierge Céphéenne, hélas! encor vivante,
Liée, échevelée, au roc des noirs îlots,
Se lamente en tordant avec de vains sanglots
Sa chair royale où court un frisson d'épouvante.

L'Océan monstrueux que la tempête évente
Crache à ses pieds glacés l'âcre bave des flots,
Et partout elle voit, à travers ses cils clos,
Bâiller la gueule glauque, innombrable et mouvante.

Tel qu'un éclat de foudre en un ciel sans éclair,
Tout à coup, retentit un hennissement clair.
Ses yeux s'ouvrent. L'horreur les emplit, et l'extase;

Car elle a vu, d'un vol vertigineux et sûr,
Se cabrant sous le poids du fils de Zeus, Pégase
Allonger sur la mer sa grande ombre d'azur.

PERSÉE ET ANDROMÈDE

Au milieu de l'écume arrêtant son essor,
Le Cavalier vainqueur du monstre et de Méduse,
Ruisselant d'une bave horrible où le sang fuse,
Emporte entre ses bras la vierge aux cheveux d'or.

Sur l'étalon divin, frère de Chrysaor,
Qui piaffe dans la mer et hennit et refuse,

Perseus and Andromeda

ANDROMEDA AND THE MONSTER

Cepheus's daughter still lives, alas,
Chained to the rock, and struggles with the chain,
Striving to tear it from her flesh in vain
As through her royal body shudders pass.

The monstrous Ocean that the winds amass
Spits at her icy feet an acrid rain,
And through half-closed eyes she sees again
The green mouth moving like a huge crevasse.

Like thunder in a sky that does not lighten,
Suddenly a neigh sounds. Her eyes widen
With horror, then are filled with joyful tears,

For she has seen, flying down steep and sure,
The son of Zeus, and Pegasus uprears
On the sea his great shadow of azure.

PERSEUS AND ANDROMEDA

The conqueror of Medusa, slayer
Of the sea monster, streaming slime and blood,
Arrests his flight, leaps in the running flood,
And clasps the virgin with the golden hair.

He lifts her in his arms, and places her
On the great stallion. And the Beloved,

Il a posé l'Amante éperdue et confuse
Qui lui rit et l'étreint et qui sanglote encor.

Il l'embrasse. La houle enveloppe leur groupe.
Elle, d'un faible effort, ramène sur la croupe
Ses beaux pieds qu'en fuyant baise un flot vagabond;

Mais Pégase irrité par le fouet de la lame,
A l'appel du Héros s'enlevant d'un seul bond,
Bat le ciel ébloui de ses ailes de flamme.

LE RAVISSEMENT D'ANDROMÈDE

D'un vol silencieux, le grand Cheval ailé
Soufflant de ses naseaux élargis l'air qui fume,
Les emporte avec un frémissement de plume
A travers la nuit bleue et l'éther étoilé.

Ils vont. L'Afrique plonge au gouffre flagellé,
Puis l'Asie . . . un désert . . . le Liban ceint de brume . . .
Et voici qu'apparaît, toute blanche d'écume,
La mer mystérieuse où vint sombrer Hellé.

Et le vent gonfle ainsi que deux immenses voiles
Les ailes qui, volant d'étoiles en étoiles,
Aux amants enlacés font un tiède berceau;

Tandis que, l'oeil au ciel où palpite leur ombre,
Ils voient, irradiant du Bélier au Verseau,
Leurs Constellations poindre dans l'azur sombre.

Confused, and still joyfully bewildered,
Laughs, and sobs, and holds him close to her.

He embraces her. Surf surrounds the group.
She, with an effort, raises to the croup
Beautiful feet a vagrant billow kisses.

Pegasus, maddened by these whips and stings,
At the Hero's call in one bound rises
And beats the sky dazzled by his flaming wings.

ANDROMEDA'S WEDDING

The great winged Horse in a silent flight,
Breathing from large nostrils smoke and air,
Carries them away, tracing a feather
Across the blue and star-bespangled night.

Africa sinks in the whipped gulf out of sight.
Asia, a desert. Lebanon likes to wear
A belt of fog. And, mysterious, there,
The sea where Hellé perished, foaming white.

The wind fills those two immense sails so,
The wings, that as from star to star they go,
They make the loving pair a wedding bed.

Their moving shadows in the sky entwine.
From Aries to Aquarius outspread
Against the night, their Constellations shine.

Stéphane Mallarmé

La Pipe

Hier, j'ai trouvé ma pipe en rêvant une longue soirée de travail, de beau travail d'hiver. Jetées les cigarettes avec toutes les joies enfantines de l'été dans le passé qu'illuminent les feuilles bleues de soleil, les mousselines et reprise ma grave pipe par un homme sérieux qui veut fumer longtemps sans se déranger, afin de mieux travailler: mais je ne m'attendais pas à la surprise que préparait cette délaissée, à peine eus-je tiré la première bouffée, j'oubliai mes grands livres à faire, émerveillé, attendri, je respirai l'hiver dernier qui revenait. Je n'avais pas touché à la fidèle amie depuis ma rentrée en France, et tout Londres, Londres tel que je le vécus en entier à moi seul, il y a un an, est apparu; d'abord les chers brouillards qui emmitouflent nos cervelles et ont, là-bas, une odeur à eux, quand ils pénètrent sous la croisée. Mon tabac sentait une chambre sombre aux meubles de cuir saupoudrés par la poussière du charbon sur lesquels se roulait le maigre chat noir; les grands feux! et la bonne aux bras rouges versant les charbons, et le bruit de ces charbons tombant du seau de tôle dans la corbeille de fer, le matin — alors que le facteur frappait le double coup solennel, qui me faisait vivre! J'ai revu par les fenêtres ces arbres malades du square désert — j'ai vu le large, si souvent traversé cet hiver-là, grelottant sur le pont du steamer mouillé de bruine et noirci de fumée — avec ma pauvre bien-aimée errante, en habits de voyageuse, une longue robe terne couleur de la poussière des routes, un manteau qui collait humide à ses épaules froides, un de ces chapeaux de paille sans plume et presque sans rubans, que les riches dames jettent en arrivant, tant ils sont déchiquetés par l'air de la mer et que les pauvres bien-aimées regarnissent pour bien des saisons encore. Autour de son cou s'enroulait le terrible mouchoir qu'on agite en se disant adieu pour toujours.

The Pipe

Yesterday I found my pipe, dreaming of a long evening of work, fine winter work. Cigarettes were discarded with all the childish joys of summer past lighted by the blue leaves of the sun, muslin dresses, and the thoughtful pipe picked up again, the pipe of a serious man who wants to smoke for a long time without being distracted, so as to work better. But I did not expect the surprise this relaxation was preparing. Scarcely had I drawn the first puff when I forgot the great books I had to write. Filled with wonder and emotion I inhaled the last winter as it returned. I had not touched the faithful friend since coming back from France, and all London appeared, London as I had lived and had it entirely to myself a year ago: first the dear fogs that wrap our brains and, over there, have a smell all their own when they seep through the casement. My tobacco smelled of a dark room with leather furniture sprinkled with the coal dust in which the thin black cat rolled; big fires! and in the morning the maid with red arms pouring coal, and the sound of coals falling from the metal pail into the iron bin — and just then the mailman giving the solemn double knock that brought me to life! I looked out again from the windows on those sick trees of the empty square. I saw the sea, so often crossed that winter . . . shivering on the bridge of the steamer drenched with drizzle and black with smoke, with my poor wandering love, dressed for travel, a long dull dress the color of road dust, a cloak that clung damply to her cold shoulders, one of those straw hats without a feather and almost without ribbons that rich ladies throw away on arriving, they are so mangled by the sea air, and which poor loves refurbish for many seasons to come. Around her neck hung the terrible kerchief that is waved in saying goodbye forever.

Brise marine

La chair est triste, hélas! et j'ai lu tous les livres.
Fuir! là-bas fuir! Je sens que des oiseaux sont ivres
D'être parmi l'écume inconnue et les cieux!
Rien, ni les vieux jardins, reflétés par les yeux
Ne retiendra ce coeur qui dans la mer se trempe
O nuits! ni la clarté déserte de ma lampe
Sur le vide papier que la blancheur défend
Et ni la jeune femme allaitant son enfant.
Je partirai! Steamer, balançant ta mâture,
Lève l'ancre pour une exotique nature!

Un Ennui, désolé par les cruels espoirs,
Croit encore à l'adieu suprême des mouchoirs!
Et peut-être, les mâts, invitants les orages
Sont-ils de ceux qu'un vent penche sur les naufrages
Perdus, sans mâts, sans mâts, ni fertiles îlots . . .
Mais, ô mon coeur, entends le chant des matelots!

Sea Breeze

The flesh is sad, alas! And I have read
All the books. To fly! To fly instead!
Birds, I know, are drunk for unknown skies.
Nothing, not old gardens mirrored in eyes,
Holds the heart that still drips with the sea,
O nights! Neither the lamplit mystery
Of a page yet white and undefiled,
Nor the nursing woman and her child.
Steamer, weigh your anchor! I shall go
To some exotic land I do not know.

Despair, whose hopes have often come to grief,
Believes the last wave of a handkerchief!
These masts may be the kind storms do not bend
Toward some greener isle, but foaming send
Onto the rocks, and roll the wreck along.
But, O my sad heart, hear the sailors' song!

Le Tombeau d'Edgar Poe

Tel qu'en Lui-même enfin l'éternité le change,
Le Poëte suscite avec un glaive nu
Son siècle épouvanté de n'avoir pas connu
Que la mort triomphait dans cette voix étrange!

Eux, comme un vil sursaut d'hydre oyant jadis l'ange
Donner un sens plus pur aux mots de la tribu
Proclamèrent très haut le sortilège bu
Dans le flot sans honneur de quelque noir mélange.

Du sol et de la nue hostiles, ô grief!
Si notre idée avec ne sculpte un bas-relief
Dont la tombe de Poe éblouissante s'orne,

Calme bloc ici-bas chu d'un désastre obscur,
Que ce granit du moins montre à jamais sa borne
Aux noirs vols du Blasphème épars dans le futur.

The Tomb of Poe

At last the Poet, changed by eternity
Into Himself, goads with a naked sword
The century, dismayed that it ignored
In that amazing voice, death's victory.

Like the vile hydra, leaping up to see
An angel give the tribe the purer word,
They shouted that the charm had been procured
From some dark potion, mixed illicitly.

You are hated by heaven and earth, O grief,
If our art cannot sculpt a bas-relief
For the tomb of Poe, so that dazzling granite,

Calm block fallen from some dark disaster,
At least may stand forever as a limit
To black flights of Blasphemy in the future.

L'Après-midi d'un faune

Églogue

LE FAUNE

Ces nymphes, je les veux perpétuer.

                       Si clair,
Leur incarnat léger, qu'il voltige dans l'air
Assoupi de sommeils touffus.

                  Aimai-je un rêve?
Mon doute, amas de nuit ancienne, s'achève
En maint rameau subtil, qui, demeuré les vrais
Bois mêmes, prouve, hélas! que bien seul je m'offrais
Pour triomphe la faute idéale de roses.
Réflechissons . . .

             ou si les femmes dont tu gloses
Figurent un souhait de tes sens fabuleux!
Faune, l'illusion s'échappe des yeux bleus
Et froids, comme une source en pleurs, de la plus chaste:
Mais, l'autre tout soupirs, dis-tu qu'elle contraste
Comme brise du jour chaude dans ta toison?
Que non! par l'immobile et lasse pâmoison
Suffoquant de chaleurs le matin frais s'il lutte,
Ne murmure point d'eau que ne verse ma flûte
Au bosquet arrosé d'accords; et le seul vent
Hors des deux tuyaux prompt à s'exhaler avant
Qu'il disperse le son dans une pluie aride,
C'est, à l'horizon pas remué d'une ride,
Le visible et serein soufflé artificiel
De l'inspiration, qui regagne le ciel.

The Afternoon of a Faun

Eclogue

THE FAUN

Those nymphs, I want to capture them.

So clear
Their light incarnation, that it floats in air,
Drowsing in leafy slumber.

Was it a dream
I loved? The shapes of ancient night that seem
Vague end, alas, in branches, and I see
That I, and I alone, was offering me
In triumph the perfect frailty of roses.
Consider . . .

whether your talk of women is
Inspired, faun, by your fabled senses.
In the cold, blue eyes of the chaster one
Like a tearful fountain, the illusion
Escapes, but then the other, when a breeze
Warms you, is she sighing on your fleece?
But no! In this torpid swooning state
Of morning almost stifled by the heat,
My flute is the only water with its stops,
Sprinkling its harmonies about the copse
Watered with music; and the only breeze
Apart from the two pipes sound quickly empties
Before dispersing in the arid plain,
Is, on the horizon's unwrinkled line,
The serene and artificial exhalation,
Returning to the sky, of inspiration.

O bords siciliens d'un calme marécage
Qu'à l'envi de soleils ma vanité saccage,
Tacite sous les fleurs d'étincelles, CONTEZ
"Que je coupais ici les creux roseaux domptés
Par le talent; quand, sur l'or glauque de lointaines
Verdures dédiant leur vigne à des fontaines,
Ondoie une blancheur animale au repos:
Et qu'au prélude lent où naissent les pipeaux
Ce vol de cygnes, non! de naïades se sauve
Ou plonge . . ."

                Inerte, tout brûle dans l'heure fauve
Sans marquer par quel art ensemble détala
Trop d'hymen souhaité de qui cherche le *la*:
Alors m'éveillerai-je à la ferveur première,
Droit et seul, sous un flot antique de lumière,
Lys! et l'un de vous tous pour l'ingénuité.

Autre que ce doux rien par leur lèvre ébruité,
Le baiser, qui tout bas des perfides assure,
Mon sein, vierge de preuve, atteste une morsure
Mystérieuse, due à quelque auguste dent;
Mais, bast! arcane tel élut pour confident
Le jonc vaste et jumeau dont sous l'azur on joue:
Qui, détournant à soi le trouble de la joue,
Rêve, dans un solo long, que nous amusions
La beauté d'alentour par des confusions
Fausses entre elle-même et notre chant crédule;
Et de faire aussi haut que l'amour se module
Évanouir du songe ordinaire de dos
Ou de flanc pur suivis avec mes regards clos,
Une sonore, vaine et monotone ligne.

O Sicilian marshes that my vanity
Parches, so that suns are filled with envy,
Silent beneath your flowering sparks, RECOUNT
"That I was cutting hollow reeds, the amount
Talent would need, when on the glaucous gold
Of green with fountains on which vines take hold,
An animal whiteness seems to undulate,
And at the slow beginning of the flute
That flight of swans, no, naiads, runs away
Or dives . . ."

                    At the fawn's time of day—
All burns, and the art by which the excess
Of hymen wished for by the one who searches
For *la* escaped is unnoticed—I shall wake
At the first transport, in an antique
Flood of light, lily, erect and alone,
And, of all of you, the innocent one.

Aside from the sweet nothings that are murmured,
The kiss, by which treachery is assured,
There is a bite mark on my breast, that was
Virgin till now. I can only suppose,
Due to some august tooth. But no more!
Only the elect know such things, taking for
Their confidant the vast twin reed beneath
The azure, that takes in the troubled breath
And in a solo dreams we were amusing
The beauty all around us, by confusing
It with our song . . . and dreams of a love so high
That it can do without the back and thigh
Of ordinary dreams, the parts I know
And, with both my eyes shut tight, can follow,
A sonorous, vain, montonous line.

Tâche donc, instrument des fuites, ô maligne
Syrinx, de refleurir aux lacs où tu m'attends!
Moi, de ma rumeur fier, je vais parler longtemps
Des déesses; et par d'idolâtres peintures,
A leur ombre enlever encore des ceintures:
Ainsi, quand des raisins j'ai sucé la clarté,
Pour bannir un regret par ma feinte écarté,
Rieur, j'élève au ciel d'été la grappe vide
Et, soufflant dans ses peaux lumineuses, avide
D'ivresse, jusqu'au soir je regarde au travers.

O nymphes, regonflons des SOUVENIRS divers.
"Mon oeil, trouant les joncs, dardait chaque encolure
Immortelle, qui noie en l'onde sa brûlure
Avec un cri de rage au ciel de la forêt;
Et le splendide bain de cheveux disparaît
Dans les clartés et les frissons, ô pierreries!
J'accours; quand, à mes pieds, s'entrejoignent (meurtries
De la langueur goûtée à ce mal d'être deux)
Des dormeuses parmi leurs seuls bras hasardeux;
Je les ravis, sans les désenlacer, et vole
A ce massif, haï par l'ombrage frivole,
De roses tarissant tout parfum au soleil,
Où notre ébat au jour consumé soit pareil."
Je t'adore, courroux des vierges, ô délice
Farouche du sacré fardeau nu qui se glisse
Pour fuir ma lèvre en feu buvant, comme un éclair
Tressaille! la frayeur secrète de la chair:
Des pieds de l'inhumaine au coeur de la timide
Que délaisse à la fois une innocence, humide
De larmes folles ou de moins tristes vapeurs.
"Mon crime, c'est d'avoir, gai de vaincre ces peurs
Traîtresses, divisé la touffe échevelée
De baisers que les dieux gardaient si bien mêlée:

Try then, you instrument of flights, malign
Syrinx, again to flower by the lake
Where you are waiting for me! I shall speak
Of goddesses at length, for I am proud
Of the fame I have in paintings with the crowd:
Making off with a girdle in a shadow,
Sucking the light out of some grapes, to show
I have no regrets. Lifting a grapeskin to blow
Into it, and look through it at the sky,
Avid for drink, and so the hours fly.

Nymphs, let us reinflate some MEMORIES.
"My eye makes holes among the reeds and pierces
Each immortal neck that would assuage
Its burning in water with a cry of rage;
And the splendid bath of hair that flashes
And shivers like a jewel vanishes.
I come running up, when on the ground
(Bruised by the taste of evil they have found
In being two) these sleepers are enlaced.
I seize without disjoining them, and haste
To a bed of roses hated by the shade
That spill their perfumes in the sun and fade
Like our folic, squandering the day."
I love you, anger of virgins, ecstasy
Of the sacred naked burden that would fly
My lips on fire drinking like a flash
Of lightning secret terror of the flesh
From the cold one's feet to the heart of the timid
That innocence gives up together, humid
With wild tears or less unhappy vapors.
"My crime is that, glad to vanquish those terrors,
I separated hair that was entangled
By kisses that the gods themselves had mingled,

Car, à peine j'allais cacher un rire ardent
Sous les replis heureux d'une seule (gardant
Par un doigt simple, afin que sa candeur de plume
Se teignît à l'émoi de sa soeur qui s'allume,
La petite, naïve et ne rougissant pas:)
Que de mes bras, défaits par de vagues trépas,
Cette proie, à jamais ingrate se délivre
Sans pitié du sanglot dont j'étais encore ivre."

Tant pis! vers le bonheur d'autres m'entraîneront
Par leur tresse nouée aux cornes de mon front:
Tu sais, ma passion, que, pourpre et déjà mûre,
Chaque grenade éclate et d'abeilles murmure;
Et notre sang, épris de qui le va saisir,
Coule pour tout l'essaim éternel du désir.
A l'heure où ce bois d'or et de cendres se teinte
Une fête s'exalte en la feuillée éteinte:
Etna! c'est parmi toi visité de Venus
Sur ta lave posant ses talons ingénus,
Quand tonne un somme triste ou s'épuise la flamme.
Je tiens la reine!

       O sûr châtiment . . .

                      Non, mais l'âme
De paroles vacante et ce corps alourdi
Tard succombent au fier silence de midi:
Sans plus il faut dormir en l'oubli du blasphème,
Sur le sable altéré gisant et comme j'aime
Ouvrir ma bouche à l'astre efficace des vins!

Couple, adieu; je vais voir l'ombre que tu devins.

For just as I was about to smother
A laugh in the folds of one (keeping the other
By just a finger, so she would take on
The rising fervor of her sister's passion,
The little unblushing one, the innocent),
From my slack arms, by deaths vaguely spent,
The two, ungrateful forever, run away
And leave me sobbing drunk at the end of day."

So what! Others will lead to happiness
My horns as with a noose tied by a tress.
You know, my passion, purple and ripening
Pomegranates burst, and bees are murmuring;
And that our amorous, responsive blood
Pours out desire in a constant flood.
At the hour when the woods are ash and gold,
The leaves that have lost all their color hold
A festival. It is Venus walking,
Etna, that sets off your lava sparkling
When sad dreams thunder or the flame is low.
I have the queen!

        I shall be punished . . .

                         No,
But the soul drained of words and this dull body
Are succumbing to the silence of midday.
Now I must sleep, forgetting blasphemy,
On the changing sand, and, as pleases me,
Open my mouth to wine's consoling star!

Adieu, you two. I shall see the shade you are.

Le vierge, le vivace, et le bel aujourd'hui

Le vierge, le vivace et le bel aujourd'hui
Va-t-il nous déchirer avec un coup d'aile ivre
Ce lac dur oublié que hante sous le givre
Le transparent glacier des vols qui n'ont pas fui!

Un cygne d'autrefois se souvient que c'est lui
Magnifique mais qui sans espoir se délivre
Pour n'avoir pas chanté la région où vivre
Quand du stérile hiver a resplendi l'ennui.

Tout son col secouera cette blanche agonie
Par l'espace infligé à l'oiseau qui le nie,
Mais non l'horreur du sol où le plumage est pris.

Fantôme qu'à ce lieu son pur éclat assigne,
Il s'immobilise au songe froid de mépris
Que vêt parmi l'exil inutile le Cygne.

Virginal, vivid, beautiful, will this be

Virginal, vivid, beautiful, will this be
The day that shatters with a drunken wing
The lake beneath the frost, still mirroring
Flights that were never made, transparency?

A swan of old remembers that it is he,
Superb but helpless, for he would not sing
Of regions where life still was beckoning
When winter spread its sterile, cold ennui.

His whole neck shakes off the white agony
Inflicted by the space he would deny,
But not the earth that grips him horribly.

Phantom, that with pure brilliance lives on,
He lies immobile, dreaming scornfully,
Such dreams as in his exile clothe the Swan.

Paul Verlaine

Chanson d'automne

Les sanglots longs
Des violons
   De l'automne
Blessent mon coeur
D'une langueur
   Monotone.

Tout suffoquant
Et blême, quand
   Sonne l'heure,
Je me souviens
Des jours anciens
   Et je pleure;

Et je m'en vais
Au vent mauvais
   Qui m'emporte
Decà, delà,
Pareil à la
   Feuille morte.

Autumn Song

Violins complain
Of autumn again,
    They sob and moan.
And my heartstrings ache
Like the song they make,
    A monotone.

Suffocating, drowned,
And hollowly, sound
    The midnight chimes.
Then the days return
I knew, and I mourn
    For bygone times.

And I fall and drift
With the winds that lift
    My heavy grief.
Here and there they blow,
And I rise and go
    Like a dead leaf.

Les Ingénus

Les hauts talons luttaient avec les longues jupes,
En sorte que, selon le terrain et le vent,
Parfois luisaient des bas de jambes, trop souvent
Interceptés — et nous aimions ce jeu de dupes.

Parfois aussi le dard d'un insecte jaloux
Inquiétait le col des belles sous les branches,
Et c'était des éclairs soudains de nuques blanches,
Et ce régal comblait nos jeunes yeux de fous.

Le soir tombait, un soir équivoque d'automne:
Les belles, se pendant rêveuses à nos bras,
Dirent alors des mots si spécieux, tout bas,
Que notre âme depuis ce temps tremble et s'étonne.

The Young Fools

High-heels were struggling with a full-length dress
So that, between the wind and the terrain,
At times a shining stocking would be seen,
And gone too soon. We liked that foolishness.

Also, at times a jealous insect's dart
Bothered our beauties. Suddenly a white
Nape flashed beneath the branches, and this sight
Was a delicate feast for a young fool's heart.

Evening fell, equivocal, dissembling.
The women who hung dreaming on our arms
Spoke in low voices, words that had such charms
That ever since our stunned soul has been trembling.

Il pleure dans mon coeur

Il pleut doucement sur la ville.
ARTHUR RIMBAUD

Il pleure dans mon coeur
Comme il pleut sur la ville.
Quelle est cette langueur
Qui pénètre mon coeur?

O bruit doux de la pluie
Par terre et sur les toits!
Pour un coeur qui s'ennuie,
O le chant de la pluie!

Il pleure sans raison
Dans ce coeur qui s'écoeure.
Quoi! nulle trahison?
Ce deuil est sans raison.

C'est bien la pire peine
De ne savoir pourquoi,
Sans amour et sans haine,
Mon coeur a tant de peine.

Tears Fall in My Heart

It rains gently on the town.
ARTHUR RIMBAUD

Tears fall in my heart
Like rain on the town.
O why did it start,
This grief in my heart?

Gentle sound of the rain
On the ground and the roofs . . .
For a heart in such pain,
O the song of the rain!

I am sad for no reason
And sickened at heart.
Why? What have I done?
This grief has no reason.

This is the worst state,
To know of no reason,
Without love, without hate,
Why my grief is so great.

Je n'ai pas de chance en femme

Je n'ai pas de chance en femme,
Et, depuis mon âge d'homme,
Je ne suis tombé guère, en somme,
Que sur des criardes infâmes.

C'est vrai que je suis criard,
Moi-même, et d'un révoltant
Caractère tout autant,
Peut-être plus, par hasard.

Mes femmes furent légères,
Toi-même tu l'es un peu,
Cet épouvantable aveu
Soit dit entre nous, ma chère.

C'est vrai que je fus coureur.
Peut-être le suis-je encore:
Cet aveu me déshonore.
Parfois je me fais horreur.

Baste! restons tout de même
Amants fervents, puisqu'en somme
Toi, bonne fille et moi, brave homme,
Tu m'aimes, dis, et que je t'aime.

I've Had No Luck With Women

I've had no luck with women
Ever since I was a lad.
Screechers are what I've had,
With a lousy reputation.

I've done a bit of scrapping
Myself, and my character
Leaves something to be desired.
Even worse. It could happen.

My women were easy. You too,
More than a little bit,
Much as I hate to say it.
Let's keep it between us two.

I've been a long time lusting
Myself, and still am, maybe.
This confession dishonors me.
Sometimes I find myself disgusting.

Enough! So what shall we do?
Stay as loving as we can.
You're a good girl, I'm . . . a man.
You love me, don't you? And I love you.

Mon Apologie

Je suis un homme étrange, à ce que l'on me dit:
Aux yeux de quelques-uns pur et simple bandit,
Pur et simple imbécile aux yeux de quelques autres;
D'autres encor m'ont mis au rang des faux apôtres,
Pourquoi? D'aucuns enfin au rang des dieux, pourquoi,
Mon Dieu? Quand je ne suis qu'un bonhomme assez coi,
Somme toute, en dépit de quelque incohérence.

Or, j'ai souffert pas mal et joui non moins: rance
Juste milieu, je t'ai toujours mal reniflé,
Malgré tout mon désir de vivre mieux réglé,
Mieux équilibré, comme parlerait un sage
De nos jours après tout sages, selon l'usage
Des jours anciens et futurs.
                                        Donc, j'ai souffert
Beaucoup et surtout de mon fait, à découvert,
Par exemple, et saignant ainsi que pour l'exemple,
Et scandaleux comme l'ilote. Oui, mais quel ample
Et bon remords me prit, par la grâce de Dieu,
De mes fautes d'antan, presque juste au milieu
De l'expiation de tant de jouissances!
Et, dès lors, j'ai vécu de toutes les puissances
Du coeur et de l'esprit bien mûris par l'été
Splendide du bonheur et de l'adversité.
Voilà pouquoi je suis ce qu'on nomme cet homme
Étrange, et qui ne l'est, encore qu'on le nomme
Tel. Au plus un original; encore, encor?
Car je ne pose pas dans tel ou tel décor,
Que je sache, et mon geste est d'un complet nature.
Triste ou gai, je concède assez vif, d'aventure,
Quand il sied, assez lent par hasard, s'il le faut.

My Apology

I am a strange man, just a criminal
In some eyes, I have been told, that's all.
To others, a pure and simple idiot.
And others have called me a false prophet,
Why? And some seem to think me a god. Why,
My God? I am a peaceful enough guy
After all, in spite of some confusion.

I have suffered, and had as much fun.
If the place I am in smells rank, I'll smell,
In spite of my desire to live well,
A more balanced life, as one of our sages
Of today would say, as through the ages
They have said, and always will.

                        I have paid
With much suffering for what I did.
It was a bleeding bad example,
And scandalous. Yes, but what ample
And good remorse came over me, by God's grace,
For faults of long standing, in the process
Of expiating so much enjoyment!
Since then, I have lived with all the bent
Of heart and spirit, ripened by the sun
That shines on happiness and misfortune.
And that is why I am the strange fellow
They call me, and who is not, although
They say he is. Let's say, original,
For I don't fit into any scene at all,
And my acts proceed from my whole being.
Sad or gay, I'm ready for anything
When I like, and if I must, I can be slow.

Donc, ô mes amis chers, prisez pour ce qu'il vaut
Mon caractère tel qu'il est: tout d'une pièce?
Non, et je ne crois pas qu'il importe en l'espèce,
Mais fort peu compliqué; et de bonne foi toujours?
Non, car je suis un homme et je ne suis pas l'ours
Des solitudes, brave bête un peu farouche,
Mais si franche! — et je mens parfois, plutôt de bouche
Qu'autrement, mais enfin je mens . . . au fond, si peu!

Eh oui, j'ai mes défauts, qui n'en a devant Dieu?
J'ai mes vices aussi, parbleu! Qui n'en a guère
Ou beaucoup? Mais à la guerre comme à la guerre!
Il faut me supporter ainsi, m'aimer ainsi
Plutôt, car j'ai besoin qu'on m'aime.
                                        Et puis ceci:
Dieu m'a béni, lui qui punit de main de maître,
Terriblement, et j'ai reconquis tout mon être
Dans le malheur tant mérité, tant médité,
Et c'est ce qui m'a fait meilleur, en vérité,
Que beaucoup d'entre ceux dont si stricte est l'enquête.

Mais, Seigneur, gardez-moi de l'orgueil, toujours bête!

O dear friends, take my character so,
For what it may be worth. All of a piece?
I don't think that applies to the human race.
But not too complicated. Always sincere?
No, for I am a man, and not a bear
Of the forest, brave, a bit unfriendly
But so frank! Sometimes I chance to lie,
But not otherwise. But I lie. Not much, really.

Ah yes, I have my failings. In God's eye
Who doesn't? And vices. Who doesn't have a few
Or many? In war, do as you have to do!
You must put up with me, love me so
Rather, for I need to be loved.
                              This also:
God has blessed me, who as the Creator
Chastises me. I have won back my nature
In misfortune so well deserved and taken,
And it has made me better than many men
Whose judgments are so severely applied.

But, Lord, keep me from the foolishness of pride!

Arthur Rimbaud

Le Mal

Tandis que les crachats rouges de la mitraille
Sifflent tout le jour par l'infini du ciel bleu;
Qu'écarlates ou verts, près du Roi qui les raille,
Croulent les bataillons en masse dans le feu;

Tandis qu'une folie épouvantable broie
Et fait de cent milliers d'hommes un tas fumant;
— Pauvres morts! dans l'été, dans l'herbe, dans ta joie,
Nature! ô toi qui fis ces hommes saintement! . . .

— Il est un Dieu, qui rit aux nappes damassées
Des autels, à l'encens, aux grands calices d'or;
Qui dans le bercement des hosannah s'endort,

Et se réveille, quand des mères, ramassées
Dans l'angoisse, et pleurant sous leur vieux bonnet noir,
Lui donnent un gros sou lié dans leur mouchoir!

Evil

When the gobs spat by flaming cannon
Whistle all day beneath a clear blue sky,
And the King cracks jokes as he looks on,
And red or green battalions march and die;

While a terrifying, pounding madness
Turns tens of thousands into smoking garbage
In the grass, in summer, in your gladness,
Nature, who made these men in His image!

There is a God, who laughs at silk and linen,
Altars, incense, and gold chalices,
Who falls asleep when choirs sing His praises,

And wakes when all the mothers shuffle in
With their old black bonnet and their grief,
And give him a big penny tied in a kerchief.

Au Cabaret-Vert

Depuis huit jours, j'avais déchiré mes bottines
Aux cailloux des chemins. J'entrais à Charleroi.
— *Au Cabaret-Vert*: je demandai des tartines
De beurre et du jambon qui fût à moitié froid.

Bienheureux, j'allongai les jambes sous la table
Verte: je contemplai les sujets très naïfs
De la tapisserie. — Et ce fut adorable
Quand la fille aux tétons énormes, aux yeux vifs,

— Celle-là, ce n'est pas un baiser qui l'épeure! —
Rieuse, m'apporta des tartines de beurre,
Du jambon tiède, dans un plat colorié,

Du jambon rose et blanc parfumé d'une gousse
D'ail, — et m'emplit la chope immense, avec sa mousse
Que dorait un rayon de soleil arriéré.

At the Green Cabaret

For eight days I wore out my shoe leather
On graveled roads, and came to Charleroi,
The Green Cabaret. I ordered bread and butter,
And ham . . . I'd prefer it cold I told her.

Happy, I stretched my legs under the table
Which was green; looked at the simple stories
On the tapestry. And it was adorable
When the girl with big breasts and lively eyes —

That one, it wouldn't be a kiss that scared her! —
Laughing, appeared with my bread and butter
And the ham, warm, on a colored plate.

Ham, rosy and white, that was flavored
With garlic, and a mug with a foaming head,
Gold in a ray of sunlight, falling late.

Le Bateau ivre

Comme je descendais des Fleuves impassibles,
Je ne me sentis plus guidé par les haleurs:
Des Peaux-Rouges criards les avaient pris pour cibles,
Les ayant cloués nus aux poteaux de couleurs.

J'étais insoucieux de tous les équipages,
Porteur de blés flamands ou de cotons anglais.
Quand avec mes haleurs ont fini ces tapages,
Les Fleuves m'ont laissé descendre où je voulais.

Dans les clapotements furieux des marées,
Moi, l'autre hiver, plus sourd que les cerveaux d'enfants,
Je courus! Et les Péninsules démarrées
N'ont pas subi tohu-bohus plus triomphants.

La tempête a béni mes éveils maritimes.
Plus léger qu'un bouchon j'ai dansé sur les flots
Qu'on appelle rouleurs éternels de victimes,
Dix nuits, sans regretter l'oeil niais des falots!

Plus douce qu'aux enfants la chair des pommes sures,
L'eau verte pénétra ma coque de sapin
Et des taches de vins bleus et des vomissures
Me lava, dispersant gouvernail et grappin.

Et dès lors, je me suis baigné dans le Poème
De la Mer, infusé d'astres, et lactescent,
Dévorant les azurs verts; où, flottaison blême
Et ravie, un noyé pensif parfois descend;

The Drunken Boat

As I went gliding down rivers that looked on
Impassively, my guides and haulers gone —
The yelling Redskins had filled them with holes
And nailed them naked to barbershop poles —

What did I care about crews that traded
In wheat from Flanders or English cotton!
When the noises made by my haulers faded
The rivers let me wander freely on.

The winter before last, at the rising tide,
I, harder of hearing than children are,
Ran too! Peninsulas that have been untied
Do not endure a greater brouhaha.

I stood my night watches blessed by tempests,
Lighter than a cork I danced on the crests
Said to roll victims eternally . . . ten nights
Without needing a lighthouse's silly lights!

Sweeter than the flesh of a sour apple
To a child, green water breached my boat,
Washing off blue wine spots and puke. The grappling
Hook went sailing, the rudder was afloat.

Since then I have bathed in the starry lactescent
Poem of the sea, devouring green azure, where
A drowned body sometimes makes its descent,
Floating palely down with a glad, pensive air;

Où, teignant tout à coup les bleuités, délires
Et rhythmes lents sous les rutilements du jour,
Plus fortes que l'alcool, plus vastes que nos lyres,
Fermentent les rousseurs amères de l'amour!

Je sais les cieux crevant en éclairs, et les trombes
Et les ressacs et les courants: je sais le soir,
L'Aube exaltée ainsi qu'un peuple de colombes,
Et j'ai vu quelquefois ce que l'homme a cru voir!

J'ai vu le soleil bas, taché d'horreurs mystiques,
Illuminant de longs figements violets,
Pareils à des acteurs de drames très-antiques
Les flots roulant au loin leurs frissons de volets!

J'ai rêvé la nuit verte aux neiges éblouies,
Baiser montant aux yeux des mers avec lenteurs,
La circulation des sèves inouïes,
Et l'éveil jaune et bleu des phosphores chanteurs!

J'ai suivi, des mois pleins, pareille aux vacheries
Hystériques, la houle à l'assaut des récifs,
Sans songer que les pieds lumineux des Maries
Pussent forcer le mufle aux Océans poussifs!

J'ai heurté, savez-vous, d'incroyables Florides
Mêlant aux fleurs des yeux de panthères à peaux
D'hommes! Des arcs-en-ciel tendus comme des brides
Sous l'horizon des mers, à de glauques troupeaux!

J'ai vu fermenter les marais énormes, nasses
Où pourrit dans les joncs tout un Léviathan!
Des écroulements d'eaux au milieu des bonaces,
Et les lointains vers les gouffres cataractant!

Where suddenly staining the bluenesses, dreams
And slow rhythms under the day's red gleams,
Stronger than alcohol, vaster than our lyres,
I saw fermenting love's red, bitter fires!

I know waterspouts, skies that burst with light,
And undertows and currents. I have been
Where the dawn rises up like doves in flight.
And at times I have seen what men think they have seen!

I saw a horribly spotted, mystic sunset
Illuminating long clots of violet,
Like actors in some very ancient play
Waves that were rolling shutters far away!

I have dreamed a green night with dazzling snow,
A kiss rising slowly to the eyes of seas,
Circulation of unknown saps, blue and yellow
Of the morning song of phosphoruses!

For months I followed the swells as they beat
Like hysterical cows on reefs in the bay,
Nor dreamed that the Marys' luminous feet
Could force those wheezing sea snouts to obey!

I ran into Floridas that were incredible,
Flowers mingled with the eyes of panthers
With human skin! Rainbows stretched like a bridle
Beneath the sea's edge with its glaucous herds!

I have seen vast, fermenting marshes
Where leviathan rots among fishnet traps,
Still places where a waterfall rushes,
Distances pouring toward deep cataracts!

Glaciers, soleils d'argent, flots nacreux, cieux de braises!
Échouages hideux au fond des golfes bruns
Où les serpents géants dévorés des punaises
Choient, des arbres tordus, avec de noirs parfums!

J'aurais voulu montrer aux enfants ces dorades
Du flot bleu, ces poissons d'or, ces poissons chantants.
— Des écumes de fleurs ont bercé mes dérades
Et d'ineffables vents m'ont ailé par instants.

Parfois, martyr lassé des pôles et des zones,
La mer dont le sanglot faisait mon roulis doux
Montait vers moi ses fleurs d'ombre aux ventouses jaunes
Et je restais, ainsi qu'une femme à genoux . . .

Presque île, ballottant sur mes bords les querelles
Et les fientes d'oiseaux clabaudeurs aux yeux blonds.
Et je voguais, lorsqu'à travers mes liens frêles
Des noyés descendaient dormir, à reculons! . . .

Or moi, bateau perdu sous les cheveux des anses,
Jeté par l'ouragan dans l'éther sans oiseau,
Moi dont les Monitors et les voiliers des Hanses
N'auraient pas repêché la carcasse ivre d'eau;

Libre, fumant, monté de brumes violettes,
Moi qui trouais le ciel rougeoyant comme un mur
Qui porte, confiture exquise aux bons poètes,
Des lichens de soleil et des morves d'azur,

Qui courais, taché de lunules électriques,
Planche folle, escorté des hippocampes noirs,
Quand les juillets faisaient crouler à coups de triques
Les cieux ultramarins aux ardents entonnoirs;

Glaciers, siver suns, nacreous waves, red skies!
Hideous wrecks that have sunk to the bottom
Where gigantic serpents being eaten by lice
Fall from twisted branches with black perfume!

I would have liked to show children fishes
In blue waves, dolphins, goldfish, the fish that sings.
Flowers of foam have cradled my wishes
And ineffable winds have given me wings.

Sometimes a martyr, weary of zone and pole,
The sea whose sobbing made me gently roll
Brought me her yellow-rooted flowers of darkness,
And I was rapt, like a woman on her knees . . .

A peninsula, cliffs white with the droppings
Of birds with shining eyes that scream or gossip.
And I was voyaging, when through my lines came drifting
Drowned men, sinking backwards down, to sleep!

Now I was a boat being driven by the gale
To entangling bays, into a birdless sky.
Neither Monitor nor Hanseatic sail
Would have saved my skin, so drunk on water was I;

Free, smoking, a violet fog overhead,
I who drove through the red sky like a wall
That bears the jam good poets like on their bread,
Mucus of azure, lichens where sunbeams fall,

Who ran, with little electric moon spots,
Wild plank, with my black sea horse escorts,
When Julys hammered with blows like cudgels
Ultramarine skies with burning funnels;

Moi qui tremblais, sentant geindre à cinquante lieues
Le rut des Béhémots et les Maelstroms épais,
Fileur éternel des immobilités bleues,
Je regrette l'Europe aux anciens parapets!

J'ai vu des archipels sidéraux! et des îles
Dont les cieux délirants sont ouverts au vogueur:
— Est-ce en ces nuits sans fonds qu tu dors et t'exiles,
Million d'oiseaux d'or, ô future Vigueur? —

Mais, vrai, j'ai trop pleuré! Les Aubes sont navrantes.
Toute lune est atroce et tout soleil amer:
L'âcre amour m'a gonflé de torpeurs enivrantes.
O que ma quille éclate! O que j'aille à la mer!

Si je désire une eau d'Europe, c'est la flache
Noire et froide où vers le crépuscule embaumé
Un enfant accroupi plein de tristesses, lâche
Un bateau frêle comme un papillon de mai.

Je ne puis plus, baigné de vos langueurs, ô lames,
Enlever leur sillage aux porteurs de cotons,
Ni traverser l'orgueil des drapeaux et des flammes,
Ni nager sous les yeux horribles des pontons.

I who at fifty leagues would shudder
At maelstroms and Behemoth's nuptials,
Eternal spinner of the still azure,
Long for old Europe and her castle walls!

I saw astral archipelagos, isles
With delirious skies for the voyager.
In those bottomless nights do you sleep out your exiles,
Million golden birds, O future vigor?

But it's true, I have wept too much! Dawns are heart-
        breaking,
Moons atrocious, the sun bitter. Acrid love swells me
With torpors that are intoxicating.
O may my keel split! I go into the sea!

If I want any water of Europe, it is
The black, cold puddle at the fragrant end of day
Where a child filled with sadness squats and releases
A boat as frail as a butterfly in May.

I can no longer, waves, bathed in your languor,
Follow in the wake of the cotton bearers,
Or traverse the pride of flame and flag, or
Swim under the prison ships' horrible stares.

Voyelles

A noir, E blanc, I rouge, U vert, O bleu: voyelles,
Je dirai quelque jour vos naissances latentes:
A, noir corset velu des mouches éclatantes
Qui bombinent autour des puanteurs cruelles,

Golfes d'ombre; E, candeurs des vapeurs et des tentes,
Lances des glaciers fiers, rois blancs, frissons d'ombelles;
I, pourpres, sang craché, rire des lèvres belles
Dans la colère ou les ivresses pénitentes;

U, cycles, vibrements divins des mers virides,
Paix des pâtis semés d'animaux, paix des rides
Que l'alchimie imprime aux grands fronts studieux;

O, suprême Clairon plein des strideurs étranges,
Silences traversés des Mondes et des Anges:
— O l'Oméga, rayon violet de Ses Yeux!

Vowels

A black, E white, I red, U green, O blue: vowels,
Some day I shall speak of your genesis:
A, corset black and hairy with flies
Heaped to bursting on atrocious smells,

Dark gulfs; E, candor of steamship and tent,
Spears of proud glaciers, white kings, shivering umbels;
I, purples, spat blood, beautiful lips
That laugh in anger or drunkenly repent;

U, cycles, divine vibrations of green seas,
Peace of pastures dotted with animals,
Lines that alchemy prints in studious faces;

O, supreme trumpet full of strange, harsh sounds,
Silences traversed by worlds and angels;
O Omega, His eyes' violet rays!

Une Saison en enfer [Extraits]

DÉLIRES: II ALCHIMIE DU VERBE

À moi. L'histoire d'une de mes folies.

Depuis longtemps je me vantais de posséder tous les paysages possibles, et trouvais dérisoires les célébrités de la peinture et de la poésie moderne.

J'aimais les peintures idiotes, dessus de portes, décors, toiles de saltimbanques, enseignes, enluminures populaires; la littérature démodée, latin d'église, livres érotiques sans orthographe, romans de nos aïeules, contes de fées, petits livres de l'enfance, opéras vieux, refrains niais, rhythmes naïfs.

Je rêvais croisades, voyages de découvertes dont on n'a pas de relations, républiques sans histoires, guerres de religion étouffées, révolutions de moeurs, déplacements de races et de continents: je croyais à tous les enchantements.

J'inventai la couleur des voyelles! — *A* noir, *E* blanc, *I* rouge, *O* bleu, *U* vert. — Je réglai la forme et le mouvement de chaque consonne, et, avec des rhythmes instinctifs, je me flattai d'inventer un verbe poétique accessible, un jour ou l'autre, à tous les sens. Je réservais la traduction.

Ce fut d'abord une étude. J'écrivais des silences, des nuits, je notais l'inexprimable. Je fixais des vertiges.

*

La vieillerie poétique avait une bonne part dans mon alchimie du verbe.

Je m'habituai à l'hallucination simple: je voyais très-franchement une mosquée à la place d'une usine, une école de tambours faite par des anges, des calèches sur les routes du ciel, un salon au fond d'un lac; les monstres, les mystères; un titre de vaudeville dressait des épouvantes devant moi.

A Season in Hell [Selections]

DELIRIOUS: II ALCHEMY OF LANGUAGE

My turn. The story of one of my crazy spells.

For a long time I had prided myself on possessing all possible landscapes, and found the celebrities of painting and modern poetry ridiculous.

I liked idiotic paintings, door panels, stage scenery, backdrops for acrobats, signs, illuminations, literature out of fashion, church Latin, erotic books with missspellings, the novels of our grandparents, fairytales, little books for children, old operas, simple songs, naive rhythms.

I dreamed of crusades, voyages of discovery of which there are no records, republics with no history, forgotten wars of religion, revolutions in customs, movements of races and continents. I believed in all enchantments.

I invented the color of vowels! *A* black, *E* white, *I* red, *O* blue, *U* green. I set the form and movement of each consonant and, with instinctive rhythms, I flattered myself that I had invented a poetic language that, one day or another, would be accessible to all the senses. I reserved the translation rights.

At first it was a subject of study. I wrote of silences, nights, I made notes of the inexpressible. I standardized the vertigos.

*

Old ideas about poetry played a considerable part in my alchemy of language.

I practiced simple hallucination: I saw very clearly a mosque in place of a factory, a school of drummers made up of angels, carriages on the roads of the sky, a drawing room at the bottom of a lake; monsters, mysteries. The title of a vaudeville raised terrors in front of me.

Puis j'expliquai mes sophismes magiques avec l'hallucination des mots!

Je finis par trouver sacré le désordre de mon esprit. J'étais oisif, en proie à une lourde fièvre: j'enviais la félicité des bêtes, — les chenilles, qui représentent l'innocence des limbes, les taupes, le sommeil de la virginité!

Mon caractère s'aigrissait. Je disais adieu au monde dans d'espèces de romances. . . .

Then I explained my magic tricks with the hallucination of language!

I ended by finding my spiritual disorder sacred. I was idle, prey to a clinging fever. I envied the happiness of animals — caterpillars that represent the innocence of limbos, moles, the sleep of virginity!

My character became embittered. I said goodbye to the world in ballads of a kind. . . .

Vies III

Dans un grenier où je fus enfermé à douze ans j'ai connu le monde, j'ai illustré la comédie humaine. Dans un cellier j'ai appris l'histoire. A quelque fête de nuit dans une cité du Nord, j'ai rencontré toutes les femmes des anciens peintres. Dans un vieux passage à Paris on m'a enseigné les sciences classiques. Dans une magnifique demeure cernée par l'Orient entier j'ai accompli mon immense oeuvre et passé mon illustre retraite. J'ai brassé mon sang. Mon devoir m'est remis. Il ne faut même plus songer à cela. Je suis réellement d'outre-tombe, et pas de commissions.

Lives III

In an attic where I was shut when I was twelve I learned about the world. I illustrated the human comedy. In a cellar I learned history. At some evening feast in a city of the North I met all the women of ancient painters. In an old passageway in Paris I was taught the classic sciences. In a magnificent dwelling surrounded by the entire Orient I finished my immense work and spent my illustrious retirement. I warmed up my blood. My assignment has been handed back. I needn't even think about that any longer. I am really a voice from beyond the grave, and at liberty.

Ouvriers

O cette chaude matinée de février. Le Sud inopportun vint relever nos souvenirs d'indigents absurdes, notre jeune misère.

Henrika avait une jupe de coton à carreau blanc et brun, qui a dû être portée au siècle dernier, un bonnet à rubans, et un foulard de soie. C'était bien plus triste qu'un deuil. Nous faisions un tour dans la banlieue. Le temps était couvert, et ce vent du Sud excitait toutes les vilaines odeurs des jardins ravagés et des prés desséchés.

Cela ne devait pas fatiguer ma femme au même point que moi. Dans une flache laissée par l'inondation du mois précédent à un sentier assez haut elle me fit remarquer de très petits poissons.

La ville, avec sa fumée et ses bruits de métiers, nous suivait très loin dans les chemins. O l'autre monde, l'habitation bénie par le ciel et les ombrages! Le Sud me rappelait les misérables incidents de mon enfance, mes désespoirs d'été, l'horrible quantité de force et de science que le sort a toujours éloignée de moi. Non! nous ne passerons pas l'été dans cet avare pays où nous ne serons jamais que des orphelins fiancés. Je veux que ce bras durci ne traîne plus *une chère image.*

Workers

Oh that warm February morning! The unseasonable South came to renew the memories of absurd poor people like us, our wretched youth.

Henrika had a cotton skirt with black and brown checks that must have been worn in the last century, a hat with ribbons, and a silk scarf. This was much sadder than mourning. We were taking a walk in the suburbs. It was overcast and this South wind called up all the nasty smells from ravaged gardens and dried up meadows.

That must not have tired my wife as much as me. In a pool left by the flood a month ago on a path that was quite high up she showed me some very small fishes.

The town with its smoke and sounds of work followed us very far on the roads. Oh the other world, the habitation blessed by sky and shade! The South brought back to my mind the miserable incidents of my childhood, my despairs in summer, the horrible amount of strength and knowledge that fate has always kept far from me. No! We shall not spend the summer in that miserly country where we shall never be anything more than orphans who are engaged. I don't want this hardened arm to drag *a dear image* along any more.

Marine

Les chars d'argent et de cuivre —
Les proues d'acier et d'argent —
Battent l'écume, —
Soulèvent les souches des ronces.
Les courants de la lande,
Et les ornières immenses du reflux,
Filent circulairement vers l'est,
Vers les piliers de la forêt,
Vers les fûts de la jetée,
Dont l'angle est heurté par des tourbillons de lumière.

Marine

The chariots of silver and copper —
The prows of steel and silver —
Beat the foam —
Tear at the roots of brambles.
The offshore currents,
And the huge paths of the ebbing tide,
Circle toward the East,
Toward the pillars of the forest,
Toward the timbers of the pier,
Where it is bending wounded with whirlpools of light.

Mouvement

Le mouvement de lacet sur la berge des chutes du fleuve,
Le gouffre à l'étambot,
La célérité de la rampe,
L'énorme passade du courant,
Mènent par les lumières inouïes
Et la nouveauté chimique
Les voyageurs entourés des trombes du val
Et du strom.

Ce sont les conquérants du monde
Cherchant la fortune chimique personnelle;
Le sport et le comfort voyagent avec eux;
Ils emmènent l'éducation
Des races, des classes et des bêtes, sur ce Vaisseau.
Repos et vertige
A la lumière diluvienne,
Aux terribles soirs d'étude.

Car de la causerie parmi les appareils, — le sang; les
        fleurs, le feu, les bijoux —
Des comptes agités à ce bord fuyard,
— On voit, roulant comme une digue au delà de la route
        hydraulique motrice,
Monstrueux, s'éclairant sans fin, — leur stock d'études;
Eux chassés dans l'extase harmonique
Et l'héroisme de la découverte.
Aux accidents atmosphériques les plus surprenants
Un couple de jeunesse s'isole sur l'arche,
— Est-ce ancienne sauvagerie qu'on pardonne?
Et chante et se poste.

Progress

The flicking shoelace of falls along the bank,
The whirlpool at the rudder,
The swiftness of the handrail,
The huge passing of the current,
Are bringing by unheard-of lights
And the latest chemistry
Travelers among waterspouts of the valley
And the stream.

These are the conquerors of the world
Seeking a personal chemical fortune;
Sport and comfort travel with them;
They are bringing the education
Of races, classes and animals, on this Vessel.
Repose and vertigo
To the diluvian light,
The terrible nights of study.

For, from talk among apparatuses — blood,
    flowers, fire, jewels —
Reports waved at this flying rail,
— You see, rolling like an embankment beyond the
    hydraulic motor road,
Monstrous, endlessly lighted — their stock of studies;
They are driven into harmonious ecstasy
And the heroism of discovery.
Among the most surprising atmospheric discoveries
A youthful couple isolate themselves on the ark,
— Is some ancient savagery being pardoned?
And sing and take their station.

Jules Laforgue

Complainte des pianos

Menez l'âme que les Lettres ont bien nourrie,
Les pianos, les pianos, dans les quartiers aisés,
Premiers soirs, sans pardessus, chaste flânerie,
Aux complaintes des nerfs incompris ou brisés.

Ces infants, à quoi rêvent-elles,
Dans les ennuis des ritournelles?

"Préaux des soirs,
Christs des dortoirs!

Tu t'en vas et tu nous laisses,
Tu nous laiss's et tu t'en vas,
Défaire et refaire ses tresses,
Broder d'éternels canevas."

Jolie ou vague? triste ou sage? encore pure?
O jours, tout m'est égal? ou, monde, moi je veux?
Et si vierge, du moins, de la bonne blessure,
Sachant quels gras couchants ont les plus blancs aveux?

Mon Dieu, à quoi donc rêvent-elles?
A des Roland, à des dentelles?

"Coeurs en prison,
Lentes saisons!

Tu t'en vas et tu nous quittes,
Tu nous quitt's et tu t'en vas!
Couvents gris, choeurs de Sulamites,
Surs nos seins nuls croisons nos bras."

Complaint of the Pianos
YOU HEAR IN BETTER NEIGHBORHOODS

Conduct the well read, carefully nurtured soul,
Pianos, pianos, through a better neighborhood
On spring evenings, no overcoat, for a chaste stroll,
To nerves that are shattered or misunderstood.

Those children, of what do they dream
With each sad repeat of the theme?

"Games at twilight,
Christs at night.

You are going away, you are leaving,
Leaving us and going away,
Redoing our hair and reweaving
The same stories every day."

Pretty or plain? Sad or wise? Still untouchable?
O life, what does it matter? World, what is it to me?
If a virgin, at least not too vulnerable,
Knowing what the end of fine avowals may be.

What are they dreaming of? The face
Of some Roland? Satin and lace?

"Hearts in prison,
A slow season!

You are going away and leaving us,
You are leaving and going away,
Gray convents, a Shulamite chorus,
Arms crossed on our breasts piously."

Laforgue / 149

Fatales clés de l'être un beau jour apparues;
Psitt! aux hérédités en ponctuels ferments,
Dans le bal incessant de nos étranges rues;
Ah! pensionnats, théâtres, journaux, romans!

Allez, stériles ritournelles,
La vie est vraie et criminelle.

"Rideaux tirés,
Peut-on entrer?

Tu t'en vas et tu nous laisses,
Tu nous laiss's et tu t'en vas,
La source des frais rosiers baisse,
Vraiment! Et lui qui ne vient pas . . ."

Il viendra! Vous serez les pauvres coeurs en faute,
Fiancés au remords comme aux essais sans fond,
Et les suffisants coeurs cossus, n'ayant d'autre hôte
Qu'un train-train pavoisé d'estime et de chiffons.

Mourir? peut-être brodent elles,
Pour un oncle à dot, des bretelles?

"Jamais! Jamais!
Si tu savais!

Tu t'en vas et tu nous quittes,
Tu nous quitt's et tu t'en vas,
Mais tu nous reviendras bien vite
Guérir mon beau mal, n'est-ce pas?"

Et c'est vrai! l'Idéal les fait divaguer toutes,
Vigne bohême, même en ces quartiers aisés.

Fatal keys of being one day having shown,
Psst! to timely fermenting inheritances
At the ball in our streets all the time going on,
Ah! boarding schools, theaters, journals, true romances!

Close the piano, that will be all,
Life is real, life is criminal.

"A drawn curtain . . .
May one come in?

You are leaving us, you are going,
And the spring that waters the tree
That bears roses is flowing
More slowly. And where is he?"

He will come! Poor hearts, yours will be the sin,
Engaged to remorse as to an endless test,
You will have money, and nothing else coming in
But routine, status, and being well dressed.

You could die. Or else knit a pair
Of socks for an uncle to wear?

"I won't! They can't
Make me! I shan't!

You are going away, you are leaving,
Leaving us and going away.
You'll be back, won't you, one evening,
To cure my refined malady?"

Idealistic! It drives all of them gaga,
Even in these neighborhoods . . . the elixir

La vie est là; le pur flacon des vives gouttes
Sera, *comme il convient*, d'eau propre baptisé.

Aussi, bientôt, se joueront-elles
De plus exactes ritournelles.

"Seul oreiller!
Mur familier!

Tu t'en vas et tu nous laisses,
Tu nous laiss's et tu t'en vas.
Que ne suis-je morte à la messe!
O mois, ô linges, ô repas!"

Of life. But the strong wine of bohemia
Will be mixed, "as is fitting," with holy water.

And soon they'll be turning the sheets
Of more explicit repeats.

"Only pillow!
Wall that I know!

You are leaving us, you will pass,
Leaving us and going away.
Why didn't I die during Mass!
O linens, O meals, every day!"

Autre Complainte

DE LORD PIERROT

Celle qui doit me mettre au courant de la Femme!
Nous lui dirons d'abord, de mon air le moins froid:
"La somme des angles d'un triangle, chère âme,
        "Est égale à deux droits."

Et si ce cri lui part: "Dieu de Dieu! que je t'aime!"
— "Dieu reconnaîtra les siens." Ou piquée au vif:
— "Mes claviers ont du coeur, tu seras mon seul thème."
        Moi: "Tout est relatif."

De tous ses yeux, alors! se sentant trop banale:
"Ah! tu ne m'aimes pas; tant d'autres sont jaloux!"
Et moi, d'un oeil qui vers l'Inconscient s'emballe:
        "Merci, pas mal; et vous?"

— "Jouons au plus fidèle!" — "A quoi bon, ô Nature!"
"Autant à qui perd gagne!" Alors, autre couplet:
—"Ah! tu te lasseras le premier, j'en suis sûre . . ."
        "Après vous, s'il vous plaît."

Enfin, si, par un soir, elle meurt dans mes livres,
Douce; feignant de n'en pas croire encor mes yeux,
J'aurai un: "Ah çà, mais, nous avions De Quoi vivre!
        "C'était donc sérieux?"

Another Complaint

The one who keeps me informed how a woman feels,
I shall say to her first, with my least frigid air,
"The sum of the angles of a triangle equals
      Two right angles, my dear."

And if this cry escapes her: "God, how I love you!"
"God rewards his own." Or sadly contemplative:
"Keyboards have a heart. My theme is always of you."
      I: "All is relative."

With blazing eyes, aware of being tedious:
"Ah, you don't love me! But so many others do!"
I with an eye racing toward the Unconscious:
      "Well enough, thanks. And you?"

"Let's see which can be more faithful." "What's the idea?"
"The one who loses wins." Then another couplet:
"Ah, you would be the first to grow tired, I swear. . ."
      "Go ahead. Place your bet."

Finally, still pretending that I don't believe,
If one evening she should die, and not make a fuss,
I shall say, "How so? We had what it takes to live!
      Then it was serious?"

Solo de lune

Je fume, étalé face au ciel,
Sur l'impériale de la diligence,
Ma carcasse est cahotée, mon âme danse
Comme un Ariel;
Sans miel, sans fiel, ma belle âme danse,
O routes, coteaux, ô fumées, ô vallons,
Ma belle âme, ah! récapitulons.

Nous nous aimions comme deux fous,
On s'est quitté sans en parler,
Un spleen me tenait exilé,
Et ce spleen me venait de tout. Bon.

Ses yeux disaient: "Comprenez-vous?
Pourquoi ne comprenez-vous pas?"
Mais nul n'a voulu faire le premier pas,
Voulant trop tomber *ensemble* à genoux.
(Comprenez-vous?)

Où est-elle à cette heure?
Peut-être qu'elle pleure . . .
Où est-elle à cette heure?
Oh! du moins, soigne-toi, je t'en conjure!

O fraîcheur des bois le long de la route,
O châle de mélancolie, toute âme est un peu aux écoutes.
Que ma vie
Fait envie!
Cette impériale de diligence tient de la magie.

Solo by Moonlight

I am smoking, sprawled beneath the sky,
On the roof of the carriage,
My carcass is jolted, my soul dances
Like an Ariel;
Without marriage or rage, my fine soul dances,
O roads, hills, smoke, O valleys,
My lovely soul, ah! let us sum up.

We were both madly in love, and
I left, and didn't speak of it.
I was depressed, and came away.
Everything was depressing me. Really.

Her eyes said, "Do you understand?
Why don't you understand?" But neither
Wanted to take the first step,
Wanting to fall on our knees together.
(Do you understand?)

Where is she at this hour?
No doubt feeling blue,
Perhaps crying. Where are you?
O at least take care of yourself, I urge you!

How fresh are the woods along the road!
Shawl of melancholy, there's a listener in every soul.
My life must be
A thing to envy,
On this magical carriage, imperial me!

Accumulons l'irréparable!
Renchérissons sur notre sort!
Les étoiles sont plus nombreuses que le sable
Des mers où d'autres ont vu se baigner son corps;
Tout n'en va pas moins à la mort.
Y a pas de port.

Des ans vont passer là-dessus,
On s'endurcira chacun pour soi,
Et bien souvent et déjà je m'y vois,
On se dira: "Si j'avais su . . ."
Mais mariés de même, ne se fût-on pas dit
"Si j'avais su, si j'avais su! . . ."?
Ah! rendez-vous maudit!
Ah! mon coeur sans issue! . . .
Je me suis mal conduit.

Maniaques de bonheur,
Donc, que ferons-nous? Moi de mon âme,
Elle de sa faillible jeunesse?
O viellissante pécheresse,
Oh! que de soirs je vais me rendre infâme
En ton honneur!

Ses yeux clignaient: "Comprenez-vous?
Pourquoi ne comprenez-vous pas?"
Mais nul n'a fait le premier pas
Pour tomber ensemble à genoux. Ah! . . .

La lune se lève,
O route en grand rêve! . . .
On a dépassé les filatures, les scieries,
Plus que les bornes kilométriques,
De petits nuages d'un rose de confiserie,
Cependant qu'un fin croissant de lune se lève,

Let us keep what cannot be undone,
Bid higher than our fate!
The stars are more numerous than the sand
Of the seas in which others have gone.
All goes to death equally, and
There is no haven.

Years will pass over it,
Each of us will harden.
Often, I can already see it,
One will say, "If I had known . . ."
But if one married, wouldn't one say,
"If I had known, if I had known! . . ." ?
Ah, that meeting was unlucky!
Ah, my heart with no exit!
I have behaved badly.

Hell-bent on happiness,
Then what shall we do? I with my soul,
She with her youthful weakness?
O you aging sinner,
How many evenings shall I make myself foul
In your honor!

Her eyes said, "Do you understand?
Why don't you?" But neither
Would take the first step
To fall on our knees together.

The moon is rising,
O road of the big dream!
Past the textile mills, the sawmills,
The milestones, so it goes,
Little clouds of a candy rose,
While a fine crescent moon is rising

O route de rêve, ô nulle musique . . .
Dans ces bois de pins où depuis
Le commencement du monde
Il fait toujours nuit,
Que de chambres propres et profondes!
Oh! pour un soir d'enlèvement!
Et je les peuple et je m'y vois,
Et c'est un beau couple d'amants,
Qui gesticulent hors la loi.

Et je passe et les abandonne,
Et me recouche face au ciel.
La route tourne, je suis Ariel,
Nul ne m'attend, je ne vais chez personne.
Je n'ai que l'amitié des chambres d'hôtel.

La lune se lève,
O route en grand rêve,
O route sans terme,
Voici le relais,
Où l'on allume les lanternes,
Où l'on boit un verre de lait,
Et fouette postillon,
Dans le chant des grillons,
Sous les étoiles de juillet.

O clair de lune,
Noce de feux de Bengale noyant mon infortune,
Les ombres des peupliers sur la route . . .
Le gave qui s'écoute . . .
Qui s'écoute chanter . . .
Dans ces inondations du fleuve du Léthé . . .

O solo de lune,
Vous défiez ma plume,

To non-existent music, road of the dream.
In these pine woods that have been
Since the world's beginning
It is always night.
The rooms are large and clean.
O why don't I just carry her off!
I can just see the people,
And the lovers, a fine couple
Of outlaws, gesticulating.

And I leave them and pass on,
And lie back, looking at the sky.
The road turns, I am Ariel,
Nothing waits for me, I am meeting no one.
My only friends are the rooms of hotels.

The moon is rising.
O road of the big dream,
Road that has no end . . .
Here is the river bank
Where the lanterns are lit,
And a glass of milk is drunk,
And the postilion cracks his whip,
To the song of the cricket
Beneath the stars of July.

O light of the moon,
Wedding of Bengal lights drowning my misfortune,
Shadows of poplars on the road,
Sound of the mountain spring
That seems to sing
In its falls of the river Lethe . . .

O solo by moonlight,
You defy my pen.

Oh! cette nuit sur la route;
O étoiles, vous êtes à faire peur,
Vous y êtes toutes! toutes!
O fugacité de cette heure . . .
Oh! qu'il y eût moyen
De m'en garder l'âme pour l'automne qui vient! . . .

Voici qu'il fait très, très frais,
Oh! si à la même heure,
Elle va de même le long des forêts,
Noyer son infortune
Dans les noces du clair de lune! . . .
(Elle aime tant errer tard!)
Elle aura oublié son foulard,
Elle va prendre mal, vu la beauté de l'heure!
Oh! soigne-toi, je t'en conjure!
Oh! je ne veux plus entendre cette toux!

Ah! que ne suis-je tombé à tes genoux!
Ah! que n'as-tu défailli à mes genoux!
J'eusse été le modèle des époux!
Comme le frou-frou de ta robe est le modèle des frou-frou.

To be on the road that night!
Stars, you fill me with terror,
There you are, all of you!
O fleetingness of that hour!
If there were only a way
To guard my soul against the coming autumn.

It is cool now, very cool.
What if at the same hour
She goes by way of the woods
To drown her misfortune
In the wedding of moonlight?
(She likes so much to walk late.)
She will have forgotten her scarf,
She will be ill, due to the beauty of the hour.
O take care of yourself, I urge you!
I don't want to hear that cough again.

Why didn't I fall on my knees!
Why didn't you? I would have been
A model husband. As the frou-frou
Of your dress is the model of frou-frous.

Légende

Armorial d'anémie!
Psautier d'automne!
Offertoire de tout mon ciboire de bonheur et de génie
A cette hostie si féminine,
Et si petite toux sèche maligne,
Qu'on voit aux jours déserts, en inconnue,
Sertie en de cendreuses toilettes qui sentent déjà l'hiver,
Se fuir le long des cris surhumains de la mer.

Grandes amours, oh! qu'est-ce encor? . . .

En tout cas, des lèvres sans façon,
Des lèvres déflorées,
Et quoique mortes aux chansons,
Apres encore à la curée.
Mais les yeux d'une âme qui s'est bel et bien cloîtrée.
Enfin, voici qu'elle m'honore de ses confidences.
J'en souffre plus qu'elle ne pense.

— "Mais, chère perdue, comment votre esprit éclairé
Et le stylet d'acier de vos yeux infaillibles,
N'ont-ils pas su percer à jour la mise en frais
De cet économique et passager bellâtre?"

— "Il vient le premier; j'étais seule près de l'âtre;
Son cheval attaché à la grille
Hennissait en désespéré . . ."

— "C'est touchant (pauvre fille)
Et puis après?
Oh! regardez, là-bas, cet épilogue sous couleur de couchant;

Legend

Armorial of anemia!
Psalter of autumn!
Offering my genius and luck, the full ciborium,
To that so feminine hostess
And the dry, malignant cough
You visit on empty days, at an obscure address,
Bent over the ashes of her wardrobe as winter approaches,
Escaping the reach of the sea's superhuman cries.

Great loves, where are they now?

They were simple in any case:
Lips that needed no introduction,
Though the song is dead and gone
Still eager for the chase.
But the eyes of a beautiful, well cloistered soul.
Finally, she is taking me into her confidence.
It is making me suffer more than she can guess.

"But, my poor dear, a person of your intelligence
And your eyes that can cut like steel,
How could they not see through the pretense
Of an opportunist, a goodlooking heel?"

"He was the first. I was alone, over there.
His horse, tied up at the gate,
Was whinnying with despair."

"Poor girl, that's touching!
And then?
Oh, look at that epilogue disguised as a sunset!

Et puis, vrai,
Remarquez que dès l'automne, l'automne!
Les casinos,
Qu'on abandonne
Remisent leur piano;
Hier l'orchestre attaqua
Sa dernière polka,
Hier la dernière fanfare
Sanglotait vers les gares . . ."

(Oh! comme elle est maigrie!
Que va-elle devenir?
Durcissez, durcissez,
Vous, caillots de souvenir!)

— "Allons, les poteaux télégraphiques
Dans les grisailles de l'exil
Vous serviront de pleureuses de funérailles;
Moi, c'est la saison qui veut que je m'en aille,
Voic l'hiver qui vient.
Ainsi soit-il.
Ah! soignez-vous! Portez-vous bien.

Assez! assez!
C'est toi qui as commencé!

Tais-toi! Vos moindres clins d'yeux sont des parjures.
Laisse! Avec vous autres rien ne dure.
Va, je te l'assure,
Si je t'aimais, ce serait par gageure.

Tais-toi! tais-toi!
On n'aimc qu'unc fois!"

Ah! voici que l'on compte enfin avec moi!

Then, it's the custom,
At the first touch of autumn . . . autumn!
The casinos
That have been abandoned
Put away their pianos.
Yesterday the orchestra
Attacked its last polka.
Yesterday the last fanfare
Went sobbing to the stations. . . ."

(Oh, how thin she has grown!
What will become of her?
You clots of memory,
Harden, be as hard as stone!)

"Come now! The telegraph poles
In the graynesses of exile
Will serve you as mourners at funerals.
As for me, it is the season that wants me to go.
Winter will soon be here.
Then so be it.
Ah, take care of yourself! Take care.

Enough, enough!
You are the one who started it!

Don't speak! The slightest blink of your eyes is a lie.
Leave off! With all of you nothing is sure.
Go! If I loved you, I swear
It would have to be on a bet.

Be quiet! Be quiet!
One loves only once!"

And that is how they settle my accounts!

Ah! ce n'est plus l'automne, alors,
Ce n'est plus l'exil.
C'est la douceur des légendes, de l'âge d'or,
Des légendes des Antigones,
Douceur qui fait qu'on se demande:
"Quand donc cela se passait-il?"

C'est des légendes, c'est des gammes perlées,
Qu'on m'a tout enfant enseignées.
Oh! rien, vous dis-je, des estampes,
Les bêtes de la terre et les oiseaux du ciel
Enguirlandant les majuscules d'un missel,
Il n'y a pas là tant de quoi saigner.

Saigner? moi pétri du plus pur limon de Cybèle!
Moi qui lui eusse été dans tout l'art des Adams
Des Édens aussi hyperboliquement fidèle
Que l'est le soleil chaque soir envers l'Occident!...

Ah, then it is no longer autumn
Or exile, but the sweetness
Of legends, once more the age of gold . . .
Legends about Antigones,
A sweetness that makes one wonder,
"Now when did that take place?"

It is legendary, like the stories I was told,
All the pearls of the nursery.
Oh, I tell you, in none of the pictures
Of birds of the sky and animals
In the missal engarlanding the capitals
Is there anything that can make you bleed like this.

Bleed? I am covered in the pure mud of Cybele!
I who would have been, with all the art of Adams
In Edens, as true to her, speaking in hyperbole,
As the sun every evening to the West.

Léon-Paul Fargue

Kiosques

En vain la mer fait le voyage
Du fond de l'horizon pour baiser tes pieds sages.
    Tu les retires
                Toujours à temps.

Tu te tais, je ne dis rien,
Nous n'en pensons pas plus, peut-être.
Mais les lucioles de proche en proche
Ont tiré leur lampe de poche
Tout exprès pour faire briller
Sur tes yeux calmes cette larme
Que je fus un jour obligé de boire.
La mer est bien assez salée.

Une méduse blonde et bleue
Qui veut s'instruire en s'attristant
Traverse les étages bondés de la mer,
Nette et claire comme un ascenseur,
Et décoiffe sa lampe à fleur d'eau
Pour te voir feindre sur le sable
Avec ton ombrelle, en pleurant,
Les trois cas d'égalité des triangles.

Kiosks

In vain the sea makes the voyage
From the far horizon to kiss your feet so sage.
      You draw them back
                    Always in time.

You are silent, I say nothing.
Perhaps we no longer think of it.
But the flashlights of the fireflies
Are coming closer. They wink
Just to illuminate
The tear in your calm eyes
That I one day was obliged to drink.
The sea has enough salt in it.

A blond and blue medusa
That wants to learn by being sad
Crosses the moving floors of the sea,
Neat and clear as an elevator,
And removes its lamp on the surface
To see you drawing in the sand
With your umbrella, crying,
Three cases of triangles being equal.

La gare se dressait contre une forteresse

La gare se dressait contre une forteresse en fête aux
portes flambantes. On entendait gronder l'orgue. —
La guerre était déclarée.— Depuis longtemps, les miens
se détournaient de moi. — Depuis quelques heures,
l'aimée n'était plus avec moi sous ces arbres. La veille,
on m'avait condamné à rester seul . . . Et j'avais encore
une côte à gravir.

J'avais dû me séparer de mon vieux cheval. Il
m'avait longtemps cherché dans la nuit, frappant du
sabot contre les massifs du palais des Ducs. — L'aube
parut. Je rôdais sur une place bruyante où les départs
posaient leurs sacs. Des machines écornées contre un
bois que longeait la route se découpaient sur un ciel en
larmes.

Tout le paysage, autour de la gare et du fort, était
d'eau et d'herbes. Des pêcheurs vigilants et tristes sur-
veillaient le cours du ciel et du fleuve.

On allait passer les ponts vers la guerre.

Nous sortîmes par une fête foraine, dans une odeur
d'acétylène, de graisse d'armes, de fusils et de gares,
avec des souvenirs de chansons parisiennes, de catastro-
phes, et d'amour frémissant sous des temps couverts. . .
On plaçait déjà des hommes à leur poste. — Ils demeu-
raient là, droits et immobiles, chacun contenant sa peine
comme un vase une plante sombre. — Ils suivaient par-
fois du regard un ami qui vous abandonne, et tous les
yeux se perdre au tournant de la route. Et ils restent là,
droits et immobiles, en attente au bord de l'inconnu qui
murmure, sous le vertige du ciel où déjà passaient des
rougeurs . . .

The Station Stood Against a Fort

The station stood against a fort lit up with blazing doors.
You heard the organ grumbling. — War was declared.
— My friends and relatives had long parted from me.
— It had been some hours since the one I loved had
been with me under those trees. The evening before, I
had been condemned to be alone. And I still had a hill to
climb.

I had to separate from my old horse. He had looked
for me in the night for a long time, striking with his hoof
against the foundations of the Ducal Palace. Dawn
appeared. I was wandering in an open space where the
departures were leaving their bags. Against a wood that
ran beside the road some battered machines were out-
lined on a weeping sky.

The whole countryside around the station and fort
was of water and grass. Some vigilant, sad fishermen
were watching the changes of the sky and river.

We were going to cross the bridges to the war.

We came out on a fairground feast, a smell of acety-
lene, of gun grease, of rifles and stations, with memo-
ries of Paris songs, catastrophes, and love shivering
beneath an overcast. Men were already being placed at
their posts. They remained there, straight and motion-
less, each containing his trouble as a vase contains a dark
plant. Sometimes they followed with a look a friend who
was abandoning them, all eyes losing touch at a bend in
the road. And they remain there, straight and motion-
less, waiting at the edge of the murmuring unknown,
beneath the vertigo of the sky where red streaks were
already flickering.

Fargue / *175*

Les mots, les mots spéciaux

Les mots, les mots spéciaux qu'elle avait faits pour moi, je l'écoutais les dire à l'Autre.

J'entends sonner son sabre sur le bois du lit. J'entendrai toutes les paroles.

Quand il l'embrasse sur les yeux, là, tout au bord de l'île où s'allume une lampe, il sent ses paupières battre sous sa bouche comme la tête d'un oiseau qu'on a pris et qui a peur.

Il s'attarde au réseau des vaisseaux délicats comme l'ombre légère d'une plante marine.

Il caresse de tout son corps les seins qu'envenime l'amour.

J'entendrai tout, dans ce couloir aux minces cloisons, tout blanc de fenêtres, avec cette odeur fade et sucrée de la boiserie que le soleil chauffe.

Quelquefois j'attendais longtemps devant sa porte et dans un décor si connu qu'il m'écoeurait. J'y frappais. J'entendais le vide bâiller derrière. On marchait bien vite, à côté, comme pour venir ouvrir.

Une heure se plaignait quelque part. Le soir tombait par les baies vitrées, sur les marches.

Et puis les houles du vent d'automne, des frissons d'arbres sur les remparts, l'odeur de la pluie dans les douves, et bien des chansons de Paris passèrent sur elle.

The Words, the Special Words

The words, the special words that she had for me, I heard her saying them to the Other.

I hear his saber ring on the wood of the bed. I shall hear all the words.

When he kisses her on the eyes, there, at the edge of the island of lamplight he feels her eyelids beating under his mouth like the head of a bird you have caught that is afraid.

He lingers at the network of delicate vessels like the light shadow of a marine plant.

He caresses with all his body the breasts inflamed with love.

I shall hear everything, in that corridor with thin partitions, whitened by windows, that bland and sugary smell of wood warmed by the sun.

Sometimes I waited a long time before her door and in a setting so familiar that it was sickening. I would knock. I heard emptiness yawn inside. Someone walked very quickly close by as though to come and open.

An hour complained somewhere. Evening was falling through the bay windows, on the stairs.

And then the gusts of the autumn wind, shivers of trees on the ramparts, the smell of rain in ditches, and many of the songs of Paris didn't mention it.

Fargue / 177

Aux longs traits du fer et des pierres

Aux longs traits du fer et des pierres. Aux lointains môles et aux bras fins et bleus de l'air. Au pan de lumière gros de larmes où les deux amis de jadis repassent, de l'autre côté des buissons de brume, sur l'ancienne route où meurt la mer . . .

Que j'enfonce ici pour toujours ce coeur obscur que fut le nôtre, entre les canons du vieux port droits dans les quais de pierre lisse au front vert penché sur la mer.

Au fond d'une ruelle, la foule se voûte sur des cages sales où battent comme un coeur et s'éteignent des bêtes étranges et grelottantes.

Plus tard les rampes de gaz de la rue aux bouges sourcilleront au vent du soir.

Un ciel fêlé du lent défaut des trolleys chanteurs, dans les quartiers neufs au souffle humide, à l'odeur crayeuse, où j'ai suivi pour une nuit de songe aux plumes de lune la traîne silencieuse de la mort où brillaient les yeux d'une femme . . .

L'homme à la cape rôde sous la fenêtre où glisse une lumière.

Dans le bassin royal, un yacht aux yeux verts attend l'idylle contre l'hôtel noir.

Long Drafts of Iron and Stones

Long drafts of iron and stones. Distant jetties and slender blue arms of air. The pane of shining tears where two friends of long ago pass again, on the other side of clumps of fog, on the ancient road where the sea dies . . .

Let me nail down here forever the dark heart that was ours, among the cannons of the old port that stand on quays of smooth stone with a green wall fronting the sea.

At the bottom of an alley the crowd stoops over dirty cages where like a heart that is dying as it beats strange animals tremble with cold.

Later the gas lamps in the street with bars will glower in the evening wind.

A sky crazed with the slow bawling of the trolley singers, in new districts with a humid breath of air, a smell of chalk, where I followed for a night of dreaming in plumes of moonlight the silent train of death where the eyes of a woman shone . . .

The man with the cape lurks beneath the window where light slips out.

In the royal basin a yacht with green eyes is waiting for romance in front of the black hotel.

Romance

Certes nous vous avons aimée,
Marie . . . Vous le saviez,
N'est-ce pas? Vous vous rappelez?

Un soir
(Nous partions dans la nuit
Arthème et moi), nous allâmes sans bruit vous voir
Sous l'abside du ciel d'été, comme à l'église.

Il y avait de la lumière et vous lisiez.

Nous avons gardé les dessins
Aux trois crayons, et les oiseaux à l'encre bleue
Que vous faisiez.

Ah! Marie, vous chantiez si bien!
C'était au temps
Où vous étiez heureuse à l'école des Soeurs,
Où la Procession toute pâle de fleurs
Chantait dans le désert du Dimanche.
Tremblant
J'étais auprès de vous qui étiez toute en blanc.

L'orgue parlait d'ombre à l'église . . .
Sur l'autel pendait le jour bleu.
Par les blessures du vitrail, l'appel de brise
Où fuse un gros bourdon d'onyx! chassait le feu
Des cierges, vers vous qui étiez grise
De lumière et de chants sages.

Romance

We certainly loved you,
Marie. You knew,
Didn't you? Do you remember?

One evening
We set off at night,
Arthème and I, going quietly to see you
Beneath the apse of the summer sky, as at church.

There was a light and you were reading.

We kept the drawings
With three crayons, and the birds in blue ink
That you made.

Ah, Marie, you sang so well!
It was during the time
When you were happy, at the Sisters' school,
When the procession of pale flowers
Sang in the desert of Sunday.
Trembling
I was near you, who were all in white.

The organ spoke of shadows . . .
On the altar the blue day hung.
Through wounds in stained glass, the call of the breeze
Fused with a loud hum of onyx, drove the fire
Of the candles toward you, tipsy
With light and sacred songs.

Guillaume Apollinaire

Le Pont Mirabeau

Sous le pont Mirabeau coule la Seine
Et nos amours
Faut-il qu'il m'en souvienne
La joie venait toujours après la peine

Vienne la nuit sonne l'heure
Les jours s'en vont je demeure

Les mains dans les mains restons face à face
Tandis que sous
Le pont de nos bras passe
Des éternels regards l'onde si lasse

Vienne la nuit sonne l'heure
Les jours s'en vont je demeure

L'amour s'en va comme cette eau courante
L'amour s'en va
Comme la vie est lente
Et comme l'Espérance est violente

Vienne la nuit sonne l'heure
Les jours s'en vont je demeure

Passent les jours et passent les semaines
Ni temps passé
Ni les amours reviennent
Sous le pont Mirabeau coule la Seine

Vienne la nuit sonne l'heure
Les jours s'en vont je demeure

The Pont Mirabeau

The Seine runs under the Pont Mirabeau
And in our loves
Must I remember so
Joy always follows on the heels of woe

Night   the hour again
The days are going   I remain

Look in my eyes while I hold your hands fast
There underneath
Our bridging arms pour past
Waves that tire of being watched at last

Night   the hour again
The days are going   I remain

Love goes away it is passing quickly
Like this current
How slow life seems to be
And Expectation can be urgent

Night   the hour again
The days are going   I remain

The days pass and the weeks together flow
None none return
Nor loves of long ago
The Seine runs under the Pont Mirabeau

Night   the hour again
The days are going   I remain

Apollinaire / 185

Zone

A la fin tu es las de ce monde ancien

Bergère ô tour Eiffel le troupeau des ponts bêle ce matin

Tu en as assez de vivre dans l'antiquité grecque et romaine

Ici même les automobiles ont l'air d'être anciennes
La religion seule est restée toute neuve la religion
Est restée simple comme les hangars de Port-Aviation

Seul en Europe tu n'es pas antique ô Christianisme
L'Européen le plus moderne c'est vous Pape Pie X
Et toi que les fenêtres observent la honte te retient
D'entrer dans une église et d'y confesser ce matin
Tu lis les prospectus les catalogues les affiches qui chantent
    tout haut
Voilà la poésie ce matin et pour la prose il y a les journaux
Il y a les livraisons à 25 centimes pleines d'aventures policières
Portraits des grands hommes et mille titres divers

J'ai vu ce matin une jolie rue dont j'ai oublié le nom
Neuve et propre du soleil elle était le clairon
Les directeurs les ouvriers et les belles sténo-dactylographes
Du lundi matin au samedi soir quatre fois par jour y passent
Le matin par trois fois la sirène y gémit
Une cloche rageuse y aboie vers midi
Les inscriptions des enseignes et des murailles
Les plaques les avis à la façon des perroquets criaillent
J'aime la grâce de cette rue industrielle
Située à Paris entre la rue Aumont-Thiéville et l'avenue des Ternes

Zone

You're weary of this ancient world at last

O Eiffel Shepherdess the flock of the bridges bleats this morning

You're tired of living in Greek and Roman styles

Antiquity has touched the automobiles
Only religion is still new religion
Still simple as the hangars of Port Aviation

In Europe Christianity alone is never ancient
The most advanced European is Pope Pius X
And you beneath the windows whom shame prevents
From entering a church and there confessing
You read prospectuses catalogues posters that sing
This morning's poetry for prose there are newspapers
Serials true stories of crime and vice
The great and famous all at a bargain price

I saw a pretty street today whose name I forget
Sparkling and clear it announced the sun like a trumpet
Managers workers and pretty typists trek
Along it four times daily six days a week
At morning three times there the siren groans
A noisy bell barks there toward noon
The writing of signs and on walls
The plaques the notices like parrots call
I like the grace of that industrial street
Between rue Aumont-Thiéville and l'Avenue des Ternes
    you'll find it

Voilà la jeune rue et tu n'es encore qu'un petit enfant
Ta mère ne t'habille que de bleu et de blanc
Tu es très pieux et avec le plus ancien de tes camarades René Dalize
Vous n'aimez rien tant que les pompes de l'Église
Il est neuf heures le gaz est baissé tout bleu vous sortez
       du dortoir en cachette
Vous priez toute la nuit dans la chapelle du collège
Tandis qu'éternelle et adorable profondeur améthyste
Tourne à jamais la flamboyante gloire du Christ
C'est le beau lys que tous nous cultivons
C'est la torche aux cheveux roux que n'éteint pas le vent
C'est le fils pâle et vermeil de la douloureuse mère
C'est l'arbre toujours touffu de toutes les prières
C'est la double potence de l'honneur et de l'éternité
C'est l'étoile à six branches
C'est Dieu qui meurt le vendredi et ressuscite le dimanche
C'est le Christ qui monte au ciel mieux que les aviateurs
Il détient le record du monde pour la hauteur

Pupille Christ de l'oeil
Vingtième pupille des siècles il sait y faire
Et changé en oiseau ce siècle comme Jésus monte dans l'air
Les diables dans les abîmes lèvent la tête pour le regarder
Ils disent qu'il imite Simon Mage en Judée
Ils crient s'il sait voler qu'on l'appelle voleur
Les anges voltigent autour du joli voltigeur
Icare Enoch Elie Apollonius de Thyane
Flottent autour du premier aéroplane
Ils s'écartent parfois pour laisser passer ceux que
       transporte la Sainte-Eucharistie
Ces prêtres qui montent éternellement élevant l'hostie
L'avion se pose enfin sans refermer les ailes
Le ciel s'emplit alors de millions d'hirondelles
A tire-d'aile viennent les corbeaux les faucons les hiboux

There's the young street and you're still just a tot
Your mother swaddles you only in blue and white
You're very pious and with your oldest friend René Dalize
The pomps of the Church are the things you mostly prize

It's nine o'clock the gas a low blue flame you slip from the
    dormitory
And all night in the college chapel pray
While the eternal adorable depth of amethyst
Shapes forever the flaming glory of Christ
The beautiful lily that we all grow there
The inextinguishable torch with the red hair
The pale and scarlet son of mother's grief
The tree of which each prayer is a leaf
Double gallows of honor and eternity
It is the star with six rays
God dying on Friday and revived on Sunday
Christ outsoaring pilots in his flight
He holds the record of the world for height

Christ pupil of the eye
Pupil of twenty centuries he can fly
And changed to a bird this age like Jesus rises
The devils look up at him from the abysses
They say he imitates Simon Magus of Judea
They cry since he is stellar call him stealer
The angels stunt around the pretty stunter
Icarus Enoch Elijah Apollonius of Thyane
Float around the first airplane
Sometimes they part making way for those borne
    by the Eucharist
Raising the Host eternally priest after priest
At last the airplane perches with open wings
A million swallows arrive the sky sings
Crows come flapping owls and hawks

D'Afrique arrivent les ibis les flamants les marabouts
L'oiseau Roc célébré par les conteurs et les poètes
Plane tenant dans les serres le crâne d'Adam la première tête
L'aigle fond de l'horizon en poussant un grand cri
Et d'Amérique vient le petit colibri
De Chine sont venus les pihis longs et souples
Qui n'ont qu'une seule aile et qui volent par couples
Puis voici la colombe esprit immaculé
Qu'escortent l'oiseau-lyre et le paon ocellé
Le phénix ce bûcher qui soi-même s'engendre
Un instant voile tout de son ardente cendre
Les sirènes laissant les périlleux détroits
Arrivent en chantant bellement toutes trois
Et tous aigle phénix et pihis de la Chine
Fraternisent avec la volante machine

Maintenant tu marches dans Paris tout seule parmi la foule
Des troupeaux d'autobus mugissants près de toi roulent
L'angoisse de l'amour te serre le gosier
Comme si tu ne devais jamais plus être aimé
Si tu vivais dans l'ancien temps tu entrerais dans un monastère
Vous avez honte quand vous vous surprenez à dire une prière
Tu te moques de toi et comme le feu de l'Enfer ton rire pétille
Les étincelles de ton rire dorent le fond de ta vie
C'est un tableau pendu dans un sombre musée
Et quelquefois tu vas le regarder de près

Aujourd'hui tu marches dans Paris les femmes sont ensanglantées
C'était et je voudrais ne pas m'en souvenir c'était au déclin
      de la beauté

Entourée de flammes ferventes Notre-Dame m'a regardé à Chartes
Le sang de votre Sacré-Coeur m'a inondé à Montmartre
Je suis malade d'ouïr les paroles bienheureuses
L'amour dont je souffre est une maladie honteuse

Ibis of Africa flamingos storks
The roc in verse and fable read
Gripping Adam's skull the first human head
The screaming eagle dives from the horizon
From America comes the little hummingbird
From China come the pihis long and supple
They have one wing only and fly in a couple
Then the dove that spirit immaculate
With the lyrebird and peacock ocellate
The phoenix that is born from his own pyre
A moment veils all with the ash of his fire
The three sirens from the perilous straits
Arrive singing their sweet notes
And all eagle phoenix and pihis of China
Fraternize with the airliner

Now you are walking in Paris in the crowd alone
On every side herds of buses groan
Love's anguish has you by the throat
As if you never should be loved again
You'd be a monk if these were the old days
You're ashamed and surprised to find yourself on your knees
You mock yourself with laughter that crackles like Hades
The sparks of your laughter gild your deepest life
It is a picture hanging in a dark museum
To look at it closely you sometimes come

Today you walk in Paris the women are bloodstained
It was and I would wish to forget it was then beauty waned

Surrounded with leaping flames Notre Dame at Chartres
        looked down on me
The blood of your Sacré Coeur at Montmartre drowned me
I'm sick of hearing the windy pieties
The love from which I suffer is a shameful disease

Et l'image qui te possède te fait survivre dans l'insomnie
        et dans l'angoisse
C'est toujours près de toi cette image qui passe

Maintenant tu es au bord de la Méditerranée
Sous les citronniers qui sont en fleur toute l'année
Avec tes amis tu te promènes en barque
L'un est Nissard il y a un Mentonasque et deux Turbiasques
Nous regardons avec effroi les poulpes des profondeurs
Et parmi les algues nagent les poissons images du Sauveur

Tu es dans le jardin d'une auberge aux environs de Prague
Tu te sens tout heureux une rose est sur la table
Et tu observes au lieu d'écrire ton conte en prose
La cétoine qui dort dans le coeur de la rose

Epouvanté tu te vois dessiné dans les agates de Saint-Vit
Tu étais triste à mourir le jour où tu t'y vis
Tu ressembles au Lazare affolé par le jour
Les aiguilles de l'horloge du quartier juif vont à rebours
Et tu recules aussi dans ta vie lentement
En montant au Hradchin et le soir en écoutant
Dans les tavernes chanter des chansons tchèques

Te voici à Marseille au milieu des pastèques

Te voici à Coblence à l'hôtel du Géant

Te voici à Rome assis sous un néflier du Japon

Te voici à Amsterdam avec une jeune fille que tu
        trouves belle et qui est laide
Elle doit se marier avec un étudiant de Leyde
On y loue des chambres en latin Cubicula locanda
Je m'en souviens j'y ai passé trois jours et autant à Gouda

The image possessing you makes life a sleepless woe
This fugitive image is with you wherever you go

Now you're on the Mediterranean shore
Under the citrus trees that all year flower
With your friends in a boat you float and bask
This one is Nissard there's a Mentonesque and two
      Turbiasques
We look at the devilfish down there with terror
And among the algae swim fishes images of the Savior

You are in a suburb of Prague in a hotel garden
You feel quite happy there's a rose on the table
Instead of writing your little tale in prose
You examine the canker that sleeps in the heart of the rose

Dismayed you see yourself outlined in St. Vith's agates
That day you were so sad you stood at death's gates
You look like Lazarus frightened by the light
The hands of the clock in the Jewish quarter turn
Backward and you also slowly return to your life
Climbing to the Hradchin you hear at night
Czech songs in the taverns

Here you are at Marseilles among the melons

Here you are at Coblenz the Hôtel du Géant

At Rome beneath a Japanese medlar tree

In Amsterdam with a girl you think is pretty
She's ugly and engaged to a student from Leyden
Rooms for rent *cubicula locanda*
Three days I remember there and as many at Gouda

Tu es à Paris chez le juge d'instruction
Comme un criminel on te met en état d'arrestation

Tu as fait de douloureux et de joyeux voyages
Avant de t'apercevoir du mensonge et de l'âge
Tu as souffert de l'amour à vingt et à trente ans
J'ai vécu comme un fou et j'ai perdu mon temps
Tu n'oses plus regarder tes mains et à tous moments
      je voudrais sangloter
Sur toi sur celle que j'aime sur tout ce qui t'a épouvanté

Tu regardes les yeux pleins de larmes ces pauvres émigrants
Ils croient en Dieu ils prient les femmes allaitent des enfants
Ils emplissent de leur odeur le hall de la gare Saint-Lazare
Ils ont foi dans leur étoile comme les rois-mages
Ils espèrent gagner de l'argent dans l'Argentine
Et revenir dans leur pays après avoir fait fortune
Une famille transporte un édredon rouge comme vous
      transportez votre coeur
Cet édredon et nos rêves sont aussi irréels
Quelques-uns de ces émigrants restent ici et se logent
Rue des Rosiers ou rue des Ecouffes dans des bouges
Je les ai vus souvent le soir ils prennent l'air dans la rue
Et se déplacent rarement comme les pièces aux échecs
Il y a surtout des Juifs leurs femmes portent perruque
Elles restent assises exsangues au fond des boutiques

Tu es debout devant le zinc d'un bar crapuleux
Tu prends un café à deux sous parmi les malheureux

Tu es la nuit dans un grand restaurant

Ces femmes ne sont pas méchantes elles ont des soucis cependant
Toutes même la plus laide a fait souffrir son amant

You are at Paris you have been arrested
And dragged to justice like a criminal

You have made grievous and joyful voyages
Before seeing through the lie and what the age is
You suffered from love at twenty and at thirty again
I have lived like a fool and sent my time down the drain
You no longer dare to look at your hands at any moment
     I could start crying
For you for the one I love for all that you found terrifying

You regard with tearful eyes the wretched emigrants
They believe in God they pray the women nurse their
     infants
They fill with their smell the station of Saint Lazare
Like the magi they have faith in their star
They hope to make some money in the Argentine
And come back to their country with a fortune
One family carries a red quilt like a heart
That eiderdown and our dreams are a world apart
Some of these emigrants will rent a hole here
On rue des Rosiers or rue des Ecouffes
I've often seen them at evening out for the air
Like checker pieces moving in starts and fits
They're mostly Jews their bewigged women sit
Like mummies in the back rooms of the stores

You stand before the counter of a crapulous bar
You take a two sou coffee with the beggars

You are the night in a large restaurant

These women are not wicked but they have their cares
All even the ugliest has made her man shed tears

Elle est la fille d'un sergent de ville de Jersey

Ses mains que je n'avais pas vues sont dures et gercées

J'ai une pitié immense pour les coutures de son ventre

J'humilie maintenant à une pauvre fille au rire horrible ma bouche

Tu es seul le matin va venir
Les laitiers font tinter leurs bidons dans les rues
La nuit s'éloigne ainsi qu'une belle Métive
C'est Ferdine la fausse ou Léa l'attentive

Et tu bois cet alcool brûlant comme ta vie
Ta vie que tu bois comme une eau-de-vie

Tu marches vers Auteuil tu veux aller chez toi à pied
Dormir parmi tes fétiches d'Océanie et de Guinée
Ils sont des Christ d'une autre forme et d'une autre croyance
Ce sont les Christ inférieurs des obscures espérances

Adieu Adieu

Soleil cou coupé

She is the daughter of a Jersey cop

I hadn't seen her hands they're hard and chapped

I am filled with pity for the seams of her belly

I now abase my mouth to a poor girl with a horrible laugh

You are alone it is almost morning
The milkmen clink their bottles in the streets

Night goes away like a beautiful Métive
Ferdine the false or Léa the attentive

And you drink this alcohol that burns like life
Your life that you are drinking like a brandy

You walk toward Auteuil you want to go home on foot
To sleep among fetishes of Oceania and Guinea
They are Christs of another form and other culture
They are the lower Christs of hopes that are obscure

Adieu Adieu

Sun neck cut

La Petite Auto

Le 31 du mois d'Août 1914
Je partis de Deauville un peu avant minuit
Dans la petite auto de Rouveyre

Avec son chauffeur nous étions trois

Nous dîmes adieu à toute une epoque
Des géants furieux se dressaient sur l'Europe
Les aigles quittaient leur aire attendant le soleil
Les poissons voraces montaient des abîmes
Les peuples accouraient pour se connaître à fond
Les morts tremblaient de peur dans leurs sombres demeures

Les chiens aboyaient vers là-bas où étaient les frontières
Je m'en allais portant en moi toutes ces armées
    qui se battaient
Je les sentais monter en moi et s'étaler les contrées
    où elles serpentaient
Avec les forêts les villages heureux de la Belgique
Francorchamps avec l'Eau Rouge et les pouhons
Région par où se font toujours les invasions
Artères ferroviaires où ceux qui s'en allaient mourir
Saluaient encore une fois la vie colorée
Océans profonds où remuaient les monstres
Dans les vieilles carcasses naufragées
Hauteurs inimaginables où l'homme combat
Plus haut que l'aigle ne plane
L'homme y combat contre l'homme
Et descend tout à coup comme une étoile filante
Je sentais en moi des êtres neufs pleins de dextérité
Bâtir et aussi agencer un univers nouveau

The Little Car

On the 31st of August 1914
I left Deauville a little before midnight
In Rouveyre's little car

With his chauffeur we were three

We said goodbye to a whole epoch
Furious giants were rising over Europe
Eagles leaving their eyrie to greet the sun
Voracious fish were rising from the abysses
Peoples running to know each other through and
     through
The dead shaking with fear in their somber dwellings

Dogs were barking over there where the frontiers were
As I went I was carrying in me all those fighting armies
I felt them climbing in me and the countries spread out
     where they were winding
With the forests the happy villages of Belgium
Francorchamps with Eau Rouge and the "pouhons"
Region where there are always invasions
Railroad arteries by which those leaving to die
Once again waved to the colors of life
Deep oceans where monsters were stirring
Among the old carcasses of wrecks
Unimaginable heights where man is fighting
Higher than the eagle soars
Man fights against man
And falls all at once like a shooting star
I felt within me new beings full of dexterity
Building and also designing a new universe

Un marchand d'une opulence inouïe et d'une taille
    prodigieuse
Disposait un étalage extraordinaire
Et des bergers gigantesques menaient
De grands troupeaux muets qui broutaient les paroles
Et contre lesquels aboyaient tous les chiens sur la route

Je n'oublierai jamais de voyage nocturne où nul de nous ne dit un mot
O
dé   o
part   nuit
sombre   tendre   o
où mouraient   d'avant   vil $_se^h\hat{a}_i$
nos 3 phares   la guerre   lages où $t_{a_i}le^n$

MARÉCHAUX-FERRANTS RAPPELÉS

ENTRE MINUIT ET UNE HEURE DU MAT^{IN}

      v

    e r s   ou bien   v

  L I S I E U X   e r s

   la très   aille

    bleu   s d'o

     e   r   pneu qui avait éclaté

et 3 fois nous nous arrêtâmes pour changer un

Et quand après avoir passé l'après-midi
Par Fontainebleau
Nous arrivâmes à Paris
Au moment où l'on affichait la mobilisation
Nous comprîmes mon camarade et moi
Que la petite auto nous avait conduits dans une époque
          Nouvelle
Et bien qu'étant déjà tous deux des hommes mûrs
Nous venions cependant de naître

A storekeeper of unheard opulence and prodigious size
Was arranging an extraordinary display
And gigantic shepherds were driving
Large mute flocks that were feeding on words
And set all the dogs along the road barking

I shall never forget that nocturnal journey where none of us said a word
O
somber   o
departure   tender
with our   night   o
3 dying   of before   vil   sehâi
headlights   the war   lages where tailer
SHOE-SMITHS CALLED UP
BETWEEN MIDNIGHT AND ONE A.M.
        t   or else   v
    owards   ers
    LISIEUX   aille
    the very   s the
        blu   gold
        e
and 3 times we stopped to change a tire that blew out

And when at afternoon's end
By Fontainebleau
We arrived at Paris
At the moment when mobilisation was posted
We understood my comrade and I
That the little car had carried us into
        a New epoch
And though we were both well on in life
Yet we had just been born

Jolie bizarre enfant chérie

28 avril 1915

Jolie bizarre enfant chérie
Je vois tes doux yeux langoureux
Mourir peu à peu comme un train qui entre en gare
Je vois tes seins tes petits seins au bout rose
Comme ces perles de Formose
Que j'ai vendues à Nice avant de partir pour Nîmes
Je vois ta démarche rythmée de Salomé plus
    capricieuse
Que celle de la ballerine qui fit couper la tête au
    Baptiste
Ta démarche rythmée comme un acte d'amour
Et qui à l'hôpital auxiliaire où à Nice
Tu soignais les blessés
T'avait fait surnommer assez justement la chaloupeuse
Je vois tes sauts de carpe aussi la croupe en l'air
Quand sous la schlague tu dansais une sorte de kolo
Cette danse nationale de la Serbie

Jolie bizarre enfant chérie
Je sens ta pâle et douce odeur de violette
Je sens la presqu' imperceptible odeur de muguet de tes
    aisselles
Je sens l'odeur de fleur de marronnier que le mystère de
    tes jambes
Répand au moment de la volupté
Parfum presque nul et que l'odorat d'un amant
Peut seul et à peine percevoir
Je sens le parfum de rose rose très douce et lointaine
Qui te précède et te suit ma rose

Pretty Bizarre Darling Child

April 28, 1915

Pretty bizarre darling child
I see your two languorous eyes
Die little by little like a train entering a station
I see your breasts your little breasts tipped with rose
Like those pearls of Formosa
That I sold at Nice before leaving for Nîmes
I see your rhythmic walk of a Salome more capricious
Than that of the ballerina who had the head of the
    Baptist cut off
Your walk as rhythmic as an act of love
That at the auxiliary hospital at Nice
Where you cared for the wounded
Made them call you with reason the motorboat
I see your leaps like a carp also your rump in the air
When under the lash you danced a sort of kolo
That national dance of Serbia

Pretty bizarre darling child
I smell your pale and sweet scent of violets
I smell the almost imperceptible scent of lily of the
    valley
I smell the scent of flowering chestnut that the mystery
    of your legs
Pours out at the moment of pleasure
Almost non-existent perfume that only a lover's sense
    of smell
Is barely able to perceive
I smell the scent of a rose a very soft and distant rose
That precedes and follows you my rose

Jolie bizarre enfant chérie
Je touche la courbe singulière de tes reins
Je suis des doigts ces courbes qui te font faite
Comme une statue grecque d'avant Praxitèle
Et presque comme une Eve des cathédrales
Je touche aussi la toute petite éminence si sensible
Qui est ta vie même au suprême degré
Elle annihile en agissant ta volonté tout entière
Elle est comme le feu dans la forêt
Elle te rend comme un troupeau qui a le tournis
Elle te rend comme un hospice de folles
Où le directeur et le médecin-chef deviendraient
Déments eux-mêmes
Elle te rend comme un canal calme changé
    brusquement
En une mer furieuse et écumeuse
Elle te rend comme un savon satiné et parfumé
Qui mousse soudain dans les mains de qui se lave

Jolie bizarre enfant chérie
Je goûte ta bouche ta bouche sorbet à la rose
Je la goûte doucement
Comme un khalife attendant avec mépris les Croisés
Je goûte ta langue comme un tronçon de poulpe
Qui s'attache à vous de toutes les forces de ses
    ventouses
Je goûte ton haleine plus exquise que la fumée
Tendre et bleue de l'écorce du bouleau
Ou d'une cigarette de Nestor Gianaklis
Ou cette fumée sacrée si bleue
Et qu'on ne nomme pas

Jolie bizarre enfant chérie
J'entends ta voix qui me rappelle
Un concert de bois musette hautbois flûtes

Pretty bizarre darling child
I touch the singular curve of your loins
I follow with my fingers those curves that make you seem
Like a Greek statue before Praxiteles
And almost like an Eve of the cathedrals
I also touch the very little raised place that is so sensitive
That is your very life to the highest degree
As it acts it annihilates your will entirely
It is like a forest fire
It turns you into a flock with staggers
It turns you into a lunatic asylum
Where the director and chief psychiatrist themselves
Have gone crazy
It turns you into a calm canal abruptly changed
To a furious and foaming sea
It turns you into a satiny and perfumed bar of soap
That suddenly lathers in the hands of the one who is
      washing himself

Pretty bizarre darling child
I taste your mouth your mouth rose sorbet
I taste it gently
Like a caliph scornfully waiting for the crusaders
I taste your tongue like the tentacle of an octopus
That attaches itself to you with all the strength of its cups
I taste your breath more exquisite than the tender
      blue smoke
Of birch bark
Or a Nestor Gianaklis cigarette
Or that so blue sacred smoke
That is not named

Pretty bizarre darling child
I hear your voice calling me
A concert of woodwinds accordion oboe flutes

Clarinettes cors anglais
Lointain concert varié à l'infini
Tu te moques parfois et il faut qu'on rie
O ma chérie
Et si tu parles gentiment
C'est le concert des anges
Et si tu parles tristement c'est une satane triste
Qui se plaint
D'aimer en vain un jeune saint si joli
Devant son nimbe vermeil
Et qui baisse doucement les yeux
Les mains jointes
Et qui tient comme une verge cruelle
La palme du martyre

Jolie bizarre enfant chérie
Ainsi les cinq sens concourent à te créer de nouveau
Devant moi
Bien que tu sois absente et si lointaine
O prestigieuse
O ma chérie miraculeuse
Mes cinq sens te photographient en couleurs
Et tu es là tout entière
Belle
Câline
Et si voluptueuse
Colombe jolie gracieuse colombe
Ciel changeant ô Lou ô Lou
Mon adorée
Chère chère bien-aimée
Tu es là
Et je te prends toute
Bouche à bouche
Comme jadis
Jolie bizarre enfant chérie

Clarinets English horn
An infinitely varied distant concert
Sometimes you joke and one has to laugh
O my darling
And if you speak softly
It is a concert of angels
And if you speak sadly a succubus
Who is complaining
Of loving in vain a young saint who is so pretty
With his vermilion halo
And who modestly lowers his eyes
With clasped hands
Who holds like a cruel rod
The palm of the martyr

Pretty bizarre darling child
So the five senses run together to create you anew
In front of me
Although you are absent and so far
O wonderful one
O my miraculous dear
My five senses photograph you in color
And you are there entirely
Beautiful
Caressing
And so voluptuous
Dove pretty graceful dove
Changing sky O Lou O Lou
My adored
Dear dear beloved
You are there
And I take all of you
Mouth to mouth
As before
Pretty bizarre darling child

Cote 146

Plaines désolation enfer des mouches fusées le vert
    le blanc le rouge
Salves de 50 bombes dans les tranchées comme
    quand à quatre on fait claquer pour en faire sortir
    la poussière un grand tapis
Trous semblables à des cathédrales gothiques
Rumeur des mouches violentes
Lettres enfermées dans une boîte de cigares venue d'Oran
La corvée d'eau revient avec ses fûts
Et les blessés reviennent seuls par l'innombrable
    boyau aride
Embranchement du Decauville
Là-bas on joue à cache-cache
Nous jouons à colin-maillard
Beaux rêves
Madeleine ce qui n'est pas à l'amour est autant de perdu
Vos photos sur mon coeur
Et les mouches métalliques petits astres d'abord
A cheval à cheval à cheval à cheval
O plaine partout des trous où végètent des hommes
O plaine où vont les boyaux comme les traces sur le bout
    des doigts aux monumentales pierres de Gavrinis
Madeleine votre nom comme une rose incertaine rose
    des vents ou du rosier
Les conducteurs s'en vont a l'abreuvoir à 7 km d'ici
Perthes Hurlus Beauséjour noms pâles et toi Ville sur
    Tourbe
Cimetières de soldats croix où le képi pleure
L'ombre est de chairs putréfiées les arbres si rares sont
    des morts restés debout
Ouïs pleurer l'obus qui passe sur ta tête

Hill 146

Plains desolation hell of flies rockets green white red
Salvos of 50 shells in the trenches as when at four you
    beat a big carpet to get out the dust
Holes like Gothic cathedrals
Murmur of violent flies
Letters kept in a cigar box from Oran
The water detail returns with its barrels
And the wounded return alone by the innumerable dry
    communication trenches
Branch line of the narrow-gauge railway
Over there they are playing hide-and-seek
We are playing blind-man's-bluff
Beautiful dreams
Madeleine whatever isn't given to love is so much
    wasted
Your photos on my heart
And the metal flies at first little stars
On horseback horseback horseback horseback
O plain everywhere of holes where men vegetate
O plain where communication trenches go like the
    traces of fingertips in the monumental stones of
    Gavrinis
Madeleine your name is like a rose uncertain rose of
    winds and the rose bush
The drivers are going to the horse pond 7 km from here
Perthes Hurlus Beauséjour pale names and you Ville
    sur Tourbe
Soldiers' cemeteries cross where the kepi weeps
The shade is of putrified flesh the rare trees are the
    dead that remain standing
Hear the weeping of the shell that passes overhead

Prologue, Les Mamelles de Tirésias

*Devant le rideau baissé, le Directeur de la Troupe, en habit,
une canne de tranchée à la main, sort du trou du souffleur.*

LE DIRECTEUR DE LA TROUPE

Me voici donc revenu parmi vous
J'ai retrouvé ma troupe ardente
J'ai trouvé aussi une scène
Mais j'ai retrouvé avec douleur
L'art théâtral sans grandeur sans vertu
Qui tuait les longs soirs d'avant la guerre
Art calomniateur et délétère
Qui montrait le péché non le rédempteur

Puis le temps est venue le temps des hommes
J'ai fait la guerre ainsi que tous les hommes

C'était au temps où j'étais dans l'artillerie
Je commandais au front du nords ma batterie
Un soir que dans le ciel le regard des étoiles
Palpitait comme le regard des nouveau-nés
Mille fusées issues de la tranchée adverse
Réveillèrent soudain les canons ennemis

Je m'en souviens comme si cela s'était passé hier

J'entendais les départs mais non les arrivées
Lorsque de l'observatoire d'artillerie
Le trompette vint à cheval nous annoncer
Que le maréchal des logis qui pointait
Là-bas sur les lueurs des canons ennemis
L'alidade de triangle de visée faisait savoir
Que la portée de ces canons était si grande

Prologue, The Breasts of Tiresias

*In front of the lowered curtain the Director, in evening dress
and carrying a swagger stick, emerges from the prompt box.*

THE DIRECTOR

So here I am once more among you
I've found my ardent company again
I have also found a stage
The theater with no greatness and no virtue
That killed the tedious nights before the war
A slanderous and pernicious art
That showed the sin but did not show the savior

Then the hour struck the hour of men
I have been at war like all other men

In the days when I was in the artillery
On the northern front commanding my battery
One night when the gazing of the stars in heaven
Pulsated like the eyes of the newborn
A thousand rockets that rose from the opposite trench
Suddenly woke the guns of the enemy

I remember as though it were yesterday

I heard the shells depart but no explosions
Then from the observation post there came
The trumpeter on horseback to announce
That the sergeant there who calculated
From the flashes of the enemy guns
Their angle of fire had stated
That the range of those guns was so great

Que l'on n'entendait plus aucun éclatement
Et tous mes canonniers attentifs à leurs postes
Annoncèrent que les étoiles s'éteignaient une à une
Puis l'on entendit de grands cris parmi toute l'armée

ILS ÉTEIGNENT LES ÉTOILES À COUPS DE CANON

Les étoiles mouraient dans ce beau ciel d'automne
Comme la mémoire s'éteint dans le cerveau
De ces pauvres vieillards qui tentent de se souvenir
Nous étions là mourant de la mort des étoiles
Et sur le front ténébreux aux livides lueurs
Nous ne savions plus que dire avec désespoir

ILS ONT MÊME ASSASSINÉ LES CONSTELLATIONS

Mais une grande voix venue d'un mégaphone
Dont le pavillon sortait
De je ne sais quel unanime poste de commandement
La voix du capitaine inconnu qui nous sauve toujours cria

IL EST GRAND TEMPS DE RALLUMER LES ÉTOILES

Et ce ne fut qu'un cri sur le grand front français

AU COLLIMATEUR À VOLONTÉ

Les servants se hâtèrent
Les pointeurs pointèrent
Les tireurs tirèrent
Et les astres sublimes se rallumèrent l'un après l'autre
Nos obus enflammaient leur ardeur éternelle
L'artillerie ennemie se taisait éblouie
Par le scintillement de toutes les étoiles

That the bursts could no longer be heard
And all my gunners watching at their posts
Announced the stars were darkening one by one
Then loud shouts arose from the whole army

THEY'RE PUTTING OUT THE STARS WITH SHELLFIRE

The stars were dying in that fine autumn sky
As memory fades in the brain
Of the poor old men who try to remember
We were dying there of the death of stars
And on the somber front with its livid lights
We could only say in despair

THEY'VE EVEN MURDERED THE CONSTELLATIONS

But in a great voice out of a megaphone
The mouth of which emerged
From some sort of supreme headquarters
The voice of the unknown captain who always saves us cried

THE TIME HAS COME TO LIGHT THE STARS AGAIN

And the whole French front shouted together

FIRE AT WILL

The gunners hastened
The layers calculated
The marksmen fired
And the sublime stars lit up again one by one
Our shells rekindled their eternal ardor
The enemy guns were silent dazzled
By the scintillating of all the stars

Voilà voilà l'histoire de toutes les étoiles

Et depuis ce soir-là j'allume aussi l'un après l'autre
Tous les astres intérieurs que l'on avait éteints
Me voici donc revenu parmi vous

Ma troupe ne vous impatientez pas

Public attendez sans impatience

Je vous apporte une pièce dont le but est de réformer les moeurs
Il s'agit des enfants dans la famille
C'est un sujet domestique
Et c'est pourquoi il est traité sur un ton familier
Les acteurs ne prendront pas de ton sinistre
Ils feront appel tout simplement à votre bon sens
Et se préoccuperont avant tout de vous amuser
Afin que bien disposés vous mettiez à profit
Tous les enseignements contenus dans la pièce
Et que le sol partout s'étoile de regards de nouveau-nés
Plus nombreux encore que les scintillements d'étoiles

Ecoutez ô Français la leçon de la guerre
Et faites des enfants vous qui n'en faisiez guère

On tente ici d'infuser un esprit nouveau au théâtre
Une joie une volupté une vertu
Pour remplacer ce pessimisme vieux de plus d'un siècle
Ce qui est bien ancien pour une chose si ennuyeuse
La pièce a été faite pour une scène ancienne
Car on ne nous aurait pas construit de théâtre nouveau
Un théâtre rond à deux scènes
Une au centre l'autre formant comme un anneau
Autour des spectateurs et qui permettra
Le grand déploiement de notre art moderne

There there is the history of all the stars

And since that night I too light one by one
All the stars within that were extinguished
So here I am once more among you

My troupe don't be impatient

Public wait without impatience

I bring you a play that aims to reform society
It deals with children in the family
The subject is domestic
And that is why it's handled in a familiar way
The actors will not adopt a sinister tone
They will simply appeal to your common sense
And above all will try to entertain you
So that you will be inclined to profit
From all the lessons that the play contains
And so that the earth will be starred with the glances of infants
Even more numerous than the twinkling stars

Hear O Frenchmen the lesson of war
And make children you that made few before

We're trying to bring a new spirit into the theater
A joyfulness voluptuousness virtue
Instead of that pessimism more than a hundred years old
And that's pretty old for such a boring thing
The play was created for an antique stage
For they wouldn't have built us a new theater
A circular theater with two stages
One in the middle the other like a ring
Around the spectators permitting
The full unfolding of our modern art

Mariant souvent sans lien apparent comme dans la vie
Les sons les gestes les couleurs les cris les bruits
La musique la danse l'acrobatie la poésie la peinture
Les choeurs les actions et les décors multiples

Vous trouverez ici des actions
Qui s'ajoutent au drame principal et l'ornent
Les changements de ton du pathétique au burlesque
Et l'usage raisonnable des invraisemblances
Ainsi que des acteurs collectifs ou non
Qui ne sont pas forcément extraits de l'humanité
Mais de l'univers entier
Car le théâtre ne doit pas être un art en trompe-l'oeil

Il est juste que le dramaturge se serve
De tous les mirages qu'il a à sa disposition
Comme faisait Morgane sur le Mont-Gibel
Il est juste qu'il fasse parler les foules les objets inanimés
S'il lui plaît
Et qu'il ne tienne pas plus compte du temps
Que de l'espace

Son univers est sa pièce
À l'intérieur de laquelle il est le dieu créateur
Qui dispose à son gré
Les sons les gestes les démarches les masses les couleurs
Non pas dans le seul but
De photographier ce que l'on appelle une tranche de vie
Mais pour faire surgir la vie même dans toute sa vérité
Car la pièce doit être un univers complet
Avec son créateur
C'est-à-dire la nature même
Et non pas seulement
La représentation d'un petit morceau
De ce qui nous entoure ou de ce qui s'est jadis passé

Often connecting in unseen ways as in life
Sounds gestures colors cries tumults
Music dancing acrobatics poetry painting
Choruses actions and multiple sets

Here you will find actions
Which add to the central drama and augment it
Changes of tone from pathos to burlesque
And the reasonable use of the improbable
And actors who may be collective or not
Not necessarily taken from humanity
But from the whole universe
For the theater must not be "realistic"

It is right for the dramatist to use
All the illusions he has at his disposal
As Morgana did on Mount Gibel
It is right for him to make crowds speak and inanimate things
If he wishes
And for him to pay no more heed to time
Than to space

His universe is his stage
Within it he is the creating god
Directing at his will
Sounds gestures movements masses colors
Not merely with the aim
Of photographing the so-called slice of life
But to bring forth life itself in all its truth
For the play must be an entire universe
With its creator
That is to say nature itself
And not only
Representation of a little part
Of what surrounds us or has already passed

Pardonnez-moi mes amis ma troupe

Pardonnez-moi cher Public
De vous avoir parlé un peu longuement
Il y a si longtemps que je m'étais retrouvé parmi vous

Mais il y a encore là-bas un brasier
Où l'on abat des étoiles toutes fumantes
Et ceux qui les rallument vous demandent
De vous hausser jusqu'à ces flammes sublimes
Et de flamber aussi

O public
Soyez la torche inextinguible du feu nouveau

Pardon me my friends my company

Pardon me ladies and gentlemen
For having spoken a little too long
It's been so long since I have been among you

But out there there's still a fire
Where they're putting out the smoking stars
And those who light them again demand that you
Lift yourselves to the height of those great flames
And also burn

O public
Be the unquenchable torch of the new fire

Valery Larbaud

Ode

Prête-moi ton grand bruit, ta grande allure si douce,
Ton glissement nocturne à travers l'Europe illuminée,
O train de luxe! et l'angoissante musique
Qui bruit le long de tes couloirs de cuir doré,
Tandis que derrière les portes laquées, aux loquets de
    cuivre lourd,
Dorment les millionnaires.
Je parcours en chantonnant tes couloirs
Et je suis ta course vers Vienne et Budapesth,
Mêlant ma voix à tes cent mille voix,
O Harmonika-Zug!

J'ai senti pour la première fois toute la douceur de vivre,
Dans une cabine du Nord-Express, entre Wirballen et
    Pskow.
On glissait à travers des prairies où des bergers,
Au pied de groupes de grands arbres pareils à des collines,
Étaient vêtus de peaux de moutons crues et sales . . .
(Huit heures du matin en automne, et la belle cantatrice
Aux yeux violets chantait dans la cabine à côté.)
Et vous, grandes places à travers lesquelles j'ai vu passer
    la Sibérie et les monts du Samnium,
La Castille âpre et sans fleurs, et la mer de Marmara sous
    une pluie tiède!

Prêtez-moi, ô Orient-Express, Sud-Brenner-Bahn, prêtez-
    moi
Vos miraculeux bruits sourds et
Vos vibrantes voix de chanterelle;
Prêtez-moi la respiration légère et facile

Ode

Lend me your great noise, your great smooth speed,
Your nocturnal gliding across lighted Europe,
O train de luxe! and the agonizing music
That hums along your corridors of gilded leather,
While behind lacquered doors with latches of heavy
    copper
Sleep the millionaires.
I wander through your corridors singing
And I follow your course toward Vienna and Budapest,
Mingling my voice with your hundred thousand voices,
O Harmonica-Zug!

I felt for the first time all the sweetness of life
In a cabin of the North Express between Wirballen and
    Pskow.
We were gliding by meadows where shepherds
At the foot of groups of great trees like hills
Were clothed in raw and dirty sheepskin . . .
(Eight o'clock on an autumn morning, and the beautiful
    singer
With violet eyes was singing in the next compartment.)
And you, great spaces across which I have seen Siberia as
    it passed and the hills of Samnium,
Harsh, unflowering Castille, and the sea of Marmara under
    a warm rain!

Lend me, O Orient Express, South-Brenner-Bahn, lend me
Your miraculous deep sounds and
Your vibrant voices like first strings;
Lend me the light and easy breathing

Des locomotives hautes et minces, aux mouvements
Si aisés, les locomotives des rapides,
Précédant sans effort quatre wagons jaunes à lettres d'or
Dans les solitudes montagnardes de la Serbie,
Et, plus loin, à travers la Bulgarie pleine de roses . . .

Ah! il faut que ces bruits et que ce mouvement
Entrent dans mes poèmes et disent
Pour moi ma vie indicible, ma vie
D'enfant qui ne veut rien savoir, sinon
Espérer éternellement des choses vagues.

Of tall, slender locomotives with such unconstrained
Movements, the express locomotives
Effortlessly preceding four yellow coaches with gold lettering
In the mountainous solitudes of Serbia,
And, further away, crossing Bulgaria with all its roses . . .

Ah! these sounds and this movement
Must enter my poems and speak
For my life that has no speech, my life
Like a child's that does not want to know anything, only
To hope eternally for vague things.

Nuit dans le port

Le visage *vaporisé* au Portugal
(Oh, vivre dans cette odeur d'orange en brouillard frais!)
A genoux sur le divan de la cabine obscure
— J'ai tourné les boutons des branches électriques —
A travers le hublot rond et clair, découpant la nuit,
J'épie la ville.
C'est bien cela; c'est bien cela. Je reconnais
L'avenue des casinos et des cafés éblouissants,
Avec la perspective de ses globes de lumière, blancs
A travers les rideaux pendants des palmiers sombres.
Voici les façades éclairées des hôtels immenses,
Les restaurants rayonnant sur les trottoirs, sous les
    arcades,
Et les grilles dorées des jardins de la Résidence.
Je connais encore tous les coins de cette ville africaine:
Voici les Postes, et la gare du Sud, et je sais aussi
Le chemin que je prendrais pour aller du débarcadère
A tel ou tel magasin, hôtel ou théâtre;
Et tout cela est au bout de cette ondulation bleue d'eau
    calme
Où vacillent les reflets des feux du yacht . . .
Quelques mois ensoleillés de ma vie sont encore là
(Tels que le souvenir me les représentait, à Londres),
Ils sont là de nouveau, et réels, devant moi,
Comme une grande boîte pleine de jouets sur le lit d'un
    enfant malade . . .
Je reverrais aussi des gens que j'ai connus
Sans les aimer; et qui sont pour moi bien moins
Que les palmiers et les fontaines de la ville;
Ces gens qui ne voyagent pas, mais qui restent
Près de leurs excréments sans jamais s'ennuyer,

Night in the Port

Face "atomized" at Portugal
(Oh to live in that odor of oranges and fresh fog!)
On my knees on the divan in the dark cabin —
Having turned off the branching lights —
Through the round, clear porthole cutting through the night
I spy out the town.
That's it, that's it. I recognize
The avenue with casinos and dazzling cafés,
With the perspective of its globes of light, white
Through the hanging curtains of somber palms.
Here are the lighted facades of immense hotels,
Restaurants casting rays on the sidewalks, beneath
    the arcades,
And the gilded grills of the Residency gardens.
Again I know all the corners of that African town:
Here is the Post Office, and the South station, and I
    also know
The road I would take to go from the docks
To such and such shop, hotel or theater;
And all that is at the end of that blue undulation of calm
    water
On which tremble reflections of the lights of the yacht . . .
Some sun-drenched months of my life are still there
(Such as memory gave them back to me in London),
They are there once more, and real, before me,
Like a big box full of toys on the bed of a sick child . . .
I would also see again people I've known
Without liking them, and who are much less to me
Than the palms and fountains of the town;
Those people who don't travel, but remain
Near their excrements without ever getting bored,

Je reverrais leurs têtes un temps oubliées, et eux
Continuant leur vie étroite, leurs idées et leurs affaires
Comme s'ils n'avaient pas vécu depuis mon départ . . .
Non, je n'irai pas à terre, et demain
Au lever du jour la "Jaba" lèvera l'ancre;
En attendant je passerai cette nuit avec mon passé,
Près de mon passé vu par un trou
Comme dans les dioramas des foires.

I would see again those heads temporarily forgotten,
    and they
Continuing their narrow lives, their ideas and their business
As if they had not lived since my departure . . .
No, I shall not go ashore, and tomorrow
At daybreak the "Jaba" will raise anchor;
In the meantime I shall pass this night with my past,
Near my past seen through a hole
As in the dioramas at country fairs.

Océan Indien

Oh, la nuit d'été tropical!
Des atolls d'étincellements émergeant d'abîmes bleuâtres!
Le Crucero flamboyant!
Oh, m'étendre sur le pont d'un grand navire
En route vers l'Insulinde,
Nu, et béer à l'infini béant sur moi.
(Mon coeur d'enfant abandonné, ô cher malade,
Mon coeur serait content de ta main à presser,
Dans cette ombre en feu des nuits
Éblouissantes où je voudrais pouvoir m'envoler.)
Sur les navires d'autrefois, tout pavoisés,
Dont la poupe était un palais aux cent fenêtres dorées,
Et que surmontait un Himalaya de toiles,
On n'avait pas, ininterrompue, cette palpitation des étoiles,
Cette vision de la Création, immensément
Silencieuse — sur la tête, tout déroulé, le firmament.
Je désire un matin de printemps, un peu grisâtre, dans
    la chambre d'hôtel,
La fenêtre ouverte en coin sur la rue de Noailles, à l'air frais,
Et voir là-bas (cinq heures, pas encore de tramways)
Le calme Vieux Port et les bateaux du château d'If.

Indian Ocean

Oh night of tropical summer!
Glittering atolls emerging from blue abysses!
The blazing Southern Cross!
Oh to lie stretched out on the deck of a great ship
En route to Malaysia,
Naked, gaping at the infinity that gapes at me.
(My heart of an abandoned child, Oh dear sick friend,
My heart would be content to press your hand
In this shadow on fire of dazzling
Nights in which I would like to take flight.)
On the ships of olden days, with their flags,
The stern a palace with a hundred gilded windows,
Surmounted by a Himalaya of sails,
One did not have, uninterrupted, this palpitation of stars,
This vision of Creation, immensely
Silent — the firmament all unrolled above one's head.
I long for a spring morning, somewhat gray, in the hotel
    room,
The corner window opening on rue Noailles, fresh air,
And to see over there (five o'clock, no trams running yet)
The calm Old Port and boats of the Château d'If.

L'Ancienne Gare de Cahors

Voyageuse! ô cosmopolite! à présent
Désaffectée, rangée, retirée des affaires.
Un peu en retrait de la voie,
Vieille et rose au milieu des miracles du matin,
Avec ta marquise inutile
Tu étends au soleil des collines ton quai vide
(Ce quai qu'autrefois balayait
La robe d'air tourbillonnant des grands express)
Ton quai silencieux au bord d'une prairie,
Avec les portes toujours fermées de tes salles d'attente,
Dont la chaleur de l'été craquèle les volets . . .
O gare qui as vu tant d'adieux,
Tant de départs et tant de retours,
Gare, ô double porte ouverte sur l'immensité charmante
De la Terre, où quelque part doit se trouver la joie de
        Dieu
Comme une chose inattendue, éblouissante;
Désormais tu reposes et tu goûtes les saisons
Qui reviennent portant la brise ou le soleil, et tes pierres
Connaissent l'éclair froid des lézards; et le chatouillement
Des doigts légers du vent dans l'herbe où sont les rails
Rouges et rugueux de rouille,
Est ton seul visiteur.
L'ébranlement des trains ne te caresse plus:
Ils passent loin de toi sans s'arrêter sur ta pelouse,
Et te laissent à ta paix bucolique, ô gare enfin tranquille
Au coeur frais de la France.

The Old Cahors Station

Traveler! O cosmopolitan! at present
Disengaged, withdrawn, retired from business.
A little set back from the road,
Old and rosy amidst the miracles of morning,
With your useless canopy
You extend your empty platform to the sun on the hills
(The platform that used to be swept
By billowing air skirts of the great expresses)
Your platform standing silent at the edge of a meadow
With the doors always closed to your waiting rooms
Where summer's heat cracks the shutters . . .
O station who have seen so many adieus,
So many departures and many returns,
Station, O double door opening on the delightful immensity
Of the Earth, on which somewhere the joy of God must
    be found
As an unexpected, dazzling thing;
From now on you rest and taste the seasons
That return bringing wind or sun, and your stones
Know the cold flash of lizards, and the tickling
Of the wind's light fingers in grass where the rails
Lie red and roughened with rust
Is your only visitor.
The shaking of trains no longer caresses you:
They pass far away without stopping on your grassy verge,
And leave you to your bucolic peace, O finally tranquil
    station
At the cool heart of France.

Yaravi

Dans ce grand souffle de vent noir que nous fendons
Exalté, j'erre en pleurant sur le pont du yacht;
Minuit en mer, pas une côte en vue.
Tout à l'heure au coucher du soleil,
Dans la brume grondaient les canons du Bosphore,
La côte d'Asie à la côte d'Europe répondant
(Pour guider les vaisseaux) de quart d'heure en quart d'heure.
Et c'est avec des bruits guerriers à la poupe que, bondissant,
Mon navire au nom bouffon, le "Narrenschiff,"
Est entré dans cette nuit de poix et ce chaos du Pont-Euxin . . .

Encore enfant, j'ai parcouru ce chemin
D'obscurité, ce déroulement du grand flot porphyréen
Tout chargé des livides fleurs d'edelweiss maritime.

O demain! le lever du jour sur les rivages
Et dans mon cher coeur plein des cloches!
A l'infini, les côtes de l'Empire ottoman
Roses et vertes, aux ondulations douces, où se cachent
Des villages couleur de la terre et de vieilles forteresses;
Ou bien l'approche d'un port russe, annoncé
Par des milliers de courges vertes flottant sur l'eau brillante
(Comme l'Ausonie parfois, plus discrètement,
S'annonce au navigateur par un fiaschetto vide que berce
Le flot tyrrhénien).

Oh, les levers du soleil d'été sur les mers retentissantes
Et le silence des rivages vus au loin!

Mais laissez-moi m'attendrir un peu sur mon enfance,
Me revoir à quinze ans dans les rues d'Odessa;

Yaraví

In this great blast of black wind we're cleaving
Exalted, I wander weeping on the deck of the yacht;
Midnight at sea and no land in sight.
A little while ago at sunset
In the fog the cannons of the Bosporous rumbled,
The coast of Asia replying to the coast of Europe
(To guide the ships) every quarter hour.
And it was with these warlike sounds astern that, bounding,
My ship with the clownish name, "Narrenschiff,"
Entered this night of pitch and chaos on the Black Sea . . .

When still a child I traversed this road
Of darkness, this unrolling of the great tide of porphyry
Heaped with livid flowers of seaboard edelweiss.

O tomorrow! the sunrise on the shores
And in my dear heart filled with bells!
To infinity, the coast of the Ottoman Empire
Rosy and green, with soft undulations, where lie concealed
Villages the color of earth and old fortresses;
Or perhaps the approach to a Russian port, announced
By thousands of green gourds floating on the brilliant water
(As Italy sometimes, more discreetly
Announces itself to the navigator by an empty flask rocking
On the Tyrrhenian tide).

Oh the rising of the sun in summer on echoing seas
And the silence of shores seen from afar!

But let me be moved a while thinking of my childhood,
See myself again at fifteen in the streets of Odessa;

Larbaud / 235

Laissez-moi pleurer dans la nuit sans savoir pourquoi,
Et chanter dans le vent ces vers:
"Ya que para mi no vives,"
Sur un air de valse entendu je ne sais où, un air des tziganes,
Chanter en sanglotant sur un air de tziganes!
Le souvenir me fait revoir des pays éblouissants:
Des rades pleines de navires et des ports bleus
Bordés de quais plantés de palmiers géants et de figuiers
Gigantesques, pareils à des tentes de peau pendues aux cieux;
Et d'immenses forêts à demi submergées,
Et les paseos ombragés de Barcelone;
Des dômes d'argent et de cristal en plein azur;
Et la Petite-Cythère, creuse comme une coupe,
Où le long des ruisseaux les plus calmes du monde,
Se jouent toutes les pastorales du vieux temps;
Et ces îles grecques qui flottent sur la mer . . .

Je ne saurais dire si c'est de désespoir or bien de joie
Que je pleure ainsi, mêlant
Mes sanglots étouffés aux cris de panique de l'aquilon,
Au rythme de la machinerie, au tonnerre et au sifflement
Des vagues tordues en masses de verre sur les flancs
Du navire, et tout à coup étalées comme un manteau de
    pierreries
(Mais tout cela est invisible) . . .

Mais ma douleur . . . Oh, ma douleur, ma bien-aimée!
Qui adoptera cette douleur sans raison,
Que le passé n'a pas connue et dont l'avenir
Ignorera sans doute le secret?
Oh, prolonger le souvenir de cette douleur moderne,
Cette douleur qui n'a pas de causes, mais
Qui m'est un don des Cieux.

Let me weep in the night without knowing why,
And sing these verses to the wind:
"Ya que para mi no vives,"
To the tune of a waltz heard I don't know where, a Gypsy
    tune!
Sobbing as I sing to a Gypsy tune!
In memory I revisit dazzling countries:
Roadsteads full of ships and blue harbors
Bordered with quays planted with giant palms and gigantic
Fig trees, like tents of hide hung in the sky;
And immense half-submerged forests,
And the shady *paseos* of Barcelona;
Domes of silver and crystal beneath an azure sky;
And Little Cytherea, as hollow as a cup,
Where, beside the smoothest streams in the world,
All the pastorals of ancient times are played;
And those Greek islands that float on the sea . . .

I couldn't say if it's despair or happiness
That makes me weep so, mingling
My stifled sobs with the terrified cries of the north wind,
The rhythm of machinery, thunder and whistling
Of waves twisted in masses of glass on the sides
Of the ship, and suddenly spread out like a mantle of
    precious stones
(But all that is invisible) . . .

But my sorrow . . . Oh my sorrow, my beloved!
Who will adopt this unreasoning sorrow
That the past has not known and whose secret
No doubt will be closed to the future?
Oh to prolong the memory of this modern sorrow,
This grief that has no reasons, but
To me is a gift from Heaven.

Le Don de soi-même

Je m'offre à chacun comme sa récompense;
Je vous la donne même avant que vous l'ayez méritée.

Il y a quelque chose en moi,
Au fond de moi, au centre de moi,
Quelque chose d'infiniment aride
Comme le sommet des plus hautes montagnes;
Quelque chose de comparable au point mort de la rétine,
Et sans écho,
Et qui pourtant voit et entend;
Un être ayant une vie propre, et qui, cependant,
Vit toute ma vie, et écoute, impassible,
Tous les bavardages de ma conscience.

Un être fait de néant, si c'est possible,
Insensible à mes souffrances physiques,
Qui ne pleure pas quand je pleure,
Qui ne rit pas quand je ris,
Qui ne rougit pas quand je commets une action honteuse,
Et qui ne gémit pas quand mon coeur est blessé;
Qui se tient immobile et ne donne pas de conseils,
Mais semble dire éternellement:
"Je suis là, indifférent à tout."

C'est peut-être du vide comme est le vide,
Mais si grand que le Bien et le Mal ensemble
Ne le remplissent pas.
La haine y meurt d'asphyxie,
Et le plus grand amour n'y pénètre jamais.

The Gift of Himself

I offer myself to everyone as a reward;
I give it to you even before you've deserved it.

There is something inside me,
At the bottom of myself, at the center of myself,
Something infinitely arid
Like the summit of the highest mountains;
Something comparable to the dead focus of the retina,
And without an echo,
And yet that sees and listens;
A being with a life of its own that nevertheless
Lives all my life, and listens impassively
To all the babblings of my conscious mind.

A being made of nothing, if that is possible,
Insensible to my physical sufferings,
That does not weep when I weep,
That does not laugh when I laugh,
That does not blush when I commit a shameful deed,
And does not groan when my heart is wounded,
That keeps still and does not give advice,
But seems to say eternally:
"I am there, indifferent to everything."

Perhaps it is of the void as the void is,
But so large that Good and Evil together
Are not able to fill it.
There hate dies of asphyxiation
And the greatest love never enters.

Prenez donc tout de moi: le sens de ces poèmes,
Non ce qu'on lit, mais ce qui paraît au travers malgré moi:
Prenez, prenez, vous n'avez rien.
Et où que j'aille, dans l'univers entier,
Je rencontre toujours,
Hors de moi comme en moi,
L'irremplissable Vide,
L'inconquérable Rien.

Then take my whole self: the meaning of these poems,
Not what you read, but the thing that comes across in
    spite of me;
Take it, take it, you have nothing.
And wherever I go, in the entire universe,
I shall always be meeting
Outside myself as in myself,
The unrefillable Void,
The unconquerable Nothing.

Images

I

Un jour, à Kharkow, dans un quartier populaire
(O cette Russie méridionale, où toutes les femmes
Avec leur châle blanc sur la tête, ont des airs de Madone!),
Je vis une jeune femme revenir de la fontaine,
Portant, à la mode de là-bas, comme du temps d'Ovide,
Deux seaux suspendus aux extrémités d'un bois
En équilibre sur le cou et les épaules.
Et je vis un enfant en haillons s'approcher d'elle et lui
    parler.
Alors, inclinant aimablement son corps à droite,
Elle fit en sorte que le seau plein d'eau pure touchât le pavé
Au niveau des lèvres de l'enfant qui s'était mis à genoux
    pour boire.

II

Un matin, à Rotterdam, sur le quai des Boompjes
(C'était le 18 septembre 1900, vers huit heures),
J'observais deux jeunes filles qui se rendaient à leurs
    ateliers;
Et en face d'un des grands ponts de fer, elles se dirent
    au revoir,
Leurs routes n'étant pas les mêmes.
Elles s'embrassèrent tendrement; leurs mains tremblantes
Voulaient et ne voulaient pas se séparer; leurs bouches
S'éloignaient douloureusement pour se rapprocher
    aussitôt

Images

I

One day at Kharkov, in a working-class area,
(O that meridional Russia where all the women
With white shawls on their heads look like Madonnas!),
I saw a young woman coming from the fountain,
Carrying as they do, just as in the time of Ovid,
Two buckets suspended from the ends of a piece
    of wood
Balanced on her neck and shoulders.
And I saw a child in rags approach and speak to her.
Then, amiably inclining her body to the right,
She let down the bucket of pure water so that it
    rested on the pavement
Level with the lips of the child that had kneeled
    to drink.

II

One morning in Rotterdam, on the quay of Boompje,
(It was the 18th of September 1900, toward eight
    o'clock),
I observed two young girls going off to their workshops;
And in front of one of the great iron bridges they were
    saying goodbye,
Their roads not being the same.
They kissed each other tenderly; their trembling hands
Wished and did not wish to separate; their mouths
Drew distant sorrowfully and came together again

Tandis que leurs yeux fixes se contemplaient . . .
Ainsi elles se tinrent un long moment tout près l'une de
l'autre,
Debout et immobiles au milieu des passants affairés,
Tandis que les remorqueurs grondaient sur le fleuve,
Et que des trains manoeuvraient en sifflant sur les
ponts de fer.

III

Entre Cordoue et Séville
Est une petite station, où, sans raisons apparentes,
Le Sud-Express s'arrête toujours.
En vain le voyageur cherche des yeux un village
Au delà de cette petite gare endormie sous les
eucalyptus.
Il ne voit que la campagne andalouse: verte et dorée.
Pourtant de l'autre côté de la voie, en face,
Il y a une hutte faite de branchages noircis et de terre.
Et au bruit du train une marmaille loqueteuse en sort.
La soeur aînée les précède, et s'avance tout près sur le quai,
Et, sans dire un mot, mais en souriant,
Elle danse pour avoir des sous.
Ses pieds dans la poussière paraissent noirs;
Son visage obscur et sale est sans beauté;
Elle danse, et par les larges trous de sa jupe couleur de
cendre,
On voit, nues, s'agiter ses cuisses maigres,
Et rouler son petit ventre jaune;
Et chaque fois, pour cela, quelques messieurs ricanent,
Dans l'odeur des cigares, au wagon-restaurant . . .

While they gazed in each other's eyes . . .
So they held each other close for a long moment
Upright and motionless among the busy passers-by,
While the tugs grumbled on the river
And trains manoeuvered whistling on the iron bridges.

III

Between Cordova and Seville
There is a small station where, for no apparent reason,
The South Express always stops.
In vain the traveler searches with his eyes for a village
Beyond that little station asleep beneath the eucalyptus
    trees.
He sees only the Andalusian countryside, green and golden.
However, on the other side of the track, facing it,
There is a hut of black branches and earth.
And at the sound of the train a swarm of ragged children
    comes out.
Their older sister precedes them, and approaches on the
    platform,
And without saying a word, but smiling,
She dances for pennies.
Her feet in the dust appear black;
Her swarthy and dirty face is without beauty;
She dances, and through large holes in her skirt the color
    of ashes
You see, nakedly, the movements of her scrawny thighs
And rolling of her little yellow stomach;
And this is why, every time, some gentlemen laugh
In the odor of cigars in the diner.

Post-scriptum

O mon Dieu, ne sera-t-il jamais possible
Que je connaisse cette douce femme, là-bas, en Petite-
    Russie,
Et ces deux amies de Rotterdam,
Et la jeune mendiante d'Andalousie
Et que je me lie avec elles
D'une indissoluble amitié?
(Hélas, elles ne liront pas ces poèmes,
Elles ne sauront ni mon nom, ni la tendresse de mon coeur;
Et pourtant elles existent, elles vivent *maintenant.)*
Ne sera-t-il jamais possible que cette grande joie me
    soit donnée,
De les connaître?
Car je ne sais pourquoi, mon Dieu, il me semble qu'avec
    elles quatre,
Je pourrais conquérir un monde!

Postscript

O my God, will it never be possible
For me to know that sweet woman over there in Little
    Russia,
And those two friends in Rotterdam,
And the young Andalusian beggar woman,
And for me to bind myself to them
In indissoluble friendship?
(Alas, they will not read these poems,
They will know neither my name nor the tenderness in
    my heart;
And yet they exist, they are living *now*.)
Will it never be possible for me to be given the great joy
Of knowing them?
For I don't know why, my God, but it seems that with
    these four
I could conquer a world.

Catherine Pozzi

Vale

La grande amour que vous m'aviez donnée
Le vent des jours a rompu ses rayons —
Où fut la flamme, où fut la destinée
Où nous étions, où par la main serrée
      Nous nous tenions

Notre soleil, dont l'ardeur fut pensée
L'orbe pour nous de l'être sans second
Le second ciel d'une âme divisée
Le double exil où le double se fond

Son lieu pour vous apparaît cendre et crainte,
Vos yeux vers lui ne l'ont pas reconnu
L'astre enchanté qui portait hors d'atteinte
L'extrême instant de notre seule étreinte
      Vers l'inconnu.

Mais le futur dont vous attendez vivre
Est moins présent que le bien disparu.
Toute vendange à la fin qu'il vous livre
Vous la boirez sans pouvoir être qu'ivre
      Du vin perdu.

J'ai retrouvé le céleste et sauvage
Le paradis où l'angoisse est désir.
Le haut passé qui grandit d'âge en âge
Il est mon corps et sera mon partage
      Après mourir.

Quand dans un corps ma délice oubliée
Où fut ton nom, prendra forme de coeur

Vale

The rays of the great love you gave to me
Are fragments that the wind of time disbands.
Where was the flame, where the destiny
Where we once stood and grasped our ecstasy
    With burning hands?

Our sun whose heat and passion thought provided,
For us the orb of being next to none,
The second heaven of a soul divided,
The twofold exile where the two are one,

To you its place seems only ash and fear,
Your eyes that turned toward it as it shone
Were blind to the enchantment of the star
That takes the highest moment that we are
    To the unknown.

But the future where you hope to live
Is less present than the vanished hour.
Whatever other vintage time may give
You shall drink and drunkenly retrieve
    A taste that's sour.

I have found again the clear, savage sky,
The paradise where anguish is desire.
The high past that grows as time goes by
That is my body and that when I die
    Shall be my share.

In the body, in the forgetful grave,
The joy your name once was shall form again

Je revivrai notre grande journée,
Et cette amour que je t'avais donnée
Pour la douleur.

A heart, and I shall live once more and have
That day again, and the great love I gave
      For grief and pain.

Nova

Dans un monde au futur du temps où j'ai la vie
Qui ne s'est pas formé dans le ciel d'aujourd'hui,
Au plus nouvel espace où le vouloir dévie
Au plus nouveau moment de l'astre que je fuis
Tu vivras, ma splendeur, mon malheur, ma survie
Mon plus extrême coeur fait du sang que je suis,
Mon souffle, mon toucher, mon regard, mon envie,
Mon plus terrestre bien perdu pour l'infini.
Evite l'avenir, Image poursuivie!
Je suis morte de vous, ô mes actes chéris
Ne sois pas défais toi dissipe toi délie
Dénonce le désir que je n'ai pas choisi.

N'accomplis pas mon jour, âme de ma folie —
Délaisse le destin que je n'ai pas fini.

Nova

In a world in the future where I shall be
That is not formed in the sky that I see,
In the newest space where schemes *gang agley,*
In the newest phase of the star that I flee,
You will live, my splendor, my self, misery,
My deepest heart of the blood that is me,
My breath, my touch, my glance and my glee,
All my world well lost for an infinity.
Avoid the future you chase knee to knee!
I am dying of you, O my jumps left alee.
Do not exist dissipate untie cast free,
Denounce the agreement I didn't agree.

Do not end my life, in my bonnet the bee —
Relinquish the fate that I have not *fini.*

Nyx

A Louise aussi de Lyon et d'Italie

O vous mes nuits, ô noires attendues
O pays fier, ô secrets obstinés
O longs regards, ô foudroyantes nues
O vol permis outre les cieux fermés.

O grand désir, ô surprise épandue
O beau parcours de l'esprit enchanté
O pire mal, ô grâce descendue
O porte ouverte où nul n'avait passé.

Je ne sais pas pourquoi je meurs et noie
Avant d'entrer à l'éternel séjour.
Je ne sais pas de qui je suis la proie.
Je ne sais pas de qui je suis l'amour.

Nyx

To Louise also of Lyon and Italy

O my nights, O shades I am awaiting
O proud country, O secrets no one sees
O long searching looks, O naked lightning
O flight permitted far beyond shut skies.

O great desire, O surprise extending
O the spirit's long enchanted flight
O worse sickness, O grace descending
O where none has passed an open gate.

I do not know why I am dying and drown
Before the eternal sojourn where I go.
I do not know who is hunting me down.
I do not know who it is who loves me so.

Pierre Reverdy

La Vie dure

Il est tapi dans l'ombre et dans le froid pendant l'hiver.
Quand le vent souffle il agite une petite flamme au bout
des doigts et fait des signes entre les arbres. C'est un
vieil homme; il l'a toujours été sans doute et le mauvais
temps ne le fait pas mourir. Il descend dans la plaine
quand le soir tombe; car le jour il se tient à mi-hauteur
de la colline caché dans quelque bois d'où jamais on ne
l'a vu sortir. Sa petite lumière tremble comme une étoile
à l'horizon aussitôt que la nuit commence. Le soleil et le
bruit lui font peur; il se cache en attendant les jours plus
courts et silencieux d'automne, sous le ciel bas, dans
l'atmosphère grise et douce où il peut trotter, le dos
courbé, sans qu'on l'entende. C'est un vieil homme
d'hiver qui ne meurt pas.

A Hard Life

He huddles in a shadow and in winter in the cold. When the wind blows he shakes a little flame at the end of his fingers and signals among the trees. He is an old man; no doubt he has always been one and bad weather doesn't make him die. He goes down into the plain when evening falls; during the day he stays halfway up the hill hidden in some wood from which he has never been seen to emerge. His little light trembles on the horizon like a star as soon as night falls. Sunlight and noise frighten him; he hides waiting for the shorter and silent days of autumn, under the lowering sky, in the gray and gentle atmosphere where he can trot, with bent back, without being heard. He is the old man of winter who never dies.

Les Corps ridicules des esprits

Un cortège de gens plus ou moins honorables. Quelques-un sourient dans le vide avec sérénité. Ils sont nus. Une auréole à la tête des premiers qui ont su prendre la place. Les plus petits en queue.

On passe entre les arbres qui s'inclinent. Les esprits qui se sont réfugiés derrière les étoiles regardent. La curiosité vient de partout. La route s'illumine.

Dans le silence digne, si quelqu'un chante c'est une douce voix qui monte et personne ne rit. La chanson est connue de tous.

On passe devant la maison d'un poète qui n'est pas là. La pluie qui tombait sur son piano, à travers le toit, l'a chassé.

Bientôt, c'est un boulevard bordé de cafés où la foule s'ennuie. Tout le monde se lève. Le cortège a grossi.

Enfin par l'avenue qui monte la file des gens s'éloigne, les derniers paraissent les plus grands. Les premiers ont déjà disparu.

Derrière un monument d'une époque oubliée le soleil se lève en rayons séparés et l'ombre des passants lentement s'efface. Les rideaux sont tirés.

The Ridiculous Bodies of Spirits

A procession of more or less honorable people. Some of them smile serenely into the void. They are naked. A halo on the head of the first who knew how to take their place. The smaller ones in line.

They pass between trees that bow down. Spirits that have taken refuge behind the stars are looking on. There is curiosity on all sides. The road lights up.

In the dignified silence, if someone sings it is with a sweet voice that rises up and no one laughs. The song is known by all.

They pass before the house of a poet who is not there. The rain that fell on his piano, through the roof, drove him away.

Soon there is a boulevard lined with cafés where the crowd is bored. Everyone stands up. The procession has grown.

Finally as the avenue climbs the file of people moves into the distance, the last appearing the biggest. The first have already disappeared.

Behind the monument to a forgotten epoch the sun rises with separate beams and the shadow of the passers-by slowly fades. Curtains are drawn.

Façade

Le chemineau aurait frappé de son bâton le sol
   durci
A cet endroit
Devant la porte un chien furieux grogne et mord
La famille protégée dort
Derrière les rideaux
Les volets clos
L'inconnu de la route où tout le monde passe
Un cri sinistre dans la nuit
Tous les voleurs du rêve se sont évanouis
Ils se sont dispersés dans quelques livres
Les chemins sont devenus plus sûrs
Et nos visages en ont pris une tranquillité incolore
On ne craint plus le danger et on connaît la mort
Au soleil
Nous imitons les gens des pays chauds
Et c'est une fausse confiance dans la nature
Que nous avons oubliée
Il est temps de sortir de ce trop long repos
Qui ressemble à la fin de tout
Nous sommes tous liés à cause de la civilisation
On comprendra trop tard le danger de cette imitation
Le combat singulier n'existe plus
Les caractères principaux se sont perdus
Mais la maison fermée est comme nous-mêmes
Une intimité que personne ne connaît
Des regards au dehors . . . la curiosité
Et notre hypocrisie
        La crainte d'autrui

Le chien de garde

Facade

The tramp would have struck the hard ground
    with his stick
At this place
Before the door a furious dog growls and snaps
The protected family sleeps
Behind curtains at night
Shutters shut tight
The stranger on the road where everyone passes
A sinister cry in the night
All the robbers in dreams have taken flight
They are scattered in some books
The roads are more secure
Our faces have taken on a tranquil lack of color
Death is understood no one fears danger any more
In the sun
We imitate the people in warm countries
This confidence in nature is a mistake
We have forgotten what it is like
It is time to wake from this long sleeping
That is like the end of everything
We are all tied together thanks to civilisation
It will be too late to see the danger of imitation
Single combat no longer exists
Extraordinary characters are lost
But the closed house is like ourselves
An intimacy that no one knows
Stares outside . . . curiosity
And our hypocrisy
           Fear of the other

The watchdog

Le nouveau venu des visages

Contre la glace éteinte les têtes se retournent
 La carte de visite pivote au bout des doigts
C'est la girouette qui grince pour indiquer la route au
 vent des ailes
Mais le nom de l'enseigne qui y est écrit on ne le voit
 pas
Celui qui entre revient avec la marée montante des
 faubourgs
Dans la dernière maison après les terrains vagues et
 avant la campagne saine et propre sans détours
Le café c'est un nuage à l'ombre plein de voix
Où le passant se glisse entre l'odeur et le friod
Contre la glace éteinte les têtes se retournent
La nuit suit son chemin
  Mais quelqu'un s'en détache et entre
Toutes les têtes se retournent pour deviner le nom
 approximatif de ce nouveau visage

The Latest Face to Arrive

Against the dull mirror heads turn around
    The calling card pivots at the end of fingers
It is the weathervane creaking to point the
    road to the wind of wings
But the name of the sign written there you do not
    see
The one who enters is returning with the rising
    tide of the suburbs
In the last house after indistinct lots and before
    the healthy open country with no detours
The café is a cloud in a shadow filled with a voice
Where the passerby slips in between the smell
    and the cold
Against the dull mirror heads turn around
Night follows its road
        But someone detaches himself and enters
All the heads turn around to guess the approximate
    name of this new face

La Tête rouge

Là-haut
Le creux marin
Au bord des hémisphères
La houle passe en bloc par-dessus les tréteaux
Les racines du monde
                    pendent
                    par delà la terre
les jambes du jockey au bord du tilbury
              Les côtés de la route changent
              les franges du ciel remuent
              Et le vent se replie derrière la forêt
              les monticules
                    à la ligne des dunes où roule le soleil
Les pins dans les barreaux de fer
renferment les bêtes immobiles
la peau des roches
              à travers les ondes des coups de tonnerre de l'orage
Il ne manque plus rien si l'horizon frémit

              Mais derrière
        Il y a sur le mur l'affiche ensanglantée
        les lambeaux de carton que la pluie fait bouger
                    le soir
        aux yeux du passant qui remonte par la plus
        longue rue
        Rue déserte encombrée de maisons qui se
        déplacent
Les arbres prisonniers s'entendent à voix basse
              Chaque vitrine a son secret

The Portrait I Am Leaving

Up there
The marine hollow
At the edge of the hemisphere
The swell passes whole above the trestles
The roots of the world
        hang
           beyond the earth
the legs of the jockey at the side of the tilbury
        The sides of the road change
        the fringes of the sky stir
        And the wind folds up the small hills
        behind the forest
           at the line of dunes where the sun rolls
The pines in bars of iron
shut in the motionless beasts
the skin of rocks
    across the waves thunderclaps of the storm
Nothing more is needed if the horizon shudders

        But behind
    On the wall there is the bloody poster
    scraps of a carton that the rain is moving
        the evening
    in the eyes of the passerby who is climbing by the
    longest road
    A deserted street encumbered with houses that
    are moving
Trees prisoners come to an understanding with
lowered voices
        Each window has its secret

Dans la nuit

Sous le ciel et une voie d'étoiles

Des gémissements

Des oscillations inquiétantes de la terre qui
change son mouvement

L'homme qui monte sans rien voir que son pas
devant

Les bruits dans les gradins du port

et les bruits des enseignes

Toutes les voix

Tous les tumultes

Les formes blanches des étages qui se plaignent

Tout luit

L'eau a lavé la pierre

Des mots glissent des toits

Un bruit sourd des lumières

Entre les deux troupeaux des trottoirs les portes
pleines qu'on pousse et qui ne s'ouvrent pas

Le langage étranger dans la tête du matelot qui va

La mémoire du poète en avant qui dicte

Et les livres dont les noms et les mots reviennent
constamment

Nuages   Tour Eiffel les noms du Dictionnaire

Et les mots étrangers et ceux de son pays

Où seront-ils passés

Et l'ombre de l'ami mort l'an dernier toujours
présente derrière sa table et dans ses promenades
et même pour signer

Cette réclame

Ce mouvement dans l'être qui agite son chapeau
au bout du même bras

Et cette face rouge

La même qui guidait le marin qui allait
la tête émerveillée des noms du Dictionnaire

In the night
Under the sky and a road of stars
Groans
Restless oscillations of the earth that is changing
its movement
The man climbing who sees nothing but the step in
front of him
The noises in the grades of the port
and noises of the signs
All the voices
All the tumults
The white forms of the stories complaining
Everything shines
The water has washed the stone
Words slide from roofs
A sound springs up from lights
Between the two flocks of sidewalks solid doors
you push that do not open
The foreign language in the head of the sailor who
is walking
The memory of the poet up in front dictating
And books whose titles and words return continually
Clouds   Eiffel Tower names in the dictionary
And foreign words and those of his country
Where will they have gone
And the shadow of the friend who died a year ago still
present behind his table and in his walks and even signing
That advertisement
That movement of the being who waves his hat at the end of
the same arm
And that red face
The same that guided the sailor who was
walking head filled with wonder at the names in the dictio-
nary

des mots de la légende et de l'astrologie
Le temps passé sous l'aile
La caresse de l'air
Le portrait que je laisse
Et tous les mots violents que je n'aurai pas dits

words from legend and astrology
Time passed under the wing
The caress of air
The portrait I am leaving
And all the violent words that I shall not have said

Tristan Tzara

La Revue Dada

cinq négresses dans une auto
ont explosé suivant les cinq directions de mes doigts,
quand je pose la main sur la poitrine pour prier dieu parfois
autour de ma tête il y a la lumière humide des vieux oiseaux lunaires
l'auréole verte des saints levée des évasions cérébrales
tralalalalalalalalalalalalala
qu'on voit maintenant crever dans les obus

il y a quelque part un jeune homme qui mange ses poumons
il fit un pet si lumineux que la maison devint minuit
comme un retour d'oiseaux qu'on chante dans les poésies
et la mort jaillie des canons coupe la conversation des vautours
le très grand voilier ouvrit son livre comme un ange cependant
on a fixé les feuilles printemps une belle page dans la typographie
zoumbaï zoumbaï zoumbaï diê
j'ai touché à tout au bien et au mal ah la joie du général
voilà pourquoi je mets sur chaque coeur une draperie et sur chaque
    draperie il y a notre seigneur et sur chaque seigneur il y a mon
    coeur
mon coeur je l'ai donné pourboire hihi

The Dada Review

five black women in a car
have exploded following the five directions of my fingers
when I place my hand on my chest to pray sometimes
around my head there is the humid light of old lunar birds
the green aureole of saints that rose from cerebral evasions
Tralalalalalalalalalalalalalala
that you now see bursting in shells

somewhere there is a young man who is eating his lungs
he made such a luminous fart that the house became midnight
like a return of birds that are sung in poems
and the death hurled by cannon cuts short the conversation of
        vultures
the very great sail-maker opened his book like an angel however
the leaves have been fixed spring a beautiful page in typography
zoumbaï zoumbaï zoumbaï diê
I have felt everything good and bad ah the joy of the general
that is why I am hanging a curtain on each heart and on each
        curtain there is our lord and on each lord there is my heart
my heart I gave it a tip hehe

Chanson Dada

La chanson d'un ascenseur
qui avait dada au coeur
Fatiguait trop son moteur
qui avait dada au coeur

L'ascenseur portait un roi
Lourd fragile autonome
Il coupa son grand bras droit
L'envoya au pape à Rome

C'est pourquoi
L'ascenseur
N'avait plus dada au coeur

Mangez du chocolat
Lavez votre cerveau
Dada
Dada

Buvez de l'eau

La chanson d'un dadaïste
qui n'était ni gai ni triste
Et aimait une bicycliste
qui n'était ni gaie ni triste

Mais l'époux le jour de l'an
Savait tout et dans une crise
Envoya au Vatican
Leurs deux corps en trois valises

Dada Song

The song of an elevator
that had dada in its heart
Was wearing out its motor
that had dada in its heart

A king heavy and fragile enough
Rode the elevator up
He cut his big right arm off
Sent it to Rome to the pope

        That is why
        The elevator
Had no more dada in its heart

Eat chocolate
        Wash your brain
        Dada
        Dada

Drink water

The song of a dadaist
who was neither happy nor sad
And loved a bicyclist
who was neither happy nor sad

But on New Year's Day her husband
Found out and in a crisis
Sent to the Vatican
Their two bodies in three valises

Ni amant
Ni cycliste
N'étaient plus ni gais ni tristes

Mangez de bons cerveaux
Lavez votre soldat
Dada
Dada

Buvez de l'eau

La chanson d'un bicycliste
qui était dada de coeur
qui était donc dadaïste
Comme tous les dadas de coeur

Un serpent portait des gants
Il ferma vite la soupape
Mit des gants en peau d' serpent
Et vint embrasser le pape

C'est touchant
Ventre en fleur
N'avait plus dada au coeur.

Buvez du lait d'oiseau
Lavez vos chocolats
Dada
Dada

Mangez du veau

Neither lover
Nor cyclist
Were happy or sad any more

Eat good brains
Wash your soldier
Dada
Dada

Drink water

The song of a bicyclist
who had dada in her heart
and so was a dadaist
Like all who have dada in their heart

A snake with gloves that was passing
Closed the valve just like this
Put the gloves in snakeskin
And went and gave the pope a kiss

That's touching
Belly flower
Had no dada in its heart any more

Drink bird milk
Wash your chocolates
Dada
Dada

Eat veal cutlets

L'Homme approximatif [Extrait]

I

dimanche lourd couvercle sur le bouillonnement
    du sang
hebdomadaire poids accroupi sur ses muscles
tombé à l'intérieur de soi-même retrouvé
les cloches sonnent sans raison et nous aussi
sonnez cloches sans raison et nous aussi
nous nous réjouirons au bruit des chaines
que nous ferons sonner en nous avec les cloches

                    *

quel est ce langage qui nous fouette nous sursautons
    dans la lumière
nos nerfs sont des fouets entre les mains du temps
et le doute vient avec une seule aile incolore
se vissant se comprimant s'écrasant en nous
comme le paper froissé de l'emballage défait
cadeau d'un autre âge aux glissements des poissons
    d'amertume

                    *

les cloches sonnent sans raison et nous aussi
les yeux des fruits nous regardent attentivement
et toutes nos actions sont contrôlées il n'y a rien de
    caché
l'eau de la rivière a tant lavé son lit
elle emporte les doux fils des regards qui ont trainé
aux pieds des murs dans les bars léché des vies
alléché les faibles lié des tentations tari des extases

Approximate Man [Selection]

PART I

sunday heavy lid of the bubbling blood
weekly weight squatting on his muscles
fallen inside his rediscovered self
the bells ring for no reason and we too
ring bells for no reason and we too
we rejoice at the sound of the chains
that we set ringing in us with the bells

*

what is this language that whips us we leap
    into light
our nerves are whips in the hands of time
and doubt comes with a single colorless wing
screwing itself squeezing crushing into us
like the crumpled paper of an opened carton
gift of another age to the glidings of the fishes
    of bitterness

*

the bells ring for no reason and we too
the eyes of fruit watch us attentively
and all our actions are controlled nothing is
    hidden
the river water has washed its bed so much
it carries away the soft threads of the looks that loitered
at the foot of walls in bars it has licked lives
enticed the weak tied up temptations dried up ecstasies

creusé au fond des vieilles variantes
et délié les sources des larmes prisonnières
les sources asservies aux quotidiens étouffements
les regards qui prennent avec des mains desséchées
le clair produit du jour ou l'ombrageuse apparition
qui donnent la soucieuse richesse du sourire
vissée comme une fleur à la boutonnière du matin
ceux qui demandent le repos ou la volupté
les touchers d'électriques vibrations les sursauts
les aventures le feu la certitude ou l'esclavage
les regards qui ont rampé le long des discrètes
    tourmentes
usé les pavés des villes et expié maintes bassesses
    dans les aumônes
se suivent serrés autour des rubans d'eau
et coulent vers les mers en emportant sur leur passage
les humaines ordures et leurs mirages

*

l'eau de la rivière a tant lavé son lit
que même la lumière glisse sur l'onde lisse
et tombe au fond avec le lourd éclat des pierres
les cloches sonnent sans raison et nous aussi
les soucis que nous portons avec nous
qui sont nos vêtements intérieurs
que nous mettons tous les matins
que la nuit défait avec des mains de rêve
ornés d'inutiles rébus métalliques
purifiés dans le bain des paysages circulaires
dans les villes préparées au carnage au sacrifice
près des mers aux balayements de perspectives
sur les montagnes aux inquiètes sévérités
dans les villages aux douloureuses nonchalances
la main pesante sur la tête

got to the bottom of old texts
and unbound the sources of imprisoned tears
the enslaved sources of daily suffocations
looks that take with dessicated hands
the clear product of day or the shadowy apparition
that give the caring richness of a smile
screwed like a flower in the buttonhole of morning
those that demand rest or voluptuousness
touches of electric vibrations starts
adventures fire certainty or slavery
looks that have crept the length of discreet
     tortures
worn the pavements of towns and expiated
     many base acts in acts of charity
follow one another closely around ribbons of water
and flow toward the seas carrying away in their passage
human excrements and their mirages

*

The river water has washed its bed so much
that even light glides on the smooth wave
and falls on the bottom like heavy breaking stones
the bells ring for no reason and we too
the cares that we carry with us
that are our inner clothing
that we put on every morning
that night takes off with the hands of dreams ornamented
with useless metal puzzles
purified in the bath of circular landscapes
in towns prepared for carnage for sacrifice
near seas with sweeping perspectives
on mountains with anxious severities
in villages with dolorous nonchalances
the hand weighing on the head

les cloches sonnent sans raison et nous aussi
nous partons avec les départs arrivons avec les
    arrivées
partons avec les arrivées arrivons quand les autres
    partent
sans raison un peu secs un peu durs sévères
pain nourriture plus de pain qui accompagne
la chanson savoureuse sur la gamme de la langue
les couleurs déposent leur poids et pensent
et pensent ou crient et restent et se nourrissent
de fruits légers comme la fumée planent
qui pense à la chaleur que tisse la parole
autour de son noyau le rêve qu'on appelle nous

*

les cloches sonnent sans raison et nous aussi
nous marchons pour échapper au fourmillement des
    routes
avec un flacon de paysage une maladie une seule
une seule maladie que nous cultivons la mort
je sais que je porte la mélodie en moi et n'en ai pas
    peur
je porte la mort et si je meurs c'est la mort
qui me portera dans ses bras imperceptibles
fins et légers comme l'odeur de l'herbe maigre
fins et légers comme le départ sans cause
sans amertume sans dettes sans regret sans
les cloches sonnent sans raison et nous aussi
pourquoi chercher le bout de la chaine qui nous relie
    à la chaine
sonnez cloches sans raison et nous aussi
nous ferons sonner en nous les verres cassés
les monnaies d'argent mêlées aux fausses monnaies
les débris des fêtes éclatées en rire et en tempête

the bells ring for no reason and we too
we leave with the departures arrive with the
    arrivals
leave with the arrivals arrive when others
    are leaving
for no reason a little dry a little hard severe
bread nourishment no more bread that accompanies
the savory song on the scale of the tongue
colors deposit their weight and think
and think or cry out and stay and feed
on fruit as light as smoke hover
that is thinking of the warmth that the word weaves
around its nucleus the dream called we

          *

the bells ring for no reason and we too
we are walking to escape the swarm on the roads
with a flask of scenery a malady just one
a single malady that we cultivate death
I know I carry the melody in me and am not
    afraid
I carry death and if I die it is death
that will carrry me in his imperceptible arms
fine and light like the smell of thin grass
fine and light like a departure for no reason
without bitterness without debts without regret
    without
the bells ring for no reason and we too
why look for the end of the chain that binds us to
    the chain
ring bells for no reason and we too
we shall make broken glasses ring inside us
silver coins mixed with counterfeit
the debris of feasts that burst in laughter and storm

aux portes desquelles pourraient s'ouvrir les gouffres
les tombes d'air les moulins broyant les os arctiques
ces fêtes qui nous portent les têtes au ciel
et crachent sur nos muscles la nuit du plomb fondu

*

je parle de qui parle qui parle je suis seul
je ne suis qu'un petit bruit j'ai plusieurs bruits en moi
un bruit glacé froissé au carrefour jeté sur le trottoir
    humide
aux pieds des hommes pressés courant avec leurs morts
autour de la mort qui étend ses bras
sur le cadran de l'heure seule vivante au soleil
le souffle obscur de la nuit s'épaissit
et le long des veines chantent les flûtes marines
transposées sur les octaves des couches de diverses
    existences
les vies se répètent à l'infini jusqu'à la maigreur
    atomique
et en haut si haut que nous ne pouvons pas voir
et avec ces vies à côté que nous ne voyons pas
l'ultra-violet de tant de voies parallèles
celles que nous aurions pu prendre
celles par lesquelles nous aurions pu ne pas venir
    au monde
ou en être déjà partis depuis longtemps si longtemps
qu'on aurait oublié et l'époque et la terre qui nous
    aurait sucé la chair
sels et métaux liquides limpides au fond des puits

*

je pense à la chaleur que tisse la parole
autour de son noyau le rêve qu'on appelle nous

at the doors of which gulfs could open
tombs of air mills grinding arctic bones
those feasts that carry us head in the sky
and spit on our muscles the night of molten lead

*

I am speaking of who speaks who speaks I am
    alone
I am only a little sound I have several sounds in me
a frozen sound crumpled at the crossroads thrown
    on the wet pavement
at the feet of hurrying men running with their deaths
around the death that extends his arms
on the face of the clock alone that lives in the sun
the obscure breath of night is thickening
and along veins marine flutes are singing
transposed on octaves of layers of diverse existences
lives are repeated to infinity up to atomic thinness
and on high so high that we cannot see
and with those lives at the side that we do not see
the ultraviolet of so many parallel roads
those that we could have taken
those by which we would have been able not to come
    into the world
or to have already left it a long time ago so long
that one would have forgotten both the epoch and the
    earth that would have sucked our flesh
salts and metals clear liquids at the bottom of
    wells

*

I am thinking of the warmth that the word weaves
around its nucleus the dream called us

Tzara / *289*

Georges Ribemont-Dessaignes

Le Coq fou

Un bienheureux flottant dans la mer des Sargasses
Napoléon aux îles malaises
Sémiramis au bal de l'Elysée
Cuisinière amoureuse d'un poteau télégraphique
Ne connaît ni neuf heures ni minuit ni l'aurore
Ignore le lieu précédent
Cantharide
Eléphant punique
Moteur coccinelle
Plésiosaure mitrailleuse nourrice
Descente de lit pour pieds de jeune mariée
Ses yeux sont montés sur tourniquet à courroie
    sympathie générale
Estomac acide
Moitié de vieille hottentote
Sirius
Froid du fond du ciel
Eunuque à râtelier d'ébonite
Ver luisant Kant ragoût niçois
Jirafe érudite
Ile des Singes potiron Ramsès
Ursule
Asphodèle prépuce hibou chauffeur de taxi
Astaroth
Pou
Sous l'aisselle qui le ramène à la basse-cour
Il découvre l'odeur de l'homme et l'univers sans
   changement
Roulette 37
Amant d'une pintade

Crazy Cock

A happy man floating in the Sargasso Sea
Napoleon at the sickly isles
Semiramis at the Elysée ball
Cook in love with a telegraph pole
Knows neither nine o'clock nor midnight nor dawn
Strike the preceding
Cantharides
Punic elephant
Ladybug motor
Plesiosaur machine gun wet nurse
Bedside rug for feet of young married woman
Her eyes have been put on revolving display sympathy
    from all
Acid stomach
Half of old Hottentot woman
Sirius
Cold of the bottom of the sky
Eunuch with vulcanized false teeth
Worm gleaming Kant stew from Nice
Erudite giraffe
Isle of Monkeys pumpkin Ramses
Ursula
Asphodel prepuce owl taxi driver
Astaroth
Louse
Under the armpit that reminds him of the farmyard
He discovers the odor of man and the universe
    unchanged
Wheel 37
Lover of a guinea fowl

Retour ivre
Mais coq seule soumission fatale et symbolique
Et tandis que les choisies ébrouent leur duvet
Dieu à bicyclette

Drunk return
But cock only fatal and symbolic transmission
And while the chosen shake their down
God on a bicycle

Trombone à coulisse

J'ai sur la tête une petite ailette qui tourne au vent
Et me monte l'eau à la bouche
Et dans les yeux
Pour les appétits et les extases
J'ai dans les oreilles un petit cornet plein d'odeur
    d'absinthe
Et sur le nez un perroquet vert qui bat des ailes
Et crie aux armes!
Quand il tombe du ciel des graines de soleil
L'absence d'acier au coeur
Au fond des vieilles réalités désossées et croupissantes
Est partiale aux marées lunatiques
Je suis capitaine et alsacienne au cinéma
J'ai dans le ventre une petite machine agricole
Qui fauche et lie des fils électriques
Les noix de coco que jette le singe mélancolie
Tombent comme crachats dans l'eau
Ou refleurissent en pétunias
J'ai dans l'estomac une ocarina et j'ai le foie virginal
Je nourris mon poète avec les pieds d'une pianiste
Dont les dents sont paires et impaires
Et le soir des tristes dimanches
Aux tourterelles qui rient comme l'enfer
Je jette des rêves morganatiques

Trombone Off

I have on my head a little blade that turns in the wind
And brings water to my mouth
And into my eyes
For appetites and ecstasies
I have in my ears a little paper cone filled with the odor
    of absinthe
And on my nose a green parrot that beats its wings
And shouts to arms!
When there fall from the sky grains of sunlight
The absence of steel in the heart
At the bottom of old boneless and putrid realities
Is partial to lunatic tides
I am the captain and an Alsatian woman at the cinema
I have in my belly a little agricultural machine
That reaps and binds electric wires
The coconuts that the monkey melancholy throws
Fall like spit in the water
Or blossom again as petunias
I have an ocarina in my stomach and I have a virgin
    liver
I nourish my poet with the feet of a piano player
Whose teeth are even and odd
And on sad Sunday evenings
To the turtledoves that laugh like hell
I throw morganatic dreams

Proverbe, no 6

Qu'est-ce que c'est beau? Qu'est-ce que c'est laid? Qu'est-ce que c'est grand, fort, faible? Qu'est-ce que c'est Carpentier, Renan, Foch? Connais pas. Connais pas, connais pas, connais pas.

Proverb No. 6

What's beautiful? What's ugly? What's great, strong, weak? What's Carpentier, Renan, Foch? Don't know. Don't know, don't know, don't know.

André Breton and Philippe Soupault

Les Champs magnétiques [Extraits]

LE PAGURE DIT:

J'AI BEAUCOUP CONNU

Le général Eblé distance
Papillotes
Les incompatibilités d'humeur suivant l'astronomie
Une personnification de Bonjour
L'ivresse triste des dégustateurs
A présent je me balance sur la chute des feuilles et je
     dors la tête dans les plumes comme une casserole
Tout m'est indifférent depuis les signaux singuliers où
     s'affirma la jalousie de la poussière

RIDEAUX

Souricières de l'âme après extinction du calorifère
     blanc méridien des sacrements
Bielle du navire
Radeau
Jolies algues échouées il y en a de toutes couleurs
Frissons en rentrant le soir
Deux têtes comme les plateaux d'une balance

DÉLIVRANCE

Faculté de se donner
Renseignements gratuits
Amendez-vous sur terre

Magnetic Fields [Selections]

THE HERMIT CRAB SAYS:

I HAVE KNOWN MUCH

General Eblé distance
Curl papers
The incompatibilities of mood following astronomy
A personification of Good Morning
The sad drunkenness of wine tasters
At present I am balancing on fallen leaves and I am
    sleeping with my head in feathers like a saucepan
Everything is indifferent to me since the singular signals by
    which the jealousy of dust was affirmed

CURTAINS

Mouse traps of the soul after extinguishing of the heater
    white meridian of sacraments
Tie-rod of the ship
Raft
Pretty algae stranded there are some of all colors
Shivers on coming home in the evening
Two heads like the pans of a pair of scales

DELIVERANCE

Faculty of giving oneself
Free information
Make amends on earth

Breton and Soupault / *303*

Heureux de faire plaisir
Voici les jolies pioches du retour en arrière inoffensif
L'or mérité
Champignon poussé dans la nuit demain il ne sera
        plus frais
Saisons animatrices de nos désirs
Ouverture des portes devant l'écuyère

AU SEUIL DES TOURS

Les ondes des miracles et des gestes
Le calcul divin des palais
Grâce pour tous ces membres
Un tapis solide une canne à épée et la gloire des exilés
Les numéros des horizons langue écarlate inclinaisons
Pourquoi baisser la tête noble ou lutteur
Les jours passent à travers les mains
Petite flamme pour aveugles-nés
Démonstration des rires école brune au bout du village
        fumée bleue des charbonniers et des forestiers alpestres
Un arc-en-ciel berger magicien
La lumière vient comme une source
La physique n'est plus rien
Ces longs fils et les télégrammes sont les fleurs de nos
        civilisations roses
Il faut s'occuper des voisins odeurs des nuits et des
        lendemains
Le collège fenêtre tapissée de lierre
Le galop des chameaux
Port perdu
La gare est à droite café de la gare Bifur C'est la peur
Préfectures océaniques
Je me cache dans un tableau historique

Happy to please
Here are the pretty pickaxes of the inoffensive withdrawal
Merited gold
Mushroom grown in the night tomorrow it will no longer
    be fresh
Quickening seasons of our desires
Opening of gates before the rider

ON THE THRESHOLD OF TOWERS

Waves of miracles and deeds
Divine calculation of palaces
Thanks for all these members
A solid covering a sword-cane and the glory of exiles
The numbers of horizons scarlet tongue angles
Why lower the noble or struggling head
Days pass through the hands
Little flame for the blind at birth
Demonstration of laughs brown school at the end of the village
    blue smoke of charcoal burners and alpine forest rangers
A rainbow shepherd magician
Light comes like a spring
Physics is no longer anything
Those long threads and telegrams are the flowers of our
    pink civilizations
You have to be concerned about neighbors smells of
    night and the next day
The college window hung with ivy
The gallop of camels
Lost harbor
The station is to the right café of the Branch station It is fear
Oceanic headquarters
I am hiding in a historic picture

Si vert qu'il va fleurir
Les feuilles sont des soupirs tendres
A la hâte coupez vos désirs trois-mâts échappés danseurs fous
La mer n'a plus de couleur venez voir la mer des algues
La giroflée mappemonde ou requin
La pauvre girafe est à droite
Le phoque gémit
Les inspecteurs ont dans leurs mains des obscurités et des
    martins-pêcheurs un graphomètre animal des villes sèches
Pour vous étamines perdues Etat-major des éternités froides

LES MASQUES ET LA CHALEUR COLORÉE

Les bouteilles de flammes sont douces si douces
Les pirates des faubourgs ont du noir aux yeux
Clarté verte adoration des paysages
Souliers vernis
Compagnie industrielle sans titre L'association chimique
    des pendules
Laxité des rongeurs sans yeux
Boulimies des couveuses pâles
Naïveté mauve des marchands de volets rapides et
    brutalement creusés
Sous l'oeil des acides adoptés les phares donnent du courage
Eau verte pour femmes
Journaux d'avant-hier les grands-mères radotent le ciel
    est bleu la mer est bleue les yeux sont bleus
Rayons musicaux quadrupèdes sabre indolent
Les guêpes déchirées sont muettes ce sont des mygales
    pleureuses Le sac des villes sous la mer les pigeons sont
    présents les lustres coupent les murs et les cervelles
Il y a toujours des réveille-matin
La basilique des secondes effrayées

So green that it is going to flower
The leaves are tender sighs
Be quick and stop your desires escaped three-masters
    crazy dancers
The sea has no more color come and see the sea of algae
Gilliflower world map or shark
The poor giraffe is at the right
The seal is groaning
The inspectors have obscurities and kingfishers in their
    hands an animal graphometer of dry towns
For you lost stamens staff-officer of cold eternities

MASKS AND COLORED HEAT

Bottles of flame are nice so nice
Pirates of the suburbs have black in their eyes
Green light adoration of scenery
Patent leather shoes
Unaccredited industrial company The chemical
    association of pendulums
Laxity of eyeless rodents
Bulimias of pale sitting hens
Mauve naivety of sellers of rapid and brutally hollowed
    shutters
Under the eye of adopted acids lighthouses give courage
Green water for women
The day before yesterday's newspapers grandmothers are
    driveling the sky is blue the sea is blue eyes are blue
Musical rays quadrupeds indolent saber
Torn wasps are dumb they are weeping tarantulas The
    sack of towns under the sea pigeons are present lusters
    cut the walls and brains
There are always reveilles
The basilica of frightened seconds

L'importance des baromètres poissons plats
Le basilic et le réséda
Danses espagnoles falaise des gestes échafaudage de torrents
Une sphère détruit tout

Importance of barometers fishes dishes
The basilisk and the mignonette
Spanish dances cliff of gestures scaffolding of torrents
A sphere destroys everything

André Breton

L'Union libre

Ma femme à la chevelure de feu de bois
Aux pensées d'éclairs de chaleur
A la taille de sablier
Ma femme à la taille de loutre entre les dents du tigre
Ma femme à la bouche de cocarde et de bouquet d'étoiles
    de dernière grandeur
Aux dents d'empreintes de souris blanche sur la terre blanche
A la langue d'ambre et de verre frottés
Ma femme à la langue d'hostie poignardée
A la langue de poupée qui ouvre et ferme les yeux
A la langue de pierre incroyable
Ma femme aux cils de bâtons d'écriture d'enfant
Aux sourcils de bord de nid d'hirondelle
Ma femme aux tempes d'ardoise de toit de serre
Et de buée aux vitres
Ma femme aux épaules de champagne
Et de fontaine à têtes de dauphins sous la glace
Ma femme aux poignets d'allumettes
Ma femme aux doigts de hasard et d'as de coeur
Aux doigts de foin coupé
Ma femme aux aisselles de martre et de fênes
De nuit de la Saint-Jean
De troène et de nid de scalares
Aux bras d'écume de mer et d'écluse
Et de mélange du blé et du moulin
Ma femme aux jambes de fusée
Aux mouvements d'horlogerie et de désespoir
Ma femme aux mollets de moelle de sureau
Ma femme aux pieds d'initiales
Aux pieds de trousseaux de clés aux pieds de calfats qui boivent

Free Union

My wife whose hair is a forest fire
Her thoughts that are hot lightning
Her hourglass waist
My wife with the waist of an otter in the teeth of a tiger
My wife with the mouth of a cockade and a bouquet of
    stars of the greatest magnitude
Her teeth are prints of white mice on white earth
Her tongue of polished amber and glass
My wife with the tongue of a stabbed host
The tongue of a doll that opens and closes its eyes
A tongue of unbelievable stone
My wife whose eyelashes are children's first letters
Eyebrows the edge of a swallow's nest
My wife with temples the slates of a greenhouse roof
And steam on the panes
My wife with shoulders of champagne
And a spring with heads of dolphins under ice
My wife with wrists of matches
My wife with fingers of chance and the ace of hearts
Her fingers of cut hay
My wife with armpits of sable and berries
And Midsummer Night
Of privet and a nest of angel fish
Whose arms are sea foam and a flood gate
And a mixture of wheat and a mill
My wife with legs that are rockets
With movements of clockwork and despair
My wife with calves the core of an elderberry tree
My wife whose feet are initials
Her feet are bunches of keys and caulkers drinking

Ma femme au cou d'orge imperlé
Ma femme à la gorge de Val d'or
De rendez-vous dans le lit même du torrent
Aux seins de nuit
Ma femme aux seins de taupinière marine
Ma femme aux seins de creuset du rubis
Aux seins de spectre de la rose sous la rosée
Ma femme au ventre de dépliement déventail des jours
Au ventre de griffe géante
Ma femme au dos d'oiseau qui fuit vertical
Au dos de vif-argent
Au dos de lumière
A la nuque de pierre roulée et de craie mouillée
Et de chute d'un verre dans lequel on vient de boire
Ma femme aux hanches de nacelle
Aux hanches de lustre et de pennes de flèche
Et de tiges de plumes de paon blanc
De balance insensible
Ma femme aux fesses de grès et d'amiante
Ma femme aux fesses de dos de cygne
Ma femme aux fesses de printemps
Au sexe de glaïeul
Ma femme au sexe de placer et d'ornithorynque
Ma femme au sexe d'algue et de bonbons anciens
Ma femme au sexe de miroir
Ma femme aux yeux pleins de larmes
Aux yeux de panoplie violette et d'aiguille aimantée
Ma femme aux yeux de savane
Ma femme aux yeux d'eau pour boire en prison
Ma femme aux yeux de bois toujours sous la hache
Aux yeux de niveau d'eau de niveau d'air de terre et de feu

My wife with a neck of unhulled barley
Her throat is the Valley of Gold
A rendez-vous in the very bed of the flood
With her breasts of night
My wife with breasts a molehill by the sea
My wife with breasts a crucible of ruby
Breasts the specter of the rose covered with dew
My wife whose belly is the opening of a fan of days
Her belly a giant claw
My wife with the back of a bird in vertical flight
A back of quicksilver
A back of light
The back of her neck crushed stone and wet chalk
And the fall of a glass from which you have just drunk
My wife with her gondola hips
Chandelier hips and arrow feathers
And shafts of white peacock feathers
Untrembling scales
My wife with buttocks of sandstone and asbestos
My wife with swansback buttocks
Buttocks of springtime
With her gladiola sex
Sex of a mine and the duck-billed platypus
My wife with her sex of seaweed and ancient candy
My wife with her sex mirror
My wife with her eyes filled with tears
Her eyes of violet armor and a magnetic needle
My wife with her savanna eyes
My wife's eyes are water to be drunk in prison
Eyes of wood always under the axe
Her eyes are the level of water of air and earth and fire

Philippe Soupault

Cinéma-Palace

à Blaise Cendrars

Le vent caresse les affiches
Rien
la caissière est en porcelaine

l'Ecran

le chef d'orchestre automatique dirige le pianola
il y a des coups de revolver
applaudissements
l'auto volée disparaît dans les nuages
et l'amoureux transi s'est acheté un faux col

Mais bientôt les portes claquent
Aujourd'hui très élégant
Il a mis son chapeau claque
Et n'a pas oublié ses gants

Tous les vendredis changement de programme

Palace Cinema

To Blaise Cendrars

The wind caresses the posters
Nothing
the cashier is made of porcelain

the Screen

the automatic leader of the orchestra conducts
    the player piano
there are revolver shots
          applause
the stolen automobile disappears in the clouds
and the timorous lover buys a detachable collar

But soon the doors bang shut
Today very elegant
He has put on his top hat
And has not forgotten his gloves

Every Friday a change of program

Articles de sport

Courageux comme un timbre-poste
il allait son chemin
en tapant doucement dans ses mains
pour compter ses pas
son coeur rouge comme un sanglier
frappait frappait
comme un papillon rose et vert
De temps en temps
il plantait un petit drapeau de satin
Quand il eut beaucoup marché
il s'assit pour se reposer
et s'endormit
Mais depuis ce jour il y a beaucoup de
      nuages dans le ciel
beaucoup d'oiseaux dans les arbres
et beaucoup de sel dans la mer
Il y a encore beaucoup d'autres choses

Sporting Goods

As courageous as a postage stamp
he went on his way
clapping his hands softly
to count his steps
his heart as red as a wild boar
was beating was beating
like a rose and green butterfly
From time to time
he planted a little satin flag
When he had walked for a long time
he sat down to rest
and went to sleep
But since that day there have been many
    clouds in the sky
many birds in the trees
and much salt in the sea
There are many other things too

Paul Eluard

L'Amoureuse

Elle est debout sur mes paupières
Et ses cheveux sont dans les miens
Elle a la forme de mes mains
Elle a la couleur de mes yeux
Elle s'engloutit dans mon ombre
Comme une pierre sur le ciel.

Elle a toujours les yeux ouverts
Et ne me laisse pas dormir.
Ses rêves en pleine lumière
Font s'évaporer les soleils,
Me font rire, pleurer et rire,
Parler sans avoir rien à dire.

The Lover

She is standing on my eyelids
And her hair is in mine.
She has the shape of my hands,
She has the color of my eyes,
She is swallowed by my shadow
Like a stone on the sky.

Her eyes are always open
And she does not let me sleep.
Her dreams in broad daylight
Make the suns evaporate,
Make me laugh, cry and laugh,
Speak with nothing to say.

Le Miroir d'un moment

Il dissipe le jour,
Il montre aux hommes les images déliées de
   l'apparence,
Il enlève aux hommes la possibilité de se
   distraire,
Il est dur comme la pierre,
La pierre informe,
La pierre du mouvement et de la vue,
Et son éclat est tel que toutes les armures, tous
   les masques en sont faussés.
Ce que la main a pris dédaigne même de prendre
   la forme de la main,
Ce qui a été compris n'existe plus,
L'oiseau s'est confondu avec le vent,
Le ciel avec sa vérité,
L'homme avec sa réalité.

The Mirror of a Moment

It dissipates daylight,
It shows men the unbound images of appearance,
It takes away from men the possibility of being
    distracted,
It is as hard as stone,
Unformed stone,
The stone of movement and sight,
And its brilliance is such that all armors, all masks are
    thereby falsified.
What the hand has seized even disdains to take the
    shape of the hand,
What has been understood no longer exists,
The bird is confused with the wind,
The sky with its truth,
Man with his reality.

Grand Air

La rive les mains tremblantes
Descendait sous la pluie
Un escalier de brumes
Tu sortais toute nue
Faux-marbre palpitant
Teint de bon matin
Trésor gardé par des bêtes immenses
Qui gardaient elles du soleil sous leurs ailes
Des bêtes que nous connaissions sans les voir

Par-delà les murs de nos nuits
Par-delà l'horizon de nos baisers
Le rire contagieux des hyènes
Pouvait bien ronger les vieux os
Des êtres qui vivent un par un

Nous jouions au soleil à la pluie à la mer
A n'avoir qu'un regard qu'un ciel et qu'une mer
Les nôtres

Fresh Air

The shore with trembling hands
Let down beneath the rain
A ladder of fog
You emerged naked
Like trembling marble
The color of morning
A treasure guarded by immense beasts
Shielding themselves from the sun with
    their wings
Beasts that we knew without seeing them

Beyond the walls of our nights
Beyond the horizon of our kisses
The contagious laughter of hyenas
Could very well be gnawing old bones
Of beings who live one by one

We were enjoying in the sun the rain the sea
Having only one look at one sky and one sea
Ours

Benjamin Péret

Petite Chanson des mutilés

Prête-moi ton bras
pour remplacer ma jambe
Les rats me l'ont mangée
à Verdun   /
　　　　　　　　bis
à Verdun   \
J'ai mangé beaucoup de rats
mais ils ne m'ont pas rendu ma jambe
c'est pour cela qu'on m'a donné la croix de guerre
et une jambe de bois   /
　　　　　　　　　　　bis
et une jambe de bois   \

Little Song of the Mutilated

Lend me your arm
to replace my leg
The rats ate it
at Verdun /
at Verdun \ *repeat*
I ate many rats
but they didn't give me back my leg
that is why I was given the *croix de guerre*
and a wooden leg /
and a wooden leg \ *repeat*

Au Bout du monde

Quand les charbons enflammés s'enfuient comme
    des lions apeurés au fond de la mine
les oiseaux de farine
se trâinent comme des timbres-poste sur des lettres
    retournées à l'envoyeur
et les escaliers branlants
bêtes comme des saucisses dont la choucroute a déjà
    été mangée
attendent qu'il fasse jour
que les pommes soient mûres
pour appeler le cheval de fiacre
qui joue à cache-cache avec son fiacre
et le détruira
avant que les orteils des concierges deviennent des
    rails de chemin de fer

At the End of the World

When fiery coals flee like frightened lions at the
    bottom of the mine
birds of flour
drag themselves along like postage stamps on letters
    returned to the sender
and shaky staircases
as stupid as sausages whose sauerkraut has
    already been eaten
wait for daylight
for apples to be ripe
to call the cab horse
that is playing hide-and-seek with its cab
and will destroy it
before the big toes of concierges become railroad
    rails

Allo

Mon avion en flammes mon château inondé de
    vin du Rhin
mon ghetto d'iris noir mon oreille de cristal
mon rocher dévalant la falaise pour écraser le
    garde champêtre
mon escargot d'opale mon moustique d'air
mon édredon de paradisiers ma chevelure d'écume
    noire
mon tombeau éclaté ma pluie de sauterelles rouges
mon île volante mon raisin de turquoise
ma collision d'autos folles et prudentes ma plate-
    bande sauvage
mon pistil de pissenlit projeté dans mon oeil
mon oignon de tulipe dans le cerveau
ma gazelle égarée dans un cinéma des boulevards
ma cassette de soleil mon fruit de volcan
mon rire d'étang caché où vont se noyer les prophètes
    distraits
mon inondation de cassis mon papillon de morille
ma cascade bleue comme une lame de fond qui fait le
    printemps
mon revolver de corail dont la bouche m'attire comme
    l'oeil d'un puits
scintillant
glacé comme le miroir où tu contemples la fuite des
    oiseaux-mouches de ton regard
perdu dans une exposition de blanc encadrée de momies
je t'aime

Hello

My plane on fire my castle inundated by Rhine wine
my ghetto of black iris my crystal ear
my rock rolling down the cliff to crush the sheriff
my opal snail my air mosquito
my eiderdown of birds of paradise my hair of black foam
my tomb burst asunder my rain of red grasshoppers
my flying island my turquoise grape
my collision of crazy and cautious cars my wild flower bed
my dandelion pistil shot in my eye
my tulip onion in the brain
my gazelle wandered into a cinema on the boulevard
my casket of sunlight my volcano fruit
my laugh of a hidden pond in which absent-minded
    prophets are going to drown
my inundation of cassis my morel butterfly
my blue waterfall like a deep wave that makes the spring
my coral revolver with a mouth that attracts me like the
    eye of a well
scintillating
frozen like the mirror in which you contemplate the flight
    of the hummingbirds of your glance
lost in an exhibition of white framed by mummies
I love you

Robert Desnos

L'Aumonyme

En attendant
en nattant l'attente.
Sous quelle tente
mes tantes
ont-elles engendré
les neveux silencieux
que nul ne veut sous les cieux
appeler ses cousins?
En nattant les cheveux du silence
six lances
percent mes pensées en attendant.

Almonymous

Waiting
braiding the moments.
Under what tent
did my aunts
engender
the silent nephews
no one beneath the sky wants
to call his cousins?
While braiding the hair of silence
six lances
pierce my thoughts waiting.

Les Gorges froides

A la poste d'hier tu télégraphieras
que nous sommes bien morts avec les hirondelles.
Facteur triste facteur un cercueil sous ton bras
va-t-en porter ma lettre aux fleurs à tire d'elle.

La boussole est en os mon coeur tu t'y fieras.
quelque tibia marque le pôle et les marelles
pour amputés ont un sinistre aspect d'opéras
Que pour mon épitaphe un dieu taille ses grêles!

C'est ce soir que je meurs ma chère Tombe-Issoire,
Ton regard le plus beau ne fut qu'un accessoire
de la machinerie étrange du bonjour:

Adieu! je vous aimai sans scrupule et sans ruse,
ma Folie-Méricourt ma silencieuse intruse.
Boussole à flèche torse annonce le retour.

Cold Throats

We died like the swallows who always are off in
A hurry, you'll wire the news yesterday.
Mailman sad mailman who carry a coffin
Take the letter I'm writing the flowers to say.

The compass is fashioned of bone, and a shin
Marks the pole, and the hopscotch amputees play
Like the opera makes a most sinister din.
May a god carve my tombstone in hail right away!

I'm dying, Tombe-Issoire, this evening I'm dying,
The most beautiful look in your eyes and your sighing
Were only a part of the meeting machine:

Adieu! Without scruple or guile I adored you,
Folie-Méricourt, silent intruder. Adieu!
The compass announces I'm back where I've been.

Rêve, nuit du 27 au 28 mai 1923

Je m'étais levé ce matin-là de bonne heure. Je suivais la rue de Rivoli encore déserte, de mon domicile (au 9), jusqu'à la Place de l'Hôtel-de-Ville. Je m'apprêtais à prendre l'autobus "Place de la République-Champ-de-Mars" qui s'arrête à cet endroit quand je réfléchis qu'il était utile d'avoir un numéro. J'allais en prendre un au distributeur accroché à un lampadaire, quand arriva un pensionnat d'orphelines en robes bleu foncé et chapeau de paille noire. Elles commencèrent une à une à prendre des numéros et, comme elles emplissaient la rue jusqu'à l'horizon, je bouillais d'impatience et les autobus se succédaient sans que je puisse monter. Tout à coup j'aperçus à ma droite Picabia — "Venez-vous en Angleterre?" me dit-il. J'acceptai et montai dans son auto qui partit à une allure assez modérée. Bientôt, nous arrivâmes en Angleterre, ce n'était autre chose que la Porte Maillot. Je ne sais comment Picabia et moi fûmes séparés, et je me trouvai sur une place petite, carrée et blanche qui figurait Trafalgar-Square. De cette place partait un corridor tapissé de rouge et faiblement éclairé qui conduisait à la fille du roi d'Angleterre. J'y parvins et emmenai celle-ci par la main jusqu'à la Madeleine où nous nous mariâmes en grande pompe: j'étais en habit de couleur et ma femme en costume de mariée. Comme nous paraissions en haut des marches, la place de la Madeleine déserte s'emplit de camelots qui vendaient des ournaux en criant: "Démission du roi d'Angleterre, édition spéciale." Nous descendîmes les marches et en bas nous aperçûmes un petit homme râblé et vulgaire habillé d'un costume de sport en cheviote foncée peu élégant qui me dit: "Je suis le roi d'Angleterre. J'ai démissionné pour me battre en duel avec vous." Je fis alors un grand geste en disant: "On ne se bat pas en duel avec les rois, on les guillotine," tout en pensant au premier acte de *Locus Solus* et à la tête de Danton.

Dream, the Night of May 27–28, 1923

I got up early that morning. I was following the rue de Rivoli, which was still deserted, from my domicile (at number 9) to the square of the Hôtel de Ville. I was meaning to take the Place de la République-Champs de Mars bus that makes this stop when I thought that it would be useful to have a number. I went to get one from the automatic machine attached to a lamp post, when girls from an orphanage began to arrive, in dark blue dresses and black straw hats. They began taking numbers one by one, and as they filled the street as far as the horizon I was steaming with impatience and buses went by one after another without my being able to climb on. Suddenly to my right I saw Picabia. "Are you coming to England?" he asked me. I accepted and got into his car which set off at a reasonable speed. Soon we arrived in England which was nothing else than Porte Maillot. Picabia and I became separated, I don't know how, and I found myself in a small white open space that appeared to be Trafalgar Square. From there ran a corridor carpeted in red and feebly lighted that went to the daughter of the King of England. I arrived and led her by the hand to the Madeleine where we were married in great pomp: I was in a colorful costume and my bride in a wedding dress. As we appeared at the top of the steps the empty square of the Madeleine filled with newsboys shouting, "Extra! Abdication of the King of England!" We went down the steps and at the bottom saw a small, stocky, common looking fellow dressed for sport in dark tweed that wasn't very elegant, who said to me, "I am the King of England. I have abdicated in order to fight a duel with you." I made a large gesture, saying, "One does not fight a duel with kings, one guillotines them," thinking of the first act of *Locus Solus* and Danton's head.

Les Espaces du sommeil

Dans la nuit il y a naturellement les sept merveilles
du monde et la grandeur et le tragique et le charme.
Les forêts s'y heurtent confusément avec des
créatures de légende cachées dans les fourrés.
Il y a toi.
Dans la nuit il y a le pas du promeneur et celui
de l'assassin et celui du sergent de ville et la lumière
du réverbère et celle de la lanterne du chiffonnier.
Il y a toi.
Dans la nuit passent les trains et les bateaux et
le mirage des pays où il fait jour. Les derniers souffles
du crépuscule et les premiers frissons de l'aube.
Il y a toi.
Un air de piano, un éclat de voix.
Une porte claque. Une horloge.
Et pas seulement les êtres et les choses et les
bruits matériels.
Mais encore moi qui me poursuis ou sans cesse me dépasse.
Il y a toi l'immolée, toi que j'attends.
Parfois d'étranges figures naissent à l'instant du
sommeil et disparaissent.
Quand je ferme les yeux, des floraisons phosphor-
escentes apparaissent et se fanent et renaissent
comme des feux d'artifice charnus.
Des pays inconnus que je parcours en compagnie
de créatures.
Il y a toi sans doute, ô belle et discrète espionne.
Et l'âme palpable de l'étendue.   `
Et les parfums du ciel et des étoiles et le chant
du coq d'il y a 2000 ans et le cri du paon dans des
parcs en flamme et des baisers.

The Spaces of Sleep

In the night there are naturally the seven wonders of the world and grandeur and tragedy and enchantment.

The forests are filled with confusion as legendary creatures hidden in the bushes collide with each other.

There is you.

In the night there is the step of the walker and that of the murderer and that of the policeman and the light of the street lamp and that of the garbage picker.

There is you.

In the night trains and ships pass and the mirage of countries where it is daylight. The last breaths of twilight and first shivers of dawn.

There is you.

A tune on the piano, burst of a voice.

A door bangs. A clock.

And not only human beings and things and material sounds.

But also I who am pursuing myself or ceaselessly going past.

There is you the sacrificed one, you I am waiting for.

Sometimes strange figures are born at the moment of sleep and disappear.

When I close my eyes, phosphorescent flowerings appear and wither and are reborn like artificial fires of flesh.

Unknown lands I traverse accompanied by creatures.

There is certainly you, O beautiful and prudent spy.

And the palpable soul of the whole.

And fragrances of the sky and stars and the cry of the cock 2000 years ago and the cry of the peacock in parks that are on fire and kisses.

Des mains qui se serrent sinistrement dans une lumière blafarde et des essieux qui grincent sur des routes médusantes.

Il y a toi sans doute que je ne connais pas, que je connais au contraire.

Mais qui, présente dans mes rêves, t'obstines à s'y laisser deviner sans y paraître.

Toi qui restes insaisissable dans la réalité et dans le rêve.

Toi qui m'appartiens de par ma volonté de te posséder en illusion mais qui n'approches ton visage du mien que mes yeux clos aussi bien au rêve qu'à la réalité.

Toi qu'en dépit d'une rhétorique facile où le flot meurt sur les plages, où la corneille vole dans des usines en ruine, où le bois pourrit en craquant sous un soleil de plomb.

Toi qui es à la base de mes rêves et qui secoues mon esprit plein de métamorphoses et qui me laisses ton gant quand je baise ta main.

Dans la nuit il y a les étoiles et le mouvement ténébreux de la mer, des fleuves, des forêts, des villes, des herbes, des poumons de millions et millions d'êtres.

Dans la nuit il y a les merveilles du monde.

Dans la nuit il n'y a pas d'anges gardiens, mais il y a le sommeil.

Dans la nuit il y a toi.

Dans le jour aussi.

Hands that grasp each other in a sinister way in a pallid light and axles that grate on astounding roads.

There is certainly you whom I do not know, whom on the contrary I know.

But who, present in my dreams, obstinately allow yourself to be sensed without appearing.

You who remain unseizable in reality and dreams.

You who belong to me by my willing to possess you in illusion but who bring your face close to mine only when my eyes are closed in a dream as well as reality.

You in spite of a facile rhetoric in which waves die on beaches, crows fly into ruined factories, the woods rot and crack under a leaden sky.

You who are the base of my dreams and who shake my spirit that is filled with metamorphoses and who leave me your glove when I kiss your hand.

In the night there are stars and the shadowy movement of the sea, rivers, forests, towns, grass, the lungs of millions and millions of beings.

In the night there are the wonders of the world.

In the night there are no guardian angels, but there is sleep.

In the night there is you.

In the dayime also.

Identité des images

Je me bats avec fureur contre des animaux et des bouteilles
Depuis peu de temps peut-être dix heures sont
    passées l'une après l'autre
La belle nageuse qui avait peur du corail ce matin s'éveille
Le corail couronné de houx frappe à sa porte
Ah! encore le charbon toujours le charbon
Je t'en conjure charbon génie tutélaire du rêve et de ma
    solitude laisse-moi laisse-moi parler encore de la
    belle nageuse qui avait peur du corail
Ne tyrannise plus ce séduisant sujet de mes rêves
La belle nageuse reposait dans un lit de dentelles et
    d'oiseaux
Les vêtements sur une chaise au pied du lit étaient
    illuminés par les lueurs les dernières lueurs du
    charbon
Celui-ci venu des profondeurs du ciel de la terre et
    de la mer était fier de son bec de corail et de ses
    grandes ailes de crêpe
Il avait toute la nuit suivi des enterrements
    divergents vers des cimetières suburbains
Il avait assisté à des bals dans les ambassades
    marqué de son empreinte une feuille de fougère
    des robes de satin blanc
Il s'était dressé terrible à l'avant des navires et les
    navires n'étaient pas revenus
Maintenant tapi dans la cheminée il guettait le
    réveil de l'écume et le chant des bouilloires
Son pas retentissant avait troublé le silence des
    nuits dans les rues aux pavés sonores
Charbon sonore charbon maître du rêve charbon

Identity of Images

I am fighting furiously with animals and bottles
In a short time perhaps ten hours have passed one
    after another
The beautiful swimmer who was afraid of coral wakes
    this morning
Coral crowned with holly knocks on her door
Ah! coal again always coal
I conjure you coal tutelary genius of dreams and my
    solitude let me let me speak again of the beautiful
    swimmer who was afraid of coral
No longer tyrannize this seductive subject of my
    dreams
The beautiful swimmer was reposing in a bed of lace
    and birds
The clothes on a chair at the foot of the bed were illum-
    inated by gleams the last gleams of coal
The one that had come from the depths of the sky and
    earth and sea was proud of its coral beak and great
    wings of crape
All night long it had followed divergent funerals toward
    suburban cemeteries
It had been to embassy balls marked white satin gowns with
    its imprint a fern leaf
It had risen terribly before ships and the ships had not
    returned
Now crouched in the chimney it was watching for the
    waking of foam and singing of kettles
Its resounding step had disturbed the silence of nights
    in streets with sonorous pavements
Sonorous coal coal master of dreams coal

Ah dis-moi où est-elle cette belle nageuse cette
    nageuse qui avait peur du corail?
Mais la nageuse elle-même s'est rendormie
Et je reste face à face avec le feu et je resterai
    la nuit durant à interroger le charbon aux ailes
    de ténèbres qui persiste à projeter sur mon
    chemin monotone l'ombre de ses fumées et le
    reflet terrible de ses braises
Charbon sonore charbon impitoyable charbon.

Ah tell me where is that beautiful swimmer the swimmer
  who was afraid of coral?
But the swimmer herself has gone back to sleep
And I remain face to face with the fire and shall remain
  through the night interrogating the coal with wings of
  darkness that persists in projecting on my montonous
  road the shadow of its smoke and the terrible reflec-
  tions of its embers
Sonorous coal coal pitiless coal

Complainte de Fantômas

1

Ecoutez . . . Faites silence . . .
La triste énumération
De tous les forfaits sans nom,
Des tortures, des violences
Toujours impunis, hélas!
Du criminel Fantômas.

2

Lady Beltham, sa maîtresse,
Le vit tuer son mari
Car il les avait surpris
Au milieu de leurs caresses.
Il coula le paquebot
Lancaster au fond des flots.

3

Cent personnes il assassine.
Mais Juve aidé de Fandor
Va lui faire subir son sort
Enfin sur la guillotine . . .
Mais un acteur, très bien grimé,
A sa place est exécuté.

Fantomas, a Complaint

1

Listen, children, and you shall hear
Of unmentionable acts,
Torture and violence, facts
About the wretched career,
Always unpunished, alas!
Of the criminal Fantomas.

2

Lady Beltham is his mistress.
He shot her husband dead
For he surprised them in bed
In the middle of a caress.
He sent the *Lancaster* too
To the bottom of the ocean blue.

3

He must have killed a hundred,
Which Juve, helped by Fandor,
Were going to make him pay for
On the guillotine with his head.
But an actor took his place
In makeup, with a rubber face.

4

Un phare dans la tempête
Croule, et les pauvres bateaux
Font naufrage au fond de l'eau.
Mais surgissent quatre têtes:
Lady Beltham aux yeux d'or,
Fantômas, Juve et Fandor.

5

Le monstre avait une fille
Aussi jolie qu'une fleur.
La douce Hélène au grand coeur
Ne tenait pas de sa famille,
Car elle sauva Fandor
Qu'était condamné à mort.

6

En consigne d'une gare
Un colis ensanglante!
Un escroc est arrêté!
Qu'est devenu le cadavre?
Le cadavre est bien vivant,
C'est Fantômas, mes enfants!

7

Prisonnier dans une cloche
Sonnant un enterrement
Ainsi mourut son lieutenant.
Le sang de sa pauv' caboche
Avec saphirs et diamants
Pleuvait sur les assistants.

4

In the storm a lighthouse crum-
bles and falls. All the boats
Are sinking, and nothing floats.
But look over there! Up come
Lady Beltham, and three more,
Fantomas, Juve, Fandor!

5

The monster has a daughter,
Hélène, fair as a lily.
She doesn't take after her family
With their love of crime and slaughter.
When Fandor's number was up,
Like Pocahontas she shouted, "Stop!"

6

Left at the station, a bloody
Suitcase . . . They've got the usual
Suspects up against the wall.
But what's become of the body?
It's alive, and going first class.
Children, it's Fantomas!

7

The prisoner in a bell
Ringing them to the graveside,
So his lieutenant died.
The blood of his poor noddle
Rained diamonds and sapphires
On the heads of the pallbearers.

8

Un beau jour des fontaines
Soudain chantèr'nt à Paris.
Le monde était surpris,
Ignorant que ces sirènes
De la Concorde enfermaient
Un roi captif qui pleurait.

9

Certain secret d'importance
Allait être dit au tzar.
Fantômas, lui, le reçut car
Ayant pris sa ressemblance
Il remplaçait l'empereur
Quand Juv' l'arrêta sans peur.

10

Il fit tuer par la Toulouche,
Vieillarde aux yeux dégoûtants,
Un Anglais à grands coups de dents
Et le sang remplit sa bouche.
Puis il cacha un trésor
Dans les entrailles du mort.

11

Cette grande catastrophe
De l'autobus qui rentra
Dans la banque qu'on pilla
Dont on éventra les coffres . . .
Vous vous souvenez de ça? . . .
Ce fut lui qui l'agença.

8

One fine day the fountains
Suddenly sang in Paris.
Now that was a surprise!
They didn't know that the sirens
Who live at the Concorde kept
A king captive, and he wept.

9

A very important secret
Meant for the ear of the Tsar
Went into Fantomas's ear.
He turned himself into the spit-
ting image of the Emperor.
Juve arrested him, without fear.

10

Toulouche, the old woman
With disgusting eyes, who killed
With her teeth, so her mouth filled
With blood, an Englishman . . .
He made her do it. Then puts
A treasure in the dead man's guts.

11

The great catastrophe
You recall, when the bus crashed
Into the bank, and they smashed
The strongboxes . . . it was he,
Acting both as principal
And agent, who arranged it all.

12

La peste en épidémie
Ravage un grand paquebot
Tout seul au milieu des flots.
Quel spectacle de folie!
Agonies et morts hélas!
Qui a fait ça? Fantômas.

13

Il tua un cocher de fiacre.
Au siège il le ficela
Et roulant cahin-caha,
Malgré les clients qui sacrent,
Il ne s'arrêtait jamais
L'fiacre qu'un mort conduisait.

14

Méfiez-vous des roses noires,
Il en sort une langueur
Epuisante et l'on en meurt.
C'est une bien sombre histoire
Encore un triste forfait
De Fantômas en effet!

15

Il assassina la mère
De l'héroïque Fandor.
Quelle injustice du sort,
Douleur poignante et amère . . .
Il n'avait donc pas de coeur,
Cet infâme malfaiteur!

12

A cholera epidemic
At sea . . . The ship all alone
In the middle of the ocean,
If you can imagine it . . . panic,
Agony and death, alas!
Who did it? Fantomas.

13

He killed a cabby, sat him
Bolt upright on the seat.
He went ambling down the street.
People swore and shook fists at him,
But the cab still wouldn't stop
That a dead man drove, clip-clop.

14

Be on guard against black roses.
They've been known to exhude
An aroma and lassitude
Many have died of. This is
Another heinous crime
He commits from time to time.

15

Fandor who is heroic
Had a mother. She was assass-
inated by Fantomas.
That was a heartless trick
That fate and the malefactor
Played on the brave Fandor!

16

Du Dôme des Invalides
On volait l'or chaque nuit.
Qui c'était? mais c'était lui,
L'auteur de ce plan cupide.
User aussi mal son temps
Quand on est intelligent!

17

A la reine de Hollande
Même, il osa s'attaquer.
Juve le fit prisonnier
Ainsi que toute sa bande.
Mais il échappa pourtant
A un juste châtiment.

18

Pour effacer sa trace
Il se fit tailler des gants
Dans la peau d'un trophée sanglant,
Dans d'la peau de mains d'cadavre
Et c'était ce mort qu'accusaient
Les empreintes qu'on trouvait.

19

A Valmondois un fantôme
Sur la rivière marchait.
En vain Juve le cherchait.
Effrayant vieillards et mômes,
C'était Fantômas qui fuyait
Après l'coup qu'il avait fait.

16

Who stole the gold every night
From the dome of the Invalides?
Who do you think? Yes, indeed!
His I.Q. is out of sight.
Isn't it a shame for a mind
To be wasted, when it's so refined!

17

He tackled the Queen of Holland!
Can you imagine it? Her?
But Juve took him prisoner,
Together with all his band.
Though there was the devil to pay,
He didn't. He got clean away!

18

Here's another smart thing he did.
He had gloves that fit perfectly
Made from the hands of an enemy
He killed. So when they discovered
Fingerprints, it was the body
The prints pointed to, not he.

19

A phantom had been seen
On the river at Valmondois,
Terrifying old men and boys.
Juve searched for it in vain.
It was Fantomas, when he flew
The scene of his latest coup.

20

La police d'Angleterre
Par lui fut mystifiée.
Mais, à la fin, arrêté,
Fut pendu et mis en terre.
Devinez ce qui arriva:
Le bandit en réchappa.

21

Dans la nuit sinistre et sombre,
A travers la Tour Eiffel,
Juv' poursuit le criminel.
En vain guette-t-il son ombre.
Faisant un suprême effort
Fantômas échappe encor.

22

D'vant le casino d' Monte-Carlo
Un cuirassé évoluait.
Son commandant qui perdait
Voulait bombarder la rade.
Fantômas, c'est évident,
Etait donc ce commandant.

23

Dans la mer un bateau sombre
Avec Fantômas à bord,
Hélène Juve et Fandor
Et des passagers sans nombre.
On ne sait s'ils sont tous morts,
Nul n'a retrouvé leurs corps.

20

In England all the policemen
Were baffled and mystified.
Finally he was captured, tried,
And hanged. But once again
He escaped, from six feet under.
Another famous British blunder . . .

21

It is a dark and stormy night.
Juve at the Eiffel Tower
Is lying in wait for a shadow,
Pursuing with all his might.
No luck! With all his main
Fantomas escapes again!

22

A battleship was cruising
Offshore at Monte Carlo.
It was going to shell the casino
Because the captain was losing.
It's obvious who the captain was,
That sore loser, Fantomas.

23

Deeper than the plummet goes
There's a liner with Fantomas,
Hélène, Juve, Fandor, and a mass
Of passengers. No one knows
If they're all dead and drowned,
For their bodies were never found.

24

Ceux de sa bande, Beaumôme,
Bec de Gaz et le Bedeau,
Le rempart du Montparno,
Ont fait trembler Paris, Rome
Et Londres par leurs exploits.
Se sont-ils soumis aux lois?

25

Pour ceux du peuple et du monde,
J'ai écrit cette chanson
Sur Fantômas, dont le nom
Fait tout trembler à la ronde.
Maintenant, vivez longtemps,
Je le souhaite en partant.

FINAL

Allongeant son ombre immense
Sur le monde et sur Paris,
Quel est ce spectre aux yeux gris
Qui surgit dans le silence?
Fantômas, serait-ce toi
Qui te dresses sur les toits?

24

His gang, young Sugarcake,
Gas Nose, and the Deacon,
Who frightened Paris and London
And kept all Rome awake,
Montparnasse's cream of crime,
Are any of them doing time?

25

I wrote this for the people,
Men and women of good will,
About the one who likes to kill,
Whose name makes the world tremble.
Wishing you a happy and long
Life, now I'll end my song.

FINALE

The huge shadow that stretches,
The specter with gray eyes
In silence starting to rise
Above the roofs of Paris
And the whole world, alas!
Can it be you, Fantomas?

Mi-Route

Il y a un moment précis dans le temps
Où l'homme atteint le milieu exact de sa vie,
Un fragment de seconde.
Une fugitive parcelle de temps plus rapide qu'un
    regard,
Plus rapide que le sommet des pâmoisons amoureuses,
Plus rapide que la lumière.
Et l'homme est sensible à ce moment.

De longues avenues entre des frondaisons
S'allongent vers la tour où sommeille une dame
Dont la beauté résiste aux baisers, aux saisons,
Comme une étoile au vent, comme un rocher aux
    lames.

Un bateau frémissant s'enfonce et gueule.
Au sommet d'un arbre claque un drapeau.
Une femme bien peignée, mais dont les bas tombent
    sur les souliers
Apparaît au coin d'une rue,
Exaltée, frémissante,
Protégeant de sa main une lampe surannée et qui fume.

Et encore un débardeur ivre chante au coin d'un pont,
Et encore une amante mord les lèvres de son amant,
Et encore un pétale de rose tombe sur un lit vide,
Et encore trois pendules sonnent la même heure
A quelques minutes d'intervalle,
Et encore un homme qui passe dans une rue se retourne
Parce que l'on a crié son prénom,
Mais ce n'est pas lui que cette femme appelle,

Halfway

There is a precise moment in time
When a man reaches the exact middle of his life,
The fraction of a second,
A fugitive fragment of time quicker than a glance,
Quicker than the lovers' climax,
Quicker than light.
And at that moment the man is fully aware.

Long avenues lined with leaves
Extend to the tower where a lady is sleeping
Whose beauty is resistant to kisses, seasons,
As a star to the wind, a rock to waves.

A ship quivers as it sinks and blares.
At the top of a tree a flag is flapping.
A woman who is well groomed but whose stockings
    are falling on her shoes
Appears at the corner of a street,
In a state of exaltation, trembling,
Protecting with her hand an antique lamp that is
    smoking.

And a drunk longshoreman is singing again in the
    corner of a bridge,
And a lover again biting the lips of her lover,
And a rose petal falling again on an empty bed,
And three clocks are again striking the same time
Several minutes apart,
And again a man passing in a street turns around
Because someone shouted his name,
But it isn't he the woman is calling,

Et encore, un ministre en grande tenue,
Désagréablement gêné par le pan de sa chemise coincé
  entre son pantalon et son caleçon,
Inaugure un orphelinat,
Et encore d'un camion lancé à toute vitesse
Dans les rues vides de la nuit
Tombe une tomate merveilleuse qui roule dans le
  ruisseau
Et qui sera balayée plus tard,
Et encore un incendie s'allume au sixième étage d'une
  maison
Qui flambe au coeur de la ville silencieuse et
  indifférente,
Et encore un homme entend une chanson
Oubliée depuis longtemps, et l'oubliera de nouveau,
Et encore maintes choses,
Maintes autres choses que l'homme voit à l'instant
  précis du milieu de sa vie,
Maintes autres choses se déroulent longuement dans le
  plus court des courts instants de la terre.
Il pressent le mystère de cette seconde, de ce fragment
  de seconde,

Mais il dit "Chassons ces idées noires,"
Et il chasse ces idées noires.
Et que pourrait-il dire,
Et que pourrait-il faire
De mieux?

And again, a minister in full regalia,
Discommoded by his shirttail being wedged between
    his trousers and shorts,
Inaugurates an orphanage,
And again from a truck starting at full speed
In the empty streets of night
Falls a marvelous tomato that rolls into the gutter
And later will be swept up,
And again a fire breaks out on the sixth floor of
    a house
Burning at the heart of the silent indifferent town,
And again a man hears a song
Forgotten long ago, and will forget it again,
And again many things,
Many other things the man sees at the exact moment
    of the middle of his life,
Many other things unroll slowly in the shortest of the
    short moments of the earth.
He senses the mystery of that second, that fraction of
    a second,

But he says, "Forget those depressing thoughts,"
And forgets those depressing thoughts.
And what could he say,
And what could he do
That would be better?

The Poets

GUILLAUME APOLLINAIRE
1880-1918

Guillaume Apollinaire's mother, Angelica Alexandrine Kostrowitzky, was a Pole. Her parents had taken part in an anti-Russian insurrection and been forced to leave Poland. They settled in Rome where Angelica's father was appointed papal chamberlain. She was placed at school in the French Convent of the Sacred Heart. She would not be obedient—one biographer speaks of "precocious sensuality." In 1880 she gave birth, out of wedlock, to the future poet. The child was registered at birth as being of a "father N. N." (*non noto*, unknown). She gave birth two years later to another male child, also of a "father N. N." She moved wth her two children to Monaco where she made a living as an *entraineuse*, one of the women in bars who encouraged customers to order drinks. Then she found a "protector," a man named Jules Weil.

In 1889 Guillaume was enrolled at the College of Saint Charles in Monaco where he was instructed by nuns. He developed a taste for literature and planned to write a novel in the manner of Jules Verne. In 1891 he took five honorable mentions at the prize distribution presided over by the Bishop of Monaco. Then the college was closed and the schoolboy commuted every day by train along the Côte d'Azur to the Stanislas College at Cannes. In February, 1897, he transferred to the lycée at Nice. By this time he was reading the poets Henri de Régnier and Mallarmé and the prose of Rémy de Gourmont. He was fond of bizarre anecdotes. He delved into rare texts and collected esoteric information, particularly Gothic mythology, with which he impressed his companions.

For some reason the student failed his *baccalauréat*. In June, 1897, he returned to Monaco, and from then on studied or idled as he wished. He had tried writing verse in classical alexandrines:

> Flora and warm Phoebus were returning to earth
> And the murmuring waves broke on Cytherea . . .

Soon, however, he tried his hand at free verse, describing the carnival at Nice:

> Songs! Bengal fires!
> Champagne! Dithyramb!
> The Carnival King is burning! . . .

In April, 1899, the Kostrowitzky ménage, including Jules Weil, moved to Paris, where they settled in Avenue MacMahon. Apollinaire delighted in Paris. He rummaged every day in the booksellers' boxes along the quays. "I imagined myself meeting one or another of the poets I loved, a prose writer I admired, a pedant I hated."

When he was nineteen he traveled with his brother and their "uncle" Weil to Stavelot in Belgium. Guillaume walked the roads, talked to the peasants, and observed Walloon customs. He fell in love with an innkeeper's daughter and wrote love poems and the greater part of a prose story, "L'Enchanteur pourissant," "The Putrefying Wizard," a tale set in medieval times. The wizard Merlin, the son of a virgin and a devil, esteems man above Christ.

Weil left Stavelot. The brothers stayed behind and ran up a long bill. Guillaume said that their mother was coming to pay it, then the brothers slipped off without paying. When Guillaume was brought up before a magistrate in Paris, his mother came to his defense with the airs of a duchess. She didn't have a high opinion of her first child, "father N. N.," and never would. After his death, having read in a newspaper about the famous poet Apollinaire, Olga Kostrowitzky appeared at the offices of the *Mercure de France* and asked for an explanation. Paul Léautaud spoke to her. Olga listened to what he had to say, then remarked, "My other son is a writer too. He writes financial articles for an important paper in New York."

Annie Playden was an English governess employed by a German family. Apollinaire took a position as tutor with the family and accompanied them to Oberpleis in the Rhineland. He proposed to Annie on a mountain top, the Drachenfels, where Siegfried was said to have slain the dragon. Annie would recall that he offered to make her a countess . . . "he came of a noble Russian family, full of generals and heaven knows what." He offered her his huge fortune. When she declined he pointed to the precipice at their feet and said that he could easily explain the accident when her body was discovered.

A year later he came to see Annie in London. This muse lived in Landor Road, Clapham. He rang the Playden doorbell late at night and flew into rages. The courtship was not a success. Annie escaped by the desperate expedient of going to the United States. "Kostro," as she called him, wrote a ballad, "La Chanson du mal-aimé" ("Song of the Unrequited Lover") and some poems about the Rhine.

In 1951 a woman named Mrs. Annie Playden Postings was interviewed in New York City by LeRoy Breunig. She remembered Kostro, but in those days on the Rhine she had not known that he was a poet. For fifty years she had not heard his name; she had been living in Texas; she had only recently discovered that he had become a famous poet named Apollinaire. She seemed to think that if she had to do it all over she would have been more romantic. But, she said, if she had been more generous maybe Kostro wouldn't have written the poems.

In the years when Apollinaire was writing the poems that would appear in *Alcools* and make him famous he supported himself by writing magazine articles and editing. He was the editor of his own magazine, *Le Festin d'Esope (Aesop's Feast)* from November, 1903, to August, 1904. In order to make money he wrote two erotic novels, *Les onze mille verges (The Eleven Thousand Strokes)* and *The Exploits of a Young Don Juan*. Picasso once pronounced *The Eleven Thousand Strokes* Apollinaire's masterpiece. He made a more conventional bid for fame in 1910 with a collection of short stories, *L'Hérésiarque et Cie. (The Heretic and Co)*. "The author of all these inventions," said the jacket blurb, which Apollinaire wrote himself, "is intoxicated by a charming erudition." This was one of the books voted on for the Prix Goncourt that year.

It was a significant moment in both modern painting and poetry when the young Apollinaire, walking along the Seine, stopped to observe a man dabbing at a canvas. This was André Derain. They became friends, and then Apollinaire met the *fauve* Vlaminck. From these friendships Apollinaire emerged as an art critic. Then one day Jean Mollet, managing editor of *Le Festin d'Esope*, brought his friend Picasso to the Criterion bar to meet Apollinaire, who at that moment was holding forth on the comparative merits of English and German beer.

In his turn Picasso brought the poet Max Jacob, and the character of artistic and poetic life in Paris was established for the following decade. It was a time of cross-fertilization of the arts, painting influencing poetry. The painters were insistent on this point . . . they had influenced the poets, not vice versa. It was a time of discussion, theorizing, innovation, and hard work.

Apollinaire buzzed about in the ateliers of Montmartre, bringing one artist to meet another. He wrote articles about artists and art exhibitions. As a critic of art he has been harshly criticized. "It is difficult," Francis Steegmuller says, "to discover in all of Apollinaire's art writings, a mention of a picture that has been seen —let alone seen as an artist's image." When we turn to Apollinaire's book, *The Cubist Painters*, the harshness seems justified. Here he is on some precubist paintings by Picasso: "Picasso's predeliction for the fugitive line changes and penetrates and produces almost unique examples of linear etchings in which the general aspect of the world is unaltered by the light which modifies its form by changing its colors."

But from his studies of the new painting Apollinaire derived ideas that could be applied to poetry. Reality has nothing to do with "realism.'" Chronology, logic, rational connections are not important. What matters is to seize a feeling and get it across. The artist must be bold—audacity above all! —reducing experience to the essential elements and representing them according to the importance they have in his mind.

He derived an idea of cubist poetry. "Cubist poetry?" said Pierre Reverdy. "A ridiculous term!" Apollinaire issued a Futurist manifesto.*

Futurist Antitradition

> Manifesto-synthesis . . . this engine has every trend . . .
> impressionism fauvism cubism expressionism path-
> eticism dramatism orphism paroxysm . . . "Mer . . . de."

He accompanied "Merde" with notes of music.

In 1912 Apollinaire read a poem that was original and moved him greatly, Blaise Cendrars's "Les Pâques à New York" ("Easter in New York"). The next year when Apollinaire's *Alcools* went to press he led off with a new poem, "Zone," that echoed Cendrars. To give his book a modern cast and emphasize the importance that originality had assumed in his mind he struck out all the punctuation in the galleys.

"Each of my poems," he would say, "commemorates an event in my life." In "Zone" he recalls events in his life from childhood to the present. He journeys and observes—like Cendrars he is an outsider and finds people and scenes fascinating. The theme of the "unrequited lover" is heard repeatedly— it is what gives a poem of wandering its coherence. (Perhaps Annie Playden was right—if she hadn't rejected him he wouldn't have written his poems.) The form is the "supple line" that he will describe in the preface to *Les Mamelles de Tirésias,* a line " based on rhythm, subject matter, and breathing." "Zone" examplifies what people before the Great War spoke of as "the New Spirit." The ideas are new, or seem to be, for they are expressed vivaciously.

Like Cendrars, Apollinaire in "Zone" sympathizes with prostitutes, vagabonds, and emigrants. He has had some experience of the lower depths himself. On August 23, 1912, the *Paris Journal* revealed that the Mona Lisa had been stolen from the Louvre. It turned out that it had been stolen by Apollinaire's secretary. Moreover, on a previous occasion he had stolen a Phoenician statuette and two other statuettes which he gave to Apollinaire, who passed them on to Picasso. (The ears of Picasso's "Les Demoiselles d'Avignon" are modeled on the stolen statuettes.)

Apollinaire was arrested, taken to prison, and interrogated by a magistrate who evidently enjoyed humiliating the Bohemian poet and friend of artists. It was clear, however, that he was innocent, that he had harbored the thief unknowingly, and he was released. But he was profoundly disturbed. A photograph of him in handcuffs had appeared in the newspapers. And he was shaken

---

*See FUTURISTS.

by the treachery of Picasso. Brought to the prison to confront Apollinaire, Picasso had denied knowing him. Rightists had demanded his expulsion from France as an undesirable alien. Some of them were anti-Semites who assumed that as he was a Pole he must be a Jew. Six brief, agonised poems in *Alcools* record the experience.

> Before I entered my cell
> I had to strip myself naked
> What sinister voice resounding
> Guillaume, what has become of you?
>
> Lazarus entering the tomb
> Instead of emerging . . .
> Adieu adieu . . .
> O my life O young women

The Mona Lisa had been taken to Italy by a patriotic Italian and was safely recovered. Louise Faure Favier comments: "Guillaume Apollinaire abruptly became famous throughout the entire world. He was thought of as the man who had stolen the Mona Lisa. Even today there are Parisians who believe it . . ."

"O my life O young women . . ." After Annie Playden his next major love was the artist Marie Laurencin. The affair ended in bitterness on both sides. Then he was in love with "Lou"—Louise de Coligny-Chatillon, a member of the aristocracy whom he met at an opium party in Nice. She kept him dangling and he enlisted in the army. They spent a week together and he wrote her letters from the front. Then Lou stopped answering—she had taken another lover.

In his play, *Les Mamelles de Tirésias,* and in statements about aesthetics, urgently, as though he sensed his approaching death, Apollinaire was predicting new forms of art. He experimented with typography in *Calligrammes*, making the poem look like an object. He learned from the Futurists and found images for poetry in airplanes, submarine cables, bombs, the telephone and phonograph, and he used the Futurist technique of *simultanéisme,* simultaneous narratives. Anticipating Surrealism, he placed objects in sudden, illogical juxtapositions He invented the word surrealism.

He foresaw a theater in which several media would be used simultaneously for new effects, and went beyond theater in his prediction of "a new art. . . an orchestration that will include the entire world, its sights and sounds, human thought and language, song, dance, all the arts and all the artifices—more mirages than Morgan le Fay conjured up on Mongibel to compose the book seen and heard by the future." He foresaw

The full unfolding of our modern art
Often connecting in unseen ways as in life
Sounds gestures colors cries tumults
Music dancing acrobatics poetry painting
Choruses actions and multiple sets

He called for:

A joyfulness voluptuousness virtue
Instead of that pessimism more than a hundred years old
And that's pretty old for such a boring thing . . . .

He served in the artillery and at his own request was transferred to the infantry. He was wounded by a shell fragment in the head. At first the wound seemed superficial, then it was found necessary to trepan—cut into the bone. He was discharged from the hospital to a desk job, censoring mail, which he did scrupulously.

The wound had changed him: he was corpulent, drowsy, given to outbursts of anger. In 1918 he married Jacqueline Kolb, the "pretty redhead" of a poem. A few days before the Armistice he contracted influenza and died. His body was laid out. Friends came by, and so did Apollinaire's mother, Olga Kostrowitzky. She began a furious quarrel with his widow.

Outside in the street people were shouting, "A bas Guillaume!"—"Down with Guillaume!" They meant Guillaume the German Kaiser. The scene was surrealistic —Apollinaire would have appreciated it.

See DADAISTS AND SURREALISTS, FUTURISTS

CHARLES BAUDELAIRE
1821–1867

the new flowers of which I dream
BAUDELAIRE

The poet's father, Joseph-François Baudelaire, had been a priest. He left the priesthood, moved in aristocratic circles, and dabbled in art—in his son's opinion he was "a detestable artist." Under the Empire he was Chief of the Praetorship of the Senate. His first wife died and he married Caroline Dufaÿs, the mother of the poet. Charles-Pierre Baudelaire was born in Paris on April 9, 1821.

In 1827 Baudelaire's father died. A year later his mother married Jacques Aupick, Chevalier of Saint-Louis and Officer of the Legion of Honor. Aupick was appointed co-guardian of Charles.

Aupick was assigned to Lyon as a staff officer. There Charles had his schooling. When he was sixteen he was awarded a second prize for Latin verse. At seventeen he was admiring Victor Hugo's plays and Sainte-Beuve's *Volupté*. The master of studies at the Collège Louis-le-Grand found Charles dutiful in his religious observances and a very good student, but a bit lacking in method. A year later M. Carrère said that Charles was setting a bad example and that he had had to punish him severely. In April of 1839 he was expelled for refusing to hand over a note that a companion had passed to him.

He took the *baccalauréat* at another school and applied to the school of law. But, my author says, " he was leading a free life," and he contracted a venereal disease.*

Baudelaire would continue to live freely and to disappoint his mother and the stepfather whom he detested. In 1840 Aupick was appointed commander of a brigade of the Paris garrison, and moved the ménage to Paris. Baudelaire joined in "the joyful life of students," and became the friend of a prostitute, Sarah, "called La Louchette." Aupick held a family council to determine what was to be done about Charles. They sent him to Calcutta. Charles got off the boat at what is now called Reunion Island and made his way back to Paris.

He came into his majority and 100,000 francs left him by his father. Then, in May, 1842, he met Jeanne Duval. She was a "quadroon." Those who have written about Baudelaire make a point of this, I think because the word quadroon sounds sinister. He began a liaison with Duval that lasted, on and off, for years. He would leave her for other women and return when he was in distress.

He ran through 45,000 francs in two years, and Aupick persuaded his wife to take legal steps to prevent her son's dissipating the rest of his fortune.

Charles Baudelaire was given a jail sentence of seventy-two hours for avoiding service in the National Guard.

He was writing poems that would appear in *Les Fleurs du mal* (*Flowers of Evil*). And some prose. He was trying to get a novel published. Between December of '44 and January of '46 he published five sonnets in *L'artiste* pseudonymously, giving the name of a friend as author. In 1845 he published articles

---

*Claude Pichois, ed., Baudelaire, *Oeuvres complètes 1* (Paris: Éditions Gallimard, 1975), xxviii.

on art: "Salon de 1845," "De la peinture moderne" ("On Modern Painting"), and "De la caricature." He published pieces under the name Baudelaire-Dufaÿs, using his mother's maiden name.

Baudelaire took an active part in the rising of 1848. He was seen, rifle in hand, coming from the barricades and shouting like a refrain, "We have to shoot General Aupick."

On June 11, 1855, *La Revue des deux mondes* published, with the title *Les Fleurs du mal*, eighteen poems by Baudelaire. Among them were "Au Lecteur" ("To the Reader") and "L'Invitation au voyage."

In 1852, the March and April issues of *La Revue de Paris* carried an essay by Baudelaire, "Edgar Allan Poe, His Life and Works," This was the first version of the preface to a translation of Poe's tales. *Histoires extraordinaires* was published on March 12, 1856. A second volume, *Nouvelles Histoires exraordinaires*, appeared in 1857 with some "New Notes on Edgar Poe." The tales went through several editions.

Poe had stated his aesthetics in his 1850 essay on "The Poetic Principle." Art was not utilitarian. It was not moral—it did not have Truth as its object. Poetry was *The Rhythmical Creation of Beauty*. In music the soul came closest to the "supernal" beauty it desired. The poet had "the immortal instinct for the beautiful which makes us consider the earth and its spectacles as a revelation, as in correspondence with Heaven."

An element of the strange was "the indispensable condiment . . . of all beauty." Above all, poetry must be constructed . . . it was not a naive outpouring: "construction, armature, so to speak, is the most important guarantee of the mysterious life of works of the mind."

Much that we think of as characteristically modern in literature is due to Baudelaire's championing of Poe's aesthetics. He said that in reading Poe he had been astonished to find his own ideas. Later poets would find that Poe, by way of Baudelaire, spoke for them.

Poe's "correspondence" of earth and Heaven would be the Symbolism of the movement that appeared in the 1880's, and his insistence on the "music" of poetry was equally important to the Symbolists—the rhythms and sounds of their poems were intended to create a mood. Poets would "construct" their works as Poe said they must, aiming at perfection. By their art they sought to prove that poetry "does not have Truth as an object; it has only itself."

Les Fleurs du mal went on sale on June 25, 1857. An article in *Figaro* attacked the book for its "immorality." The Public Prosecutor began legal proceedings against Baudelaire and his editors for "outraging public morality." Baudelaire was fined 300 francs, the two editors 100 francs each, and six of the poems were suppressed. Baudelaire was unable to pay the fine. He appealed to the Empress to have it reduced, and after many delays it was, to fifty francs. Sick and discouraged, Baudelaire planned to leave Paris and go with his mother to Honfleur.

Flaubert had been prosecuted for outraging public morality in his novel *Madame Bovary*. Flaubert was more fortunate than Baudelaire: he was acquitted. One might assume that it was the content of their writing that was being accused: adultery in *Madame Bovary* and the poems about lesbians in *Les fleurs du mal*. But the cause went deeper. The ruling class had no objection to "immorality" if it were served up as something else: for example, the sculpture of a naked woman lying on her back, titled "Woman Bitten by a Snake." What it found intolerable was the attitude of these writers and artists: they showed society in the worst possible light. Their contempt for the status quo smelled of republicanism . . . of revolution.

The charge that they were encouraging immorality is ironic in view of their stated intention to rise above morality, good or bad. For Baudelaire, art must be disconnected from the passions: in one of his poems Beauty says, "Never do I weep, and never laugh." He seems to be writing with the positivist philosophy of the age. Taine had said that virtue and vice were merely products, like vitriol and sugar. In his descriptions of the modern city Baudelaire is objective, impersonal, appalling.

But he is not a "realist" of the kind associated with Duranty, Champfleury, and their school of Realism that gave trivial accounts of everyday life. At one time Baudelaire contemplated writing an essay in which he would give reasons for disassociating himself from the school. Baudelaire's writing can be realistic in that his descriptions are accurate, but the objects and actions he shows are significant. At times they seem symbolic. The view opens and lifts to sweep across space and time.

There are poems in which Baudelaire is not at all impersonal. He speaks to angels and demons, to a vampire. He speaks of using opium, and of his "spleen," times

> When the sky, low and heavy, weighs like a lid
> On the groaning spirit, prey to long ennuis . . .

This is the Baudelaire who would be aped toward the end of the century by the so-called Decadents.

The greatness of Baudelaire, however, is not in passages that merely express his ennuis. It is in poetry such as the following.

I think of the negress, gaunt, tubercular,
Trudging in the mud, and looking around her
With haggard eyes for the palms of Africa
Behind the huge wall of fog that surrounds her;

Of those who have lost what can never again
Be found. Never! . . .

Is this realism? Symbolism? The writing breaks through the limits of such terms. In his power of vision, and his pity for human suffering, Baudelaire is one of the great poets of the world.

ANDRÉ BRETON
1896-1966

André Breton was born at Tinchebray in Normandy in 1896. The family moved to Lorient on the coast of Brittany. Anna Balakian in her biography of Breton says that he liked to think of himself as "a man of the North," and that he attributed to the North "his propensity for the Gothic notion of beauty, his fascination with the effects of dreams and with the powers of imagination."*

He was an only child, much attached to his father who was a "small businessman," and to his grandfather. But it is hardly an exaggeration to say that he hated his mother. She would not let him play with chldren she considered "lower class." When he did something of which she disapproved she would stand him before her and strike him in the face. She was an extraordinary prude, on guard against any interest in sex on the part of her son. When Breton was a man he would remark sardonically that he had been "a well brought up little boy."

He was fascinated by the picture of a revolutionary hero, General Hoche, on a friend's bedroom wall, and he loved Paris . . . the idea of Paris. There was a boy who read aloud Chénier's poem, "La Jeune Captive," ("The Young Captive") and Breton chose him as a friend for that reason. He had outbursts of the anger that, in later years, would be characteristic, and in the games children play he was always the leader.

He attended the Lycée Chaptal in Paris, graduating in 1907. He tells us in *Entretiens* that his "lucid life" began in 1913 when he was a medical student at the Sorbonne. He was reading the Symbolist poets . . . also Rimbaud, Valéry,

---

*Anna Balakian, *André Breton* (New York: Oxford University Press, 1971), 8.

and Apollinaire. In Rimbaud he found a justification for writing poetry: it was not an end but a means to an end. The poet does not write "to fill the leisure of his fellow man" but "to find solutions to the problems of life itself." He published his first poem in *La Phalange,* and wrote to Valéry, who wrote back offering advice and encouragement.

Breton was conscripted in 1915 and assigned to a hospital in Nantes as a medical assistant. At Nantes there was a wounded soldier, Jacques Vaché, who was "in his rebellion against society, the embodiment of Lautréamont and the Marquis de Sade combined, and in his escape through absinthe he brought back Alfred Jarry. . . ." Balakian says that "the image of Vaché" may have been a figment of Breton's imagination, the projection of his own desires. "Breton promoted a legend around this rather ordinary youth who, seized with dissent, became the symbol of his generation, immortalized by his friend Breton. A precursor of the Dada image, Vaché was to die just before Tristan Tzara came into Breton's horizon." *

From Nantes Breton was transferred to the psychiatric center of Saint-Dizier. He had some knowledge of Freudian psychology and used it in the treatment of soldiers suffering from neurosis. While at Saint-Dizier he began a correspondence with Apollinaire, who warned him against paying too much attention to style, a habit he had fallen into by imitating Mallarmé.

At the performance of Apollinaire's *Les Mamelles de Tirésias* in Paris in 1917, Jacques Vaché turned up with a revolver and was threatening to fire into the crowd. He wanted to show the difference between the "rearguard," represented by Apollinaire, and the brave avant-garde of people like himself. Breton restrained him, but he approved of the revolver—it was the emblem of protest. "The simplest surrealist act," he would write, "consists of going down into the street, revolver in hand, and shooting at random." He explained that the important word was "simplest." The only way to resist "vilification and cretinization" was "to possess the sense of revolution so totally as to be willing to be shooting-mad." He didn't mean that you were actually to shoot.

In the spring of 1918 Louis Aragon spoke to Breton about *Les Chants de Maldoror* (*The Songs of Maldoror*) and was surprised to find that he did not know it. This book by Isidore Ducasse, who used the pseudonym Le Comte de Lautréamont, was first printed in 1868-69 but not noticed until, in 1890, there was a second printing. Huysmans, Fargue, Larbaud, and Rémy de Gourmont thought highly of it. The work, written in poetic prose, was hallucinatory and savage—Lautréamont's visions might have been painted by Hieronymus Bosch. "O, if only instead of being a hell, this universe had been an immense, celestial anus!"

---

* Balakian, 24.

Maldoror anticipated by fifty years the Surrealist method of making an image—bringing together the most distant realities in order to create a new, hitherto unseen reality. "Beautiful," Lautréamont wrote, "as the chance meeting on a dissecting table of a sewing machine and an umbrella." When Breton read *Maldoror* he was overwhelmed. He said, "We now know that poetry must lead somewhere."

Breton also read Lautréamont's *Poésies* and there found a list of "Great Soft-Heads" such as Rousseau, Poe, George Sand and other Romantics for whom Lautréamont had nothing but contempt. This was right in line with Breton's own iconoclasm, his revulsion from the Great War and the prevailing spirit of nationalism. "For the next several months Lautréamont worked like a narcotic, clouding all of Breton's waking thoughts. 'I can think of nothing but Maldoror,' he wrote Fraenkel in July.'" *

A group that included Breton, Réne Crevel, Robert Desnos, Paul Eluard, Max Ernst, Max Morise, Benjamin Péret, and Francis Picabia were experimenting in "psychic automatism." They adopted a word for these experiments, "surrealism," that had been invented by Apollinaire. They induced sleep by hypnosis—Surrealist visions, Breton said, were seen with closed eyes—and they used "automatic writing" to report what they saw. In the spring of 1919 Breton, Philippe Soupault, and Louis Aragon founded a review, *Littérature*, and Breton and Soupault collaborated to write the first specifically Surrealist text, *Les Champs magnétiques* (*Magnetic Fields*).

In composing this work Breton and Soupault brought to bear what they had learned of psychology and aesthetics. "The rules were simple: they would give themselves a total of one week to 'blacken some paper' with whatever came into their heads, with, as Breton said, 'a praiseworthy disdain for what might result from a literary point of view. The ease of execution did the rest.'" Breton would call *Les Champs magnétiques* "the first attempt to 'adapt a moral attitude, and the only one possible, to a writing process.' " Automatic writing was neither a literary technique nor pure therapy—"it was both an entry into the innermost mechanism of the poetic image and, because of the challenge automatism posed to notions of responsibility, an unprecedent moral and psychological upheaval." **

The movement called Dada was taking place in Zurich. Tristan Tzara, Hugo Bal, Richard Huelsenbeck, and Hans (later Jean) Arp gathered at the Cabaret Voltaire to recite absurd poems, exhibit paintings that were "anti-art," and put on sketches that held the bourgeoisie up to ridicule. They sent their

* Mark Polizzotti, *Revolution of the Mind: The Life of André Breton* (New York: Farrar, Straus and Giroux, 1995), 75.
** Polizzotti, 104-105.

manifestos abroad . . . to Marcel Duchhamp in New York, Ernst in Cologne, Picabia in Switzerland. Tzara was writing to Breton. In January, 1919, Tzara moved to Paris. The *Littérature* group welcomed Tzara and threw themselves wholeheartedly into Dada "manifestations."

In 1921 Breton married Simone Kahn. Her father had given her a small dowry. With this they bought a few paintings which they sold for a profit. They took up buying and selling paintings, and rented an apartment in Montmartre, on the hill below Place Blanche. This would be Breton's permanent address.

The collaboration between Surrealists and Dadaists lasted until 1922, then they quarreled and separated. Dada called for self-expression and rejection of principles of any kind, a clean sweep of all social values and systems of thought . . . "DADA SIGNIFIES NOTHING . . . " while Breton and his group wanted to explore the unconscious systematically.

In 1922 Breton paid a visit to Freud in Vienna. Two years later he issued a "Manifesto of Surrealism."

> SURREALISM, n. m. Pure psychic automatism by which it is proposed to express, whether verbally, or in writing, or in any other way, the real functioning of thought. Dictated by thought, in the absence of any control exercised by reason, outside any aesthetic or moral preoccupation.

Breton read Trotsky on Lenin and was impressed. In 1925 he took over the editing of *La Révolution surréaliste* and argued for social action. In 1926 he joined the Communist Party. But he was opposed to any attempt to control "inner life"—in the "Second Manifesto of Surrealism" (1929) he would say, "The problem of social action is only one of the forms of a more general problem Surrealism set out to deal with, and that is the problem of human expression in all its forms."

The "Second Manifesto of Surrealism" has been described as an enquiry into Surrealist philosophy and "a severe recall to order in the face of all literary or opportunistic deviations,"* but it reads like a vindictive, personal attack by Breton on Surrealists who were no longer willing to accept his direction. He denounced Soupault, saying that Soupault had retailed gossip about him and had accused him of theft. He castigated Ribemont-Dessaignes for writing "odious little detective stories" and Desnos for his journalism—he would not "sit idly by while this person or that thinks he is free to abandon it [the Surre-

---

*Jean-Louis Bédouin, *La Poésie surréaliste* (Paris: Seghers, 1964), 79.

alist group] under the vague, the odious pretext that he has to live." He praised the Marquis de Sade for "the impeccable integrity " of his life and thought.

In 1930 he launched and directed the review, *Le Surréalisme au service de la révolution*. He found it impossible to take orders from the Communist Party, and in 1935 he broke with them finally. There was a split among the Surrealists: Aragon and other Surrealists left the group and adhered to the Party.

Breton traveled to Prague and the Canary Islands to take part in Surrealist demonstrations. In 1938 he visited Mexico and, with Diego Riviera and Leon Trotsky, founded the International Federation of Independent Revolutionary Art, writing the manifesto in collaboration with Trotsky.

He was conscripted in 1939. When the Germans invaded France he made his way to Martinique, and from there to the United States where he stayed until the war was over.

In 1945 Breton visited Haiti to give some lectures and establish good relations with intellectuals in the French Antilles. Due to postwar inflation life for the Haitians could be miserable. The government was unpopular—the President, Elie Lescot, was said to be too friendly with the hated Trujillo. There was repressive censorship. In his first lecture Breton spoke of the philosophy of Surrealism and the liberty he prized above all. The newspaper *La Ruche* devoted a special number to Breton and reported the lecture. The newspaper was suspended by the government. There were demonstrations protesting the suspension, the workers called a general strike, and Lescot was forced to flee the country—"as a result of a revolution touched off by—of all things—a lecture on Surrealism."* This was only a "palace revolution"—there would be no change in conditions under the new government. But the "Haitian Renaissance" in art and literature that began in 1946 was influenced by Surrealism.

Breton returned to France in 1946 and put together a new Surrealist group. The next year he organized an international exposition of Surrealism. From 1948 to 1958 he supported the "Citizens of the World" movement. He launched or had a hand in launching several reviews: *Néon, Médium, Le Surréalisme même, La Brèche,* and from 1952 to 1954 he ran the A l'Étoile Scellée gallery. He died in Paris on September 28, 1966.

See DADAISTS AND SURREALISTS

---

* Helena Lewis, *The Politics of Surrealism* (New York: Paragon House Publishers, 1988), 163–164.

DADAISTS AND SURREALISTS

You will stay a few days and then go back on line . . .
So goodbye gentlemen try to return
But there's no way of knowing what will happen
               APOLLINAIRE, "Le Vigneron champenois"

There were poets who refused to take part in the Great War that was killing a generation. From Zurich in neutral Switzerland they held up to ridicule the clichés that had plunged Europe into war. "We destroyed," says Hans Richter, "we insulted, we despised—and we laughed. We laughed at everything. We laughed at ourselves just as we laughed at Emperor, King and country, fat bellies and baby-pacifiers. We took our laughter seriously; laughter was the only guarantee of the seriousness with which, on our voyages of self-discovery, we practised anti-art."*

The word Dada is said to have been discovered at the Cabaret Voltaire in Zurich on February 8, 1916, by Tristan Tzara, Hans Arp, and Richard Huelsenbeck. They pushed a paper knife into a dictionary at random. Some said that Dada meant a rocking horse, others the tail of an African cow, but Tzara who organized Dada "manifestations" and edited *Dada* said, "DADA SIGNIFIES NOTHING."** The poets and artists who frequented the Cabaret Voltaire produced anti-art, some of it inspired babble. "Kaspar is dead," Hans Arp declared,

> alas our good kaspar is dead
> who will now carry the burning banner hidden in the
>   pigtail of clouds
> to play the daily black joke . . .
> now the black bowling alley thunders behind the sun
> and there's no one to wind up the compasses and the
> wheels of the handbarrows any more. . . .

Hugo Ball composed "abstract poetry." Dressed in a special costume, a cylinder of shiny blue cardboard and a high "witch-doctor's hat," he had himself carried to the platform—an obelisk cannot walk—and recited, slowly and majestically,

---

* Hans Richter, *Dada: Art and Anti-Art*, tr. David Britt (London: Thames and Hudson, 1965), passim.
** "Dada Manifesto 1918." Read by Tzara at the Zur Meise in Zurich on July 23, 1918. Published in *Dada 3* in December.

gadji beri bimba glandridi laula lonni cadori
gadjama gramma berida bimbala glandri galassassa laulitalomini
gadji beri bin blassa glassala laula lonni cadorsu sassala bim

The Dadaists, Richter says, "reserved their enthusiasm for the SELF, working out its own laws, its own form and its own justification free from guilt and remorse." They trusted to Chance—it was the key to self-expression. "Coincidences of sound or form were the occasion of wild leaps that revealed connections between the most apparently unconnected ideas." Tristan Tzara cut words out of newspaper articles, put them in a bag, and shook them out at random. The ensuing pattern constituted a Tzara "poem." Arp made collages in similar fashion. He would say, however, that chance was only a point of departure—the images were afterwards consciously rearranged.

After the war Dada moved to Paris. A "First Friday" was held there on January 20, 1920. Tzara, André Breton, Louis Aragon, Philippe Soupault and other Dadaists and future Surrealists took part. Tzara read his poems. There were exhibitions of art by Juan Gris, Ribemont-Dessaignes, de Chirico, Léger and other painters . . . music by Satie, Auric, Milhaud, Poulenc, and Cliquet.

> The astonished citizens of the *quartier* were shown what they had to expect from now on. Tzara read out a newspaper article to the accompaniment of clangings, tinklings and other noises. Picabia executed a large drawing on a slate, wiping out each section as he finished it, before going on to the next. So it went on. But the Parisians, less patient than the people of Zurich, started a riot—and the whole thing ended in pandemonium.*

Dada "manifestations" were more hectic versions of performances given by Marinetti and other Futurists before the war, and in fact much that happened in the postwar years was a resumption of prewar experiments. Dadaist poetry resembled the Futurists' "words at liberty."

André Breton had served during the war at the neurological center in Nantes where he used psychiatry and psychotherapy in the treatment of wounded soldiers. In 1921 he traveled to Vienna to see Freud. Subsequently he translated works by Freud into French and publicized Freud's ideas in periodicals. Breton wanted to study the unconscious as it was manifested in dreams and by "free association." This brought about a division between those who wanted to study the unconscious methodically and those like Tzara who wanted to express themselves spontaneously.

At a mock "trial of Barrès"—Maurice Barrès was a member of the

---

* Richter, 173

Académie Française who stood for nationalism and tradition—the rift between Tzara and Breton became apparent. Breton wanted to bring various avant-garde elements together in a common purpose. Tzara, who said that the only principle was to have none, appeared to know nothing about Barrès and treated the whole affair as a joke. In February and March of 1922, at a Congress held in Paris "to determine the policy and defense of the Modern Spirit," there was an open break between Tzara and Breton.

The year 1924 saw the official founding of Surrealism. Breton directed the Surrealist group and wrote a "Manifesto of Surrealism." They had their own premises, "Bureau de recherches surréalistes, 15 rue de Grenelle," and, beginning on December 1, their own organ, *La Révolution surréaliste*. The Surrealists experimented with dreams and automatic writing. Robert Desnos could dream at the drop of a hat and, Louis Aragon says, if you nudged him he would speak and prophesy.

Surrealism was not conceived as literature—it was to be a discovery of the hidden self. But as the Surrealists wrote down their dreams and hallucinations, some of the "Surrealist texts" were felt to be more significant than others. These effects were sought—therefore they were literature.

Dadaists and Surrealists came together again in 1929. Tzara published a part of his poem *L'Homme approximatif* in the last number of Breton's review, *La Révolution surréaliste*. The poem has been said to be Tzara's most important contribution to Surrealism. In 1931 Tzara contributed an essay to Breton's *Le Surréalisme au service de la révolution*, placing Surrealism in the tradition of revolution. But Tzara and Breton would again go their separate ways in 1935 when Breton severed his connections with the Communist Party. Tzara supported the Party.

Surrealism, Aragon declares, consisted of "the unruly and ardent use of the stupefying image. . . . Every image forces you to revise the entire universe." Breton explains how the Surrealist image was put together: "To compare two subjects as distant as possible one from the other, or, by any other method, to bring them face to face, remains the highest task to which poetry can aspire" (*Les Vases communicants*). In their writings and paintings the Surrealists continually brought "distant subjects" together: a guitar with epaulettes, a stool with feminine legs, a laundry iron bristling with spikes—"all objects deflected from their sense, rendered inappropriate to their technical end in order to bring to light that end without end that according to Kant is proper to beauty."*

The Symbolist image had been taken from the tangible, natural world to

---

* Ferdinand Alquié, *The Philosophy of Surrealism* (Ann Arbor:University of Michigan Press, 1969), 77.

evoke a "supernal" unity of sense and feeling. The image of the Imagists was an instant of sense-perception that triggered an intuition. The image of the Surrealists was a pure invention, a surprise: "My wife with shoulders of champagne/ And a spring with heads of dolphins under ice" (André Breton); "Stupid like sausages whose sauerkraut has already been eaten away" (Benjamin Péret); "Hands that grasp each other in a sinister way in a pallid light and axles that grate on frightening roads" (Robert Desnos).

The Surrealist image was often suggested by a coincidence of sounds. Michel Leiris composed a glossary: "ingénu: le génie nu" ... "langage: baggage lent de l'esprit" ... "révolution: solution de tout rêve." We notice a certain method—there is not the "absence of any control exercised by reason" that Breton in his manifesto defined as Surrealism. Leiris's "coincidences" make sense.

The image," Pierre Reverdy said, "is a pure creation of the mind. It cannot be born from a comparison but from a juxtaposition of two more or less distant realities. The more the relationship between the two juxtaposed realities is distant and true, the stronger the image will be—the greater its emotional power and poetic reality."* The word "true" implies that Surrealism may have a kind of logic. And, indeed, when we look at paintings by René Magritte or Max Ernst, or read a poem by Philippe Soupault or Robert Desnos, we are conscious of a mind working with a purpose—there is a logic to their dreaming. The Surrealism of less gifted artists seems mechanical, just bringing together in words or paint objects that have no connection. We soon come to expect the merely unexpected.

Alquié observes: "If Surrealism wishes to bring together in its images the most distant realities, is it not because of its unlimited confidence in the powers of the spirit? ... man is the creator of values, which have their sense only from him and relative to him."** I am reminded of the high value the Romantics placed on imagination. Wordsworth said there were moments, "spots of time," in which he had felt that "the mind is lord and master."

But the Dadaists laughed at the kind of mind that thinks it is "lord and master." Ribemont-Dessaignes said, "I have on my head a little blade that turns in the wind." When Soupault and Breton reread what they had written in *Les Champs magnétiques*, Soupault recalls, "What astounded André was, more than the images, the involuntary and extraordinary humor that sprung out at the turn of a phrase. We burst out laughing."***

---

* *Nord-Sud*, March 1918. Cited by Breton in "Manifesto of Surrealism," 1924.
** Alquié, 101-102
*** Mark Polizzotti, *Revolution of the Mind: The Life of André Breton* (New York: Farrar, Straus and Giroux, 1995), 107.

Breton said that the Surrealist image had to be "a chance encounter of two distant realities." Can Groucho Marx and Margaret Dumont be far behind?

See GUILLAUME APOLLINAIRE, PIERRE REVERDY, TRISTAN TZARA, GEORGES RIBEMONT-DESSAIGNES, ANDRÉ BRETON, PHILIPPE SOUPAULT, PAUL ELUARD, BENJAMIN PÉRET, ROBERT DESNOS

MARCELINE DESBORDES-VALMORE
1786-1859

Marie Félicité Josèphe Desbordes, who would assume the name Marceline Desbordes-Valmore, was born in 1786 at Douai in Flanders. In the middle ages Douai belonged to the counts of Flanders. It passed by marriage to the dukes of Burgundy, to Austria, and in 1556 to Philip II of Spain. In the sixteenth century Douai was a center of religious and political propaganda by exiled English Roman Catholics. This is what Desbordes-Valmore is referring to in "Intermittent Dream of a Sad Night" when she speaks of "soldiers of the cross." Douai was ceded to France by the treaty of Aix-la-Chapelle in 1668.

She would look back at her childhood as idyllic. The people were attached to simple things and led uneventful lives.* There were four children. Their father painted cabinets and made church ornaments. But Joseph Desbordes lost his clientele in the Revolution—the Terror came even to Douai and the church porch was destroyed. The Desbordes family was reduced to poverty.

In her autobiographical novel, *The Studio of a Painter*, Desbordes-Valmore tells how a swallows' nest is broken and the mother takes refuge on a neighboring roof. The father of the four young birds—"alas! there were four children"—flies plaintively around her, then returns and takes the children one by one and throws them in the courtyard where they die. Marceline adds, "a short time after, I took ship with my mother, only my mother—to America—where no one was expecting us." In her poem, "Les Sanglots," "Sobs," the mother is identified with the escaping swallow:

> Ah! it will be my mother courageous and mild,
> Descending to reclaim her punished child! . . .
>
> And my mother, flying, will take me with her,
> Will carry me alive into the future!

---

*Yves Bonnefoy, ed., *Marceline Desbordes Valmore, Poésies* (Paris:Gallimard, 1983), passim.

The mother, Catherine Desbordes, decided to go to Guadeloupe where she had a cousin who was a rich planter. Apparently she was planning not to return. Her oldest daughter Marceline, now fifteen, did not want to be separated from her. They spent a few months putting together enough money for the journey. They had a long, rough crossing, and arrived in Guadeloupe to find that there was an epidemic of yellow fever and that the rich cousin had just died.

In a fortnight Catherine Desbordes died of the fever. Her daughter managed to survive for eight months in the strange country where she knew no one. Sainte-Beuve says that she endured "frightful sufferings."* On the voyage back there was a storm. She tied herself in the shrouds in order to look at the waves rushing towards the ship.

She returned to her father's house in Douai. She had had some experience of acting and was engaged by the local theater, then by the theater in Rouen. She succeeeded rapidly and acted in Paris in several theaters. She was also writing poems that were published in song books and almanacs.

Yves Bonnefoy speaks of the obstacles to be faced by a woman who wished to make a name in the arts. Marceline had an uncle in Paris, Constant Desbordes, who was a painter. She came to know artists at his studio. When she wrote an autobiographical novel, *The Studio of a Painter*, she made the heroine a young woman who wants to paint. Her uncle encourages her but tells her that as a woman she is not expected to do more than minor work. "Keep your apron, my child. Women will never be more than gleaners, but their weak arms have grace and they are forgiven much because they seem to pray." He advises her to take as her model not Raphael and the sublime but the "charming pictures" of Mlle Lescot.

Marceline did not want to be a painter, but the attitude expressed by the uncle in the novel applies to her ambition as a writer. The Church with its story of the Fall taught that women were inherently weak—men ran things and decided what art and literature should be. Under the Empire there was a vogue for heroic, classical subjects—her uncle Constant painted "The Funeral of Atala." The poetry of the inner voice could not compete with panoramas.

In 1808 Marceline met Henri de Latouche. He was the editor of André Chenier's poems and had adopted Romantic attitudes. He was the kind of poseur who would be satirized by Flaubert in *Madame Bovary* as the clerk Léon. To impress Emma, Léon says that he likes to lie with a book by a wood and watch the sunset. He says that he adores the sea and mountain scenery. And Emma is . . . impressed.

In Desbordes-Valmore's poems Latouche appears as "Olivier" who did

---

*Sainte-Beuve, *Mme D.V., sa vie et sa correspondance* (Paris: Levy, 1870), n. pag.

not reciprocate her love. He came and went—in her poems one can almost hear him saying, "I won't be tied down." And yet she loved him . . . he was charming. Two years after their meeting she had a child by Latouche, a boy who died at the age of five.

Latouche would be a formative influence. She would be disillusioned, not with romance but the fake versions of feeling that Romanticism provided. Her experience of Latouche gave her poetry about love its realism. To love can be painful . . . love and sorrow at the loss of love are inseparable. But there is another side to this—as she says in "Intermittent Dream of a Sad Night," if love brings sorrow, sorrow brings with it the memory of love.

> Love was my life, so I was often sad,
> But love was mingled with the grief I had.

The love restored in memory may be lifted to an overview that is religion, philosophy, or art It is a consoling thought, and I do not think anyone else has stated it so succinctly. Proust says as much, but he is not succinct.

The man with whom Marceline made her life was very different from Latouche. Prosper Lanchantin, known as "Valmore," was an actor, a man of the theater, "without any mystery," Bonnefoy remarks, "and even without much charm." As an actor he was sometimes whistled and Marceline had to reassure him.

She would speak in letters of "the friendship of marriage." This does not mean that it was a "loveless marriage"—it just wasn't a Bovarist's idea of love. She and her husband shared the hardships of a life in the theater, moving from place to place and not having a home of their own. There were days when money was lacking, and there were children to be cared for. There were days when Marceline was too pressed to write and her talent seemed to be going to waste. But her poems reflect a capacity for love that grew stronger with the passing of time.

In 1819, two years after they were married, she published her first book of poems, *Elegies, Marie et romances*. The forms and style of her early poems are conventional—she is limited by what is expected of women. The religion she expresses is the Christianity that advises women to be resigned. But there are flashes of poetry in her descriptions of ordinary things. "My soul," she writes, "still like a bird skimmed the days as they passed."

Her strength is in the poems of her maturity where she speaks of a life close to nature. The central impulse is love of the father whose house she left as a girl to begin her terrible journey. The fields and woods of Douai were an extension of her father's life. She loves the place of her birth and writes about nature as though it were a living thing.

The sensual or erotic passages are not merely personal, they do not announce a "secret of the flesh." They are fused with the cry of a bird, the sound of a brook, "the gifts of life that men and women share and that ceaselessly the dream abandons but love renews." There is nothing further from her mind than the idea of a poetry that is exclusively feminine. "If she speaks constantly and profoundly of events that affect her as a woman, her way of making poetry out of them, by forgetting the self, by love, is not specifically feminine, and Baudelaire and Rimbaud will take the same path."*

Literary history has not known what to make of Marceline Desbordes-Valmore. She has been forgotten, rediscovered, and forgotten again. Shortly after her death Jules Janin remarked that she had already been forgotten. "Forgotten by whom, I ask you?" said Baudelaire. "By those who, feeling nothing, remember nothing." He said, "No poet was ever more natural; none was ever less artificial. No one has been able to imitate that charm, for it is entirely originial and naive." **

If scholars have not known what to make of her works, they have been understood by poets. Her poetry is visionary, as Rimbaud's would be; it is Mallarmé's language that does not refer but *is*. Her poetry has the living immediacy of a lyric by Verlaine.

Desbordes-Valmore's "Dans la rue," "In the Street," a realistic description of the aftermath of a massacre in Lyon, must surely have been read by Rimbaud before he wrote the poem he titled "Le Mal," "Evil." Rimbaud brought her poetry to the attention of Verlaine. Proust by way of Montesquiou discovered her poems and borrowed the name Albertine for his novel. His reveries about "young girls in blossom" evoke the wonderful opening lines of Desbordes-Valmore's "Intermittent Dream of a Sad Night":

> Land of our fathers where at eventide
> Across the fields like waves young women glide!

Yves Bonnefoy in his edition of Desbordes-Valmore's poems suggests a reason for their neglect. Poetry is still being read from the point of view of Romanticism, which remains "the greatest example of poetry that is profoundly masculine." Those who read from this point of view are impervious to the breakthrough her poetry represents. The poetry of Desbordes-Valmore rejects illusion and "the pretensions of the Me that are typical of Romanticism." ***

---

* Bonnefoy, 29.
** Charles Baudelaire, "Réflexions sur quelques-uns de mes contemporains," *Oeuvres complètes II* (Paris: Gallimard, 1976), 147, 146.
*** Bonnefoy, 31.

ROBERT DESNOS
1900-1945

Robert Desnos was born in Paris on July 4, 1900. His father, a fat, jovial little man, was in charge of fowl and game at Les Halles. His mother was a pale, blond, self-effacing woman.* Robert attended a communal school, then a lycée. He clerked in a drugstore and began making notes of his dreams. His first poems appeared in a socialist review, *La Tribune des jeunes*. These were followed by other poems, and he was often seen in Left Bank bars and cafés.

In 1920 he served with the army in Morocco. On his return he joined the Surrealists and became known for his ability to fall asleep under hypnosis and . . . but let Louis Aragon tell it: "At the café in the hubbub of voices, in plain daylight, and the elbowing, Robert Desnos has only to shut his eyes, and he speaks, and in the midst of the bocks, the saucers, the whole place collapses with a prophetic roar. . . . Let those who question this formidable sleeper merely give him a nudge and immediately prophecy, the voice of magic, of revelation, of Revolution, the tone of the fanatic and the apostle rises to the surface. In other circumstances Desnos, little as he lends himself to that delirium, would become the leader of a religion, the founder of a city, the tribune of a liberated people. He speaks, he draws, he writes." **

In December of 1922 he published "Rrose Selavy" in *Littérature*. The idea was borrowed from Marcel Duchamp—people frequently borrowed from Duchamp. Duchamp was in New York but Desnos claimed to be in telepathic communication with him. "Rose Selavy" was a word-game: you used the sound of words as a springboard for free-association. In those days when Freudian psychology was new, Rrose Selavy attracted some attention. Associations that depend entirely on sound cannot be translated . . . for example: "Perdue sur la mer sans fin Rrose Selavy mangera-t-elle du fer après avoir mangé ses mains?"

Desnos became a journalist. In 1922 his first articles appeared in *Paris Journal*. He wrote about movies for that newspaper—several of the Surrealists had a keen interest in movies. Not, however, André Breton, the leader and organizer of Surrealism . . . Breton had a churchly view of the movement. Desnos on the other hand enjoyed all the things you could read about in newspapers. He wrote for *Le Soir* and *Paris matinal*. Besides movies he liked popular music. He

---

* Théodore Fraenkel and Samy Simon, "Biographie de Robert Desnos," in Marie-Claire Dumas, ed., *Robert Desnos* (Paris: l'Herne, 1987), 317.
** Fraenkel and Simon, 315.

wrote articles about the mannequins of Paris, the infrequency of buses, and Jack the Ripper, and now and then he managed to get in something about a poet.

For ten years he was devoted to a "chanteuse," Yvonne George. He worked as a combination of editor and accountant at the Baillère medical library. In 1928 we find him making a film, *L'Étoile de mer,* in collaboration with Man Ray. He published movie scenarios. In 1929 he attended a press conference in Havana. Along with these and other activities he was writing poems: 1930 saw the publication of *Corps et biens,* a collection of all his poems since 1919.

For some time André Breton had been saying that the Surrealists should work to bring about a revolution. He wanted Surrealists to work together with the Marxists. But Marti, the head of the Communist Party, said, "Why do you need Surrealism?" To be a Communist would be enough . . . it should be everything. So Breton broke with the Communists. But some of the Surrealists, among them Aragon and Desnos, would not follow—they were committed to Marx. Breton and Desnos quarreled, and Desnos left the Surrealist group.

In his "Second Manifesto of Surrealism" (1930) Breton attacked Desnos. He said that Desnos's journalism had made him unable to respond to the serious question Surrealism had raised, whether or not to go along with Marxism. His journalistic activity had completely consumed the Surrealist part of himself—he was now even writing alexandrines!

True, there is a difference in the kind of poetry Desnos wrote after his break with Breton's group. He is using ordinary language, reaching out to the kind of people who listen to the radio and read newspapers. From 1932 on he did his journalism over the radio. The broadcast of his poem, "Complainte de Fantômas," written in rhyme and meter, reached a large audience.

When Yvonne George died he became devoted to Youki, the wife of the Japanese painter Foujita. One day Foujita went out for cigarettes and didn't come back, and Desnos and Youki were married.

In '39 Desnos was called up for military service. When the Germans invaded France his regiment, along with the rest of the French army, packed it in. After a short spell as a prisoner of war he made his way back to Paris and Youki.

Then he began his own war with the Germans. As a member of the press he was able to meet with the Nazi who gave out the news, and he passed it on, uncensored, to his contacts in the Resistance. He made speeches in bars about the ridiculous Occupation. He wrote poems against the collaborationists, using an assumed name, and these were passed around. He was practically asking to be arrested, and one day the Gestapo came and took him away. He was placed in a camp at Compiègne.

One day, so the story goes, a Nazi high official was having dinner with some sympathetic Frenchmen. The Nazi said that among the prisoners at Compiègne there were several interesting men, even a poet, Desnos. He would probably not be deported. "Desnos!" one of the French guests shouted, a man named Alain Laubreaux. "Not deported!. You ought to shoot him. He is a dangerous man, a terrorist, a Communist."

Desnos was sent to Buchenwald and from there to other concentration camps. At Auschwitz, in May of 1944, the poet André Verdet, who was also a prisoner, saw Desnos standing in the rain in the crowd of men who were emaciated and dying of hunger. The crematoria were belching smoke, and the S.S. guards as they walked by would say, "You are all going to die." Verdet saw Desnos going from one group to another. Taking a man by the arm, he would read the lines in his hand. Then, Verdet said, a miracle happened: Desnos spoke to the men of their future with such confidence that they forgot where they were and their faces lit up with hope.

After Germany surrendered, a young Czech medical student named Josef Stuna volunteered to attend to the prisoners at the Terezin concentration camp. Among the names of prisoners he came upon the name Desnos, and he recalled that before the war he had seen the name as that of a French poet whose poems had been translated into Czech. He went to the man who was lying on a paper mattress, among a hundred others. He opened his eyes. Stuna asked him, "Do you know the poet Robert Desnos?" Stuna would not forget the extraordinary expression on his face as he said, "I am the poet Robert Desnos!"

He had contracted typhus and was still running a fever. There were no medical supplies in the camp, not even enough water. He died on the 8th of June. His ashes were sent to Prague where meetings were held in his honor. They were then sent on to France.

See DADAISTS AND SURREALISTS

PAUL ELUARD
1895-1952

Eugène Grindel, who would change his name to Paul Eluard, was born in 1895 at Saint-Denis in Paris. His father was a bookkeeper, his mother a dressmaker. The family moved to Aulnay-sur-Bois, then back to Paris. They made holiday trips to Switzerland and England. Paul had a scholarship to a school nearby in the rue Clignancourt. His schooldays were pleasant and uneventful.

He spent two years at Davos in Switzerland being treated for incipient tuberculosis. There he met Hélène Dimitrovnie Diakonova, the "Gala" of his poetry. In 1913 he published his *Premiers Poèmes (First Poems)* at his own expense. Anthony Levi remarks that Eluard's early poetic style was noticeably eclectic as well as derivative. He had clearly read Lamartine, Banville, Laforgue, and Verlaine.*

In 1914 on his return to France he was called up for military service. He served in the Medical Corps, then the infantry. In 1917 he and Gala were married. The following year they had a daughter and Eluard published two more books of verse, *Le Devoir et l'Inquiétude (Duty and Anxiety)* and *Poèmes pour la paix (Poems for Peace)*. *Duty and Anxiety* shows the influence of Whitman.

In May, 1919, Eluard had a poem in *Littérature*, the review just launched by Louis Aragon, André Breton, and Philippe Soupault. Eluard started a review of his own, *Proverbe*.

He was not present at the big Dada evening organized by *Littérature* on January 23, 1920, but he took an active part in the Dada Festival that March at the Salle Gaveau. He became a friend of Breton and collaborated with Dada and the *Littérature* group.

Eluard shared Breton's interest in Freud and "automatic writing," as shown by Eluard's *Les Nécessités de la vie et les conséquences des rêves (The Necessities of Life and Consequences of Dreams)*, a collection of poems and prose poems. In 1922 Eluard and Breton broke with Tristan Tzara, the moving spirit of Dada. Tzara considered psychoanalysis a bourgeois activity. He rejected all theories and systems and called for spontaneous self-expression.

Other collections of poetry by Eluard at this time, *Répetitions* and *Mourir de ne pas mourir (To Die of Not Dying)* show him searching for a point of view. He made a voyage around the world. He collaborated with Max Ernst on *Les Malheurs des Immortels (The Misfortunes of the Immortals)* and with Benjamin Péret on *152 Proverbes mis au goût du jour (152 Proverbs for the Taste of the Times)*. Levi says that Eluard was "the principal poet" of the Surrealist movement. He was certainly the most published.

In 1924 Eluard and his wife Gala lived in a ménage à trois with Max Ernst at Eaubonne near Paris. Then Gala, without the consent of her husband, lived with Salvador Dali. In 1929 Eluard met Maria Benz, the "Nusch" of his poems, and the following year he separated from Gala. Gala married Dali. Eluard and Nusch were married in 1934.**

---

* Anthony Levi, *Guide to French Literature: 1789 to the Present* (Chicago and London: St. James Press, 1992), 221 and passim.
** For an intimate view of Eluard, Gala, Max Ernst, Dali, and life among the Surrealists, see the autobiography of Max's son, Jimmy Ernst, *A Not-So Still Life* (New York: St. Martin's/Marek, 1984).

Breton read Trotsky and was converted to Trotskyite Communism. In 1925 he assumed editorship of *La Révolution surréaliste* and called for social action. In 1926 he joined the Communist Party. Eluard too joined the Party. He contributed to *La Révolution surréaliste* and Breton's *Le Surréalisme au service de la révolution*. Surrealism was now to be "in the service of the revolution." But Breton and Eluard found it difficult to reconcile their belief in freedom of thought with Communist propaganda. Eluard broke with the Party in 1933, and so did Breton two years later.

During the Second World War Eluard rejoined the Party. He was active in the Resistance and wrote poems about it. He would be a devoted Party member for the rest of his life and propagandist for Stalin. "Stalin," he wrote, "dispels misfortune."

> Thanks to him we live without knowing autumn
> The horizon of Stalin is always renascent . . .
> For life and humanity have elected Stalin
> To represent on earth their limitless hopes.
>   "Joseph Staline"

After the war he traveled to Czechoslovakia, Italy, Yugoslavia, Greece and Poland. In Prague he spoke on "Poetry in the Service of Truth." He took part in conferences in Milan. In Rome he gave a reading of his poems of the Resistance. In 1948 with Picasso he attended the Warsaw Congress for Peace.

Nusch died. In 1951 Eluard married Dominique Lemor. In 1952 he represented France in Moscow at the celebrations on the 150th anniversary of the birth of Victor Hugo and the 100th anniversary of the death of Gogol.

In September of 1952 he had a heart attack. He died two months later.

Apart from his early Surrealist poetry, and the political poems he wrote after rejoining the Communist Party, Eluard wrote about his feelings of joy or grief. His poetry has had a wide appeal, especially the poems about women and love. He wrote about Gala, Nusch, and Dominique. Michael Benedikt says,

> The central motif of his mature work is the ability of
> Woman to act as the "Philosopher's Stone"—the reality-
> transforming, quasi-alchemical agent for which Surreal-
> ism is partly a quest. Woman is seen as Man's most
> intimate yet most mysterious equal, capable of revealing
> the best nature of individual men to themselves, as well
> as the best nature of humankind to itself.*

---

* Michael Benedikt, *The Poetry of Surrealism* (Boston, Toronto: Little, Brown and Company, 1974), 168.

Benedikt speaks of Eluard's "technical approach which places great faith in the power of sight." Eluard believes that the power of vision can fuse what one desires to see and what one "realistically" sees, so that the reality is improved. Both reader and poet can collaborate in the process.

See DADAISTS AND SURREALISTS

LÉON-PAUL FARGUE
1876-1947

Léon-Paul Fargue was born in Paris near Les Halles. His father, Louis Fargue, was a chemical engineer and the owner of a ceramics factory. One of his floral decorations may be seen at the *brasserie* Lipp at Saint Germain des Près.

Léon-Paul was illegitmate. Not until he was sixteen did Louis Fargue acknowledge him as his son. The mother was a dressmaker. It is said that her people were peasants and for that reason Louis Fargue's bourgeois family were opposed to the marriage. Young Léon-Paul was well provided for, but Sabatier in his account of Fargue's life suggests that the secrecy surrounding his birth made him anxious and "hypersensitive" as a man.*

He had some extraordinary teachers: Emile Faguet at the Janson de Sailly lycée and Stéphane Mallarmé at Condorcet. In the Ecole Normale Henri IV he had Henri Bergson as a teacher (Bergson advised him to drop out of school). Alfred Jarry, the future author of *Ubu Roi,* was a schoolmate.

In 1894 he collaborated with Jarry in publishing *L'art littéraire.* Henri Régnier brought him to one of Mallarmé's Tuesdays and Fargue was accepted by this inmost circle of the avant-garde.

He began publishing early . . . in 1895, *Tancrède,* a small collection of narratives in prose followed by poems. The following year the *Mercure de France* published most of the poems he would publish in 1914 with the title *Pour la musique (For Music).*

In spite of this early start Fargue was reluctant to publish his poems—it was said that you practically had to tear them out of his hands. Modesty, or fear, or revulsion . . . some poets have a feeling of privacy about their work. There is a secret, not about themselves but about the poem, a mystery surrounding its birth. It is no great pleasure to see it dragged into the light and exposed to praise or blame.

---

*Robert Sabatier, *Histoire de la poésie française: la poésie du XXe siècle* (Paris: Albin Michel, 1982), passim.

After the war Fargue was honored in an issue of *Feuilles libres*. Among the contributors who said that Léon-Paul Fargue was a great poet were Claudel, Picasso, Ravel, and Rilke. These testimonials may have been received by Fargue with mixed feelings, for his poetry had few readers. He had to be content with friends such as Larbaud who were able to appreciate originality, those readers whom Stendhal called "the happy few."

Fargue was a key figure in the literary life of Paris. He organized lectures and readings at Adrienne Monnier's bookshop in rue Odéon. "A dazzling conversationalist, maker of puns and epigrams, always amusing, sometimes disenchanted, he would be all of his life a joyful figure . . ." Anecdotes went around Paris about the comical things Léon-Paul said or did, but his writing reveals a different side, tender and often sad.

He was a traveler, alone or with Larbaud. He traveled in Germany, Italy, England and Central Europe.

He published poems in *Espaces* (*Spaces*) 1929; musings on "cosmological themes" in *Sous la lampe* (*Under the Lamp*) 1930; reminiscences of the Paris of horse-drawn days and a rising Eiffel Tower in *D'après Paris* (*After Paris*) 1932; a book about Paris between wars, *Le Piéton de Paris* (*The Walker in Paris*) 1939, and other works . . . mainly prose.

Fargue's prose poems are as haunting as the novels of Proust, and they are original. Max Jacob said, "Without stilts of any kind, without a shop full of poetic accessories, with neither dictionaries nor pastiches, he expressed an entirely new sensibility. At the time when all the poets—except perhaps Salmon and Henry Hertz—were still symbolists, Fargue taught us to sublimate the life of every day and make the highest poetry out of it."

Sabatier observes that Fargue inherited the Symbolists' art of half-tints and "fluidity." He doesn't aim to be modern in the usual sense of the word—he doesn't write like Paul Morand about a taste for speed or cosmopolitism. Fargue's travels take place in imagination, "a universe of memory, visions, contiguous realities intended to retain indefinable feelings, regrets, foggy illusions, to fix the unsayable, wonderings before the beauty that suddenly appears at a turn in the road."* In the *Poèmes* of 1905 he writes about childhood, love, remorse, urban scenes with modern touches, real streets and avenues in dreams, trains and stations. He is writing music in words.

With *Pour la musique* there is a change. The writing is less elegiac and more concrete. The poem loses "interiority," nuances and intimacy, in order to experiment with the force of language, the "stones" of vocables." It is drier, direct, explosive.

---

*Sabatier, 128.

A manifesto appeared in *Le Figaro* of Paris on February 20, 1909.

MANIFESTO OF FUTURISM

1. We intend to sing the love of danger, the habit of energy and fearlessness.
2. Courage, audacity, and revolt will be essential elements of our poetry.
3. Up to now literature has exalted a pensive immobility, ecstasy, and sleep. We intend to exalt aggressive action, a feverish insomnia, the racer's style, the mortal leap, the punch and the slap.
4. We say that the world's magnificence has been enriched by a new beauty, the beauty of speed. A racing car whose hood is adorned with great pipes, like serpents of explosive breath—a roaring car that seems to ride on grapeshot—is more beautiful than the *Victory of Samothrace.* . . .*

The manifesto was written by Filippo Tommaso Marinetti, poet, novelist, and impresario. The Futurists had come from Italy to take Paris by storm.

"Time and Space," they announced, "died yesterday. . . . we have created eternal, omnipresent speed." They glorified the automobile, the aeroplane, the battleship, the cannon, and expressed contempt for "moralism, feminism, every opportunistic or utilitarian cowardice." "Come on! set fire to the library shelves! Turn aside the canals to flood the museums!" They glorified war, "the world's only hygiene."

The leading Futurist artists were Umberto Boccioni, Luigi Russolo, and Carlo Carrà. Others came forward: Giacomo Balla and Gino Severini. Futurist paintings had "force lines," curves and angles intended to show the energy of life and draw the observer into the painting. They showed movement, as in Balla's "Dynamism of a Dog on a Leash," the leash and the dog's legs drawn in successive positions. They also attempted to suggest movement with abstract patterns. "Boccioni," Lynton says, "was undoubtedly the most gifted artist among them, and also the most inventive. . . . At times . . . he seems to give perfect expression to the basic themes of Futurism: metropolis, light, en-

---

*R. W. Flint, ed., *Marinetti: Selected Writings.* Translated by R. W. Flint and Arthur A. Coppotelli (New York: Farrar, Straus and Giroux, 1971), 41.

ergy, mechanical movement and noise, urban pleasure-seeking, all fused into one visual experience."*

Sant'Elia made drawings of Futurist architecture. His drawing of "The New City" showed buildings made of reinforced concrete, iron, glass, and textiles, materials with elasticity and lightness, replacing stone and wood to meet the demands of growing populations in an age of rapid transport.

Russolo was also a composer. He invented noise machines and composed pieces for them, "The Awakening City" and "The Meeting of Aeroplanes and Motors." Concerts of his music aroused the anger of audiences and critics.

The Futurists held an exhibition of their paintings in Paris on February 5, 1912, and traveled with it to London, Berlin, and Brussels. Twenty-four of the paintings were bought by a banker who showed them in other cities. The banker's collection was exhibited in Chicago.

There were Futurist demonstrations throughout Italy. Marinetti would recite his poem, "The Battle of Adrianople," with machine-gun and cannon sounds, whinnying like a horse, yelling. He traveled to Moscow and gave lectures on Futurism. The Russians were greatly impressed—they would use Futurist ideas in their post-Revolutionary architecture. Until he killed himself in 1930 the Russian poet Mayakovsky would say that he was a Futurist.

Futurist ideas about literature were the antithesisis of Symbolism. The words in the first manifesto about "pensive immobility, ecstasy, and sleep" were aimed at those who held that writing should not be explicit, that it should only suggest, for "suggestion makes the dream." The Futurists were loudly explicit.

They claimed to have invented "words at liberty," writing without syntax, without sentences: "the new Italian style . . . a synthesizing, rapid, simultaneous, incisive style completely freed from the decoration and solemn mantles of classical art. . . . Destruction of the rhetorical period with its steps, festoons, and drapery. Short sentences without a verb. Punctuation used only to avoid ambiguity. Words isolated by two dots so that they can become ambience or atmosphere."**

But for all their talk of speed, Futurist writing was static . . . at the worst, a list of nouns. This by Folgore is typical:

> A small terrace on the west side: an iron and slate
> footbridge to explore the bit of sea painted on the doormat
> on the balcony in front.

---

*Norbert Lynton, "Futurism." Nikos Stangos, ed., *Concepts of Modern Art* (New York: Harper and Row, 1981), passim .
**R. W. Flint, 164-165.

So is this, by Cangioullo:

> Outside in the square an automobile flies by, spraying.
> A rain desert.
> A desert of city squares sizzling with rain.

The manifestos of the Futurists were livelier than their writing. And some of their ideas proved useful—other writers who were not limited by Futurist theory used them to good effect. Writing about machines, for example, automobiles, airplanes, factories. . . . When Apollinaire addresses the Eiffel Tower in the opening lines of his poem, "Zone," and when he speaks of aviators, he is being Futurist—though he parts company with Futurism when he says that religion is perenially new. The American poet Hart Crane is Futurist when he apostrophizes the Brooklyn Bridge.

The Futurists spoke of *simultanéisme,* simultaneous narratives. Did they invent the technique? There are passages in James Joyce's *Ulysses,* T. S. Eliot's *The Waste Land,* Ezra Pound's *Cantos,* and Virginia Woolf's novels that could be described as simultaneous narratives—different times, places, and occurrences overlapping in a "stream of consciousness."

There was a great deal of experiment in the years leading up to the Great War and directly after. An idea would be in the air and people would come upon it . . . simultaneously.

The Futurists plunged joyously into the war. Boccioni fell off a horse at drill and died as a result of his fall. Sant'Elia was killed in combat. Marinetti and Russolo were wounded. After the war Marinetti and other Futurists who had survived "the world's only hygiene" picked up where they left off.

Then, and this is hardly surprising, Marinetti joined the Fascists. In 1933 he was awarded the Mussolini Prize for an interpretation of Dante.

Due to the association of Futurism with Fascism, after the Second World War the works of the Futurists were withdrawn from public view. But in recent years there has been a revival of interest. A conference on "Futurism and the Avant-Garde" was held in Venice in September, 1986. Futurist paintings, sculpture, and publications were brought together from several countries.

Jacob Epstein's sculpture, "Rock Drill" was on display. The legs had gone missing and had to be restored to look like the legs of a skeleton, the whole reassembled from memory. It stood then, a trunk with big arms, a metal head and snout, leaning forward as though peering into the future. It was luckily extinct.

THÉOPHILE GAUTIER

1811-1872

Théophile Gautier was born on August 31, 1811, at Tarbes in Gascony. The family moved to Paris in 1814. He attended the Collège Charlemagne— Gérard de Nerval was a fellow student and his friend. Gautier studied painting but chose poetry as his vocation, supporting the Romantic movement—he was in Hugo's faction at the performance of *Hernani* in 1830.

He published a narrative poem, *Albertus,* followed by a poem about death, *La Comédie de la mort.* In the preface to *Albertus* and the preface to a novel, *Mademoiselle de Maupin* (1835-1836), he argued for "Art for Art's sake" and advocated the classical, Greek ideal of beauty, placing it above morality. He traveled widely. A journey to Spain in 1845 gave him a book of poems, *España,* on Spanish themes, and a prose book, *Voyage en Espagne.*

On December 2, 1851, Louis Napoleon, President of the National Assembly, dissolved the government. Then he had himself elected Emperor by a referendum. The bourgeoisie and the National Guard came down firmly on the side of law and order.

What could you do if you had republican sympathies and—the two went together—rejected bourgeois ideas of culture? It seemed futile to try to change the status quo. You could believe in art . . . not as a means to an end but an end in itself. As journalist, editor, and author Gautier urged the autonomy of art. The Romantics had used art and literature as vehicles for political, philosophic, and religious ideas. Writing in *L'Artiste* he said,

> As for our principles, they are well enough known: we
> believe in the autonomy of art; art for us is not the means
> but the end; any artist who intends anything but beauty is
> not an artist in our eyes . . .

He argued the importance of form:

> we have never been able to understand the separation of
> idea and form, any more than we understand the body
> without the soul or the soul without the body, at least in
> our sphere of existence; a beautiful form is a beautiful
> idea, for what kind of form would it be that expressed
> nothing?

These ideas were current. Flaubert said that he wanted to write "a book . . . dependent on nothing external, which would be held together by the strength of its style." Baudelaire explained Poe's "poetic principle" by which he separated "poetic sentiment" from reason and passion. For Poe the object of poetry was solely the creation of beauty. The artists and writers of Paris discussed these ideas, but no other writer was in as favorable a position to advance them as Gautier, and he made the most of it, as journalist, editor, and author speaking for the "modern."

He wrote poems that described the impressions made by works of art. He was passionately addicted to painting and sculpture—so much so, he admitted, that when he wrote he was straining at the limits of language and in danger of "turning the dictionary into a palette."

He was a work of art himself, in person. " . . . a vest of intense cerise burst out on his chest; it was buttoned like a doublet under a jacket or frock coat—a bizarre vestment, nameless, fantastically shaped, belonging to no era of the monarchy, the republic, or the empire; trousers in a light color, usually a greenish or rosy gray, completed this costume, which always sent shudders through the bourgeoisie."*

In 1866 Gautier was one of the contributors to *Le Parnasse contemporain.* The Parnassians carried poetry in the direction of painting and sculpture—a Parnassian poem might be a succession of pictures. They were criticized for being *impassible*—impassive, unemotional. For Gautier *Le Parnasse* must have been too much of a good thing—there are human beings in his poems, dramatic situations, and he wrote with humor.

He traveled to England, Algeria, Italy, Turkey, Greece and Russia, and wrote books about his travels. He had a son by Eugénie Fort and two daughters by Ernesta Grisi, and supported his two sisters.

He wrote prose fiction and plays. He was a hardworking journalist, writing weekly articles—his criticism of art and drama fills volumes. He edited *L'Artiste.* He wrote ballet criticism and composed ballets—in collaboration with Vernoy de Saint-Georges, *Giselle,* and for Carlotta Grisi with whom he was in love, *La Peri.*

Baudelaire dedicated *Les Fleurs du mal* to Gautier. Flaubert, Banville, Sainte-Beuve, and the Goncourt brothers were his friends. When "le bon Théo" was old, Princess Mathilde found him a post as librarian. He died at Neuilly on October 23, 1872.

Théophile Gautier is an important figure in American as well as French literature. When Amy Lowell took over the Imagist movement from Ezra Pound

---

* Description by Alexandre Dumas appended to a photograph of Gautier by Nadar. The Metropolitan Museum of Art, New York City, June 15, 1995.

and printed some sprawling free verse in her anthologies of Imagist poets, Pound and Eliot thought it was time to back away from free verse and write in strict forms. They wrote quatrains in the manner of Gautier's *Emaux et Camées*. It wasn't just Gautier's formal ingenuity that appealed to them but his air of a man-about-town, at ease in drawing rooms, blasé and above it all.

The quatrains in Pound's *Hugh Selwyn Mauberley* (1919) are patterned on Gautier's, and there are echoes and transcriptions of his lines. Gautier writes, in "Le Château du souvenir":

> Daphné, les hanches dans l'écorce,
> Etend toujours ses doigts touffus . . .

Pound says:

> "Daphne with her thighs in bark
> Stretches toward me her leafy hands" . . .

In Eliot's *Poems* of 1920 "The Hippopotamus" and "Whispers of Immortality" paraphrase poems by Gautier. "Whispers of Immortality" changes Gautier's wiry, vivacious "Carmen" into a blowsy Russian emigrée, Grishkin, whose uncorseted bust "Gives promise of pneumatic bliss."

See JOSÉ-MARIA DE HEREDIA

JOSÉ-MARIA DE HEREDIA
1842-1905

In 1866 a group of poets published a collection of their poems, *Le Parnasse contemporain*. They were led by Théophile Gautier, then in his sixties, Leconte de Lisle, François Coppée, and Théodore de Banville. A second, younger generation comprised Catulle Mendès, Sully Prudhomme, Paul Verlaine, and José-Maria de Heredia.

The Parnassians were reacting against Romanticism. They were opposed to inspiration, spontaneity, facility, egotism, "tearful loves"—the kind of poetry Alfred de Musset wrote. The poet Lamartine had wished to guide the nation; the poet Alfred de Vigny and the novelist George Sand had both studied saint-simonianism—the Parnassians rejected all social or humanitarian causes. They subscribed to the point of view of Gautier, a program of "total art." Art did not serve any "useful" purpose—it was an end, complete in itself.

Works were created in the struggle of the artist with the material. In his poem titled "L'Art" Gautier said,

> Yes, artwork is better
> When the means used rebel:
> Meter,
> Marble, onyx, enamel.

Writing in *L'Artiste* in 1856 he said, "we have always left, as anyone can see, literature for pictures and libraries for museums. . . . our greatest pleasure has been to bring over into our own art monuments, frescoes, pictures, statues, bas-reliefs, frequently at the risk of straining the language and changing the dictionary into a palette."

The poetry of Heredia has been said to enclose "the very quintessence of Parnassian doctrine." He was born at La Fortuna near Santiago de Cuba, on November 22, 1842. His father was of Spanish descent, his mother French. He attended the Collège Saint Vincent at Senlis near Paris. In 1859 he returned to Cuba. There, after reading Leconte de Lisle, he began writing verse. He returned to Paris in 1861 and met the poets François Coppée, Sully Prudhomme, Paul Verlaine, and Leconte de Lisle. With the Hellenist Louis Ménard he studied Greek literature and mythology.

Heredia published verse in *Le Parnasse contemporain* in 1866, 1871, and 1876. His only book of verse, *Les Trophées,* did not appear until 1893—118 sonnets that he had been polishing over the years. The book had a great success. "Both friends and adversaries saw in it the most complete realisation of the Parnassian ideal. The form and labor of the work were superior to the idea and matter, but that form and labor were of a quality that, truly, one could only admire." *

Heredia's poetry makes its effect through language and rhythm, the sonority of words, richness of rhyme, grouping of sounds, harmony of the poem. "The way to understand Heredia's poetry," Martino observes, " is to see what it is not." It is not at all symbolic. Though Heredia writes on mythologic subjects, he is concerned only with the imagery—mythic or philosophic disquisitions concern him very little. Nor is he preoccupied with history. The sonnets do not have a grand design. "He has only given impressions, delicious or strong, gathered from his reading."

Finally, the poet does not have the least desire to be or appear original. Like

---

*Pierre Martino, *Parnasse et Symbolisme* (Paris: Armand Colin, n.d.), 74 and passim. Martino's is the standard work on the Parnassians.

André Chenier, his pleasure is in translating, adapting, remembering. "The sonnets are small pictures inspired by one or two lines of an ancient text, by a fragment of history, ornamented by the voluptuous sensibility of a lover of art. Heredia had exuberant taste. Only vivid and intense sensations appealed to him."

See THÉOPHILE GAUTIER

VICTOR HUGO
1802–1885

Victor (Marie) Hugo was born at Besançon on February 26, 1802, the youngest of three brothers. His mother was a royalist. His father was made a general and count under the new Spanish monarchy established by Napoleon Bonaparte. Victor's boyhood was spent mostly in Corsica, Italy, and Spain. His parents separated and Victor went to live with his mother and brothers in Paris. In 1815, after the defeat of Napoleon, Victor's father gave his allegiance to Louis XVIII.

When Victor was only seventeen and still at school his poems were noticed by the Académie Française and took two prizes at the Jeux Floraux of Toulouse. That year, together with his brother Abel, he founded *Le Conservateur littéraire.* The review became one of the principal organs of the Romantics with Hugo as spokesman for the movement. He and other like-minded writers held meetings, *cénacles,* with Charles Nodier at the Arsenal Library, at Hugo's house, or Sainte-Beuve's.

In 1822 Hugo published *Odes et Poésies diverses,* for which he was awarded a pension of 1000 francs by Louis XVIII. The next year he received a second pension of 1000 francs for his novel, *Hans d'Islande.* In 1824 he published *Nouvelles Odes* and two years later, *Odes et Ballades.* He wrote a romantic manifesto as the preface to his play, *Cromwell.* When his novel, *Bug-Jargal,* gave rise to controversy, he attacked "classicism." In 1830 his play, *Hernani,* caused riots in the theater, the Romantics applauding vigorously, members of the older generation hooting and shouting insults. Blows were exchanged. In France they take art seriously: they see a new movement in art as reflecting a change in the social order. They may very well be right.

Hugo was engaged for three years to Adèle Foucher. They married in 1822 on the strength of his first pension. They would have three sons and two daughters, but in 1831 Adèle began an affair with Sainte-Beuve. Then Hugo moved in with Juliette Drouet. He would continue to live with her, more or less, until her death in 1883.

He founded a paper, *L'Événement du peuple* (*The People's News*). In 1840 he was elected to the legislative assembly. In 1841 he was elected to the Académie, and in 1845 he was created a peer for his support of Louis-Philippe. During these years harvests failed throughout Europe and there was widespead discontent. Hugo took the side of the liberals. He spoke for the recall of the Bonapartes, but in the uprising of '48 he did his best to save the July monarchy.

Louis Philippe was forced to abdicate, the Second Republic was established, and Prince Louis Napoleon, the nephew of Napoleon Bonaparte, was elected President of the National Assembly. On December 2, 1851, he carried out a *coup d'état* and dissolved the government. Hugo had turned against Louis Napoleon—it has been said that he was disgruntled at not being appointed to a high political office. He helped to organize a futile resistance to the coup.*

The nation was promised that a new constitution would be drawn up and everyone would be asked to vote for or against it. There were protests, barricades were raised, and some republican deputies were arrested. On December 4 troops were fired on from a window and in the confusion they shot and killed more than a hundred men, women, and children, most of whom were law-abiding passersby. Louis Napoleon was elected Emperor by a referendum, but no one forgot that his regime had begun with a massacre.**

On January 9, 1852, sixty-six deputies of the National Assembly were expelled from France by decree, "for reasons of general security." The poet Victor Hugo was one of the exiled deputies.

Parliament, the army, and the press were subject to Louis Napoleon. Christiansen describes the Second Empire as "a quiet tyranny," sustained "more by propaganda than by active repression." The prosperous and self-interested could ignore the tyranny—"there was such fun, such profit to be had from doing so." The Second Empire was successful in some respects. The bureaucracy was centralized, which made for increased efficiency. Trading controls were liberalized, making for growth and productivity. And, above all, there was glamor. The nation was entertained by "a constant bustle of advertised novelty and munificence."***

---

* Anthony Levi, *Guide to French Literature: 1789 to the Present* (Chicago and London: St. James Press, 1992), 309.
** Rupert Christiansen, *Paris Babylon: The Story of the Paris Commune* (New York: Viking, 1994), 23.
*** Christiansen, 18.

All this was as gall to Victor Hugo, fuming in exile on the island of Guernsey in the Channel. He attacked "Napoleon the Little" in verse and prose. Hugo remained in exile until 1870. In that year France went to war with Prussia. The French army suffered a disastrous defeat at Sedan, and Louis Napoleon, who had placed himself at the head of the army, was captured. The Republic was restored and Hugo returned to Paris, to "an indescribable welcome."

He was immediately elected to the National Assembly, but he resigned on account of its rightist tendencies. In 1876 he was made a senator of the Third Republic. He published *Histoire d'un crime* in an attempt to prevent an anticipated coup by the right. In 1878 he had a stroke and wrote nothing more, but his works continued to appear.

He was given a state funeral. His body lay in state under the Arc de Triomphe and was carried across Paris—on a pauper's hearse, in accordance with his wishes—and buried in the Panthéon.

Victor Hugo's father said that he was conceived on the highest peak of the Vosges, and it would have been fitting: Hugo is one of the giants of literature. He embodies the best and the worst of Romanticism. The worst is easy to find—he wrote with facility and was not inhibited by a sense of humor. Consider the bombast in *L'Année terrible,* or the poem in which he sees himself as one at whose approach flowers are flirtatious and trees bow down in homage.

M. Gaëtan Picon, in his preface to Hugo's poetry in the Pléiade edition, remarks that Hugo's popularity may stand in the way of our seeing him for the great poet that he is. Modern poetry is indebted to Victor Hugo. Valéry thought that Hugo toward the end of his life was writing "prodigious verses" to which no verse compared "in reach, interior organisation, resonance, plenitude." Léon-Paul Fargue hailed Hugo as "a poet of the future." *

Hugo's greatest poetry was written in the years of exile: the satire of *Les Châtiments*, the deeply moving poetry of *Les Contemplations*, the metaphysical poetry of *La Légende des siècles*.

The "daily bread" of Hugo's poetry, Picon observes, is far removed from what is currently thought to be poetic: Nerval, Mallarmé, Baudelaire, Verlaine, Rimbaud, with "their rigor and purity, their avoidance of abstraction or emotion, their free drift of imagination or fine probing."

See ROMANTICS

---

* Victor Hugo, *Oeuvres poétiques I* (Paris: Gallimard, 1964), xi-xii.

JULES LAFORGUE
1860-1887

Jules Laforgue was born in Montevideo, Uruguay, on August 16, 1860, the second son of Charles and Pauline Lacolley Laforgue. The poet's father was a native of Tarbes in France—he came to Montevideo as a child. He had a small school and gave private lessons in French, Greek, and Latin. His wife was the daughter of a French bootmaker and former legionnaire.

In 1866 Pauline Laforgue traveled with five of the children and their grandparents to Tarbes, leaving her husband in Montevideo. He was now employed in a bank. Two years later he brought his family back to Montevideo, all but the two oldest boys, Emile and Jules. From 1869 to 1876 they were in a boarding school in Tarbes. Jules was awarded one first prize, in religious education.

In 1875 the parents and the eight younger children returned to France. An eleventh child was born at Tarbes. The family moved to Paris and Jules entered the Lycée Fontanes. In 1877 Pauline Laforgue died of a miscarriage.

Jules studied philosophy and rhetoric. He failed to pass the *baccalauréat* examination three times. His first poems appeared in little magazines in Tarbes and Toulouse. One was a "Song of Death," the other a dialogue between a son and his father about having to choose an occupation.

He was planning a book of "philosophical" poems. He took part in a carnival following the dedication of the Lion of Belfort, and had the idea of using a popular song, the "complaint," as a literary form. He submitted poems and stories to Paul Bourget for criticism and attended lectures by Taine on aesthetics and art at the Ecole des Beaux Arts. He worked as an assistant to Charles Ephrussi, an art historian and editor.

On the recommendation of Bourget and Ephrussi he was appointed "reader" to the Empress Augusta of Germany. He would travel with the court to Berlin in the winter. Between May and August he took his vacations in Paris. He accompanied the Empress to Baden-Baden, Coblenz, Homburg, and Babelsberg Castle near Potsdam.

In later years he traveled on his own to see exhibitions of paintings and wrote "chronicles" for Ephrussi's *Gazette des beaux arts*. We are told that he was "romantically involved with 'R.,' enigmatic personage attached to Court." In 1885 he published *Les Complaintes de Jules Laforgue*.

*

T. S. Eliot said that he traced his beginnings as a poet to two influences, the later Elizabethans and the poems of Laforgue. He said that Laforgue spoke to his generation more intimately than Baudelaire seemed to do, and he ranked Laforgue with Donne and Baudelaire as "the inventor of an attitude, a system of feeling or of morals."* Some of Eliot's early poems, notably "Portrait of a Lady" and "The Love Song of J. Alfred Prufrock," are modeled on Laforgue's "complaints."

Laforgue is important in the literature of English-speaking countries, for the poems Eliot based on Laforgue have been widely imitated. But the French do not make much of Laforgue. In the years immediately following his death his reputation stood high among readers of poetry in France, but this did not last. Scholars and critics did not write about him—he was "marginalized" as scholars and critics say. Why?

Laforgue's subject matter was original. In "Solo de lune" ("Solo by Moonlight") a young man has failed to propose marriage and is having long thoughts about this in the carriage on his way home. Poets had not thought fit to write about such common experiences. "Laforgue attempted to write a new kind of poetry drawn directly from the prosaic and from that daily life which he found deplorably 'quotidienne.'"* He was not only writing poetry with a new content, the form and style were original. "'Make a work which is alive and the rest will take care of itself,' was one of the counsels he offered..." He would seem to be just thinking out loud. Rhythms and line lengths varied. Rhymes appeared and disappeared like themes in Wagnerian music.

This was all too different for scholars and critics—it broke with tradition. But for a young American in the 1920's, Laforgue's poetry was wonderfully innovative... it was "modern." Malcolm Cowley says, "First of all, we were impressed by his subject matter. . . . we were young and yearning, and we found it exciting to read a poet who regarded adolescence as a time of life that deserved as much serious attention as any other time." Woman in a poem by Laforgue was "Weak and irresistible, compassionate, pitiless. . . . She would snatch us from our lonely divagations under the moon and make us the daylight prisoners of convention'." And there was Laforgue's style, "a literary attitude applied to life: it was irony, paradox, and a parade of learning." **

Laforgue is usually listed among the Symbolists. The term has to be stretched considerably to include him. He was certainly not a Symbolist of Mallarmé's kind—but neither was Rimbaud, nor Verlaine, nor other poets who were said to be of the Symbolist "school."

---

* Henri Peyre, "Laforgue Among the Symbolists," in Warren Ramsay, ed., *Jules Laforgue: Essays on a Poet's Life and Work* (Carbondale and Edwardsville: Southern Illinois Press, 1969), 47.
** Malcolm Cowley, "Laforgue in America: A Testimony," in Warren Ramsay, 7-8.

In January of 1886 Laforgue began taking lessons in English pronunciation from Leah Lee, the daughter of an Englishman who ran a ladies' and gentlemen's outfitting business in Teignmouth, England. Leah had held a post in Berlin as governess to the Empress Augusta's children, but was no longer employed at the court when Jules came to her for lessons.

Jules gave up his job as reader and set about earning a living by writing. His translations from "the astonishing American poet Walt Whitman" appeared in *La Vogue,* a periodical edited by Léo d'Orfer and Gustave Kahn. Between June and November *La Vogue* published five of the tales he would call *Moralités légendaires.*

In December Jules and Leah were married at Saint Barnabas Church in Kensington, London.* A book he had been writing about his experiences in Berlin was declined by a publishing house. They would consider it again if he shortened the parts about the town, and wrote more fully about life at the court in Berlin, and would have his name and court function on the cover. In July of 1887 he was correcting proofs for *Moralités légendaires.*

But a "three-months' cold" he had been nursing was worse, and on August 20 he died. Leah Laforgue died of tuberculosis in June of the following year.*

> . . . for Laforgue, life was *consciously* divided into thought and feeling; but his feelings were such as required an intellectual completion, a *beatitude*, and the philosophical systems which he embraced were so much felt as to require a sensuous completion. They did not fit. Hence the metaphysicality of Laforgue reaches in two directions: the intellectualising of the feeling and the emotionalizing of the idea. Where they meet they come into conflict, and Laforgue's irony, an irony always employed against himself, ensues.
>
> T. S. Eliot**

---

* For an account of Laforgue's marriage and Leah Lee's part in his work, see the "informal biography" of Laforgue by David Arkell, *Looking for Laforgue* (New York: Persea Books, 1979), 203 ff.

** "The Clark Lectures," *The Varieties of Metaphysical Poetry,* ed. Ronald Schuchard (New York: Harcourt Brace and Company, 1993), 212–213.

VALERY LARBAUD
1881-1957

Valery Larbaud was born at Vichy on August 29, 1881. He was the only child of Nicolas Larbaud, a landowner and Catholic, and Isabelle Bureau des Etrivaux, who came of an old Huguenot family. Isabelle's father was a man of strong republican convictions—he had removed his family to Geneva in Switzerland for the duration of Louis Napoleon's Second Empire. Isabelle attended a school in Geneva that catered to the daughters of aristocratic families. When her son Valery was five years old she made a trip with him back to Geneva where she had been a schoolgirl.

Then she took him to Paris. He was ailing and the best doctors were in Paris. Valery and his mother stayed at the Hotel of the Louvre for three months. In later years he would often return there, to the hotel, he said, of his finest memories. His love of travel may have originated in these early years of traveling with his mother.

When he was eight his father died. Valery's health continued to be a matter of concern, so that he was kept at home for two years before he was sent to the Carnot school. He liked Victor Hugo's poetry and Pierre Loti's prose. He read Jules Verne and books of travel and adventure, and felt an urge to write. His mother entered him in the College of Sainte-Barbe-des-Champs at Fontenoy-aux-Roses. The students were from different backgrounds. Marcel Arland, the editor of Larbaud's works, says that this nourished Larbaud's incipient "cosmopolitanism."* At this time he became interested in Catholicism. However, he took instruction for two years in the Protestantism of his mother's side of the family.

He was tutored in German and English, and showed a talent for drawing. At school his favorite subjects were Latin, French poetry, geography, and geology. He read Verlaine and so was introduced to contemporary literature. In 1894 his health was still precarious, so he did not return to school but moved about between Vichy, Paris, and the family property at Valbois.

In 1895 he accompanied his mother and his aunt to Nice. They made excursions to Monaco, Menton, and Bordighera, and he made a trip by himself to San Remo and learned some Italian. On their return to Vichy his mother entered him in the Henry IV lycée. He began to write verse.

There was a man named Max Lebaudy, the son of a very rich sugar refiner, whose extravagant manner of life was the talk of Paris. Lebaudy died in 1896.

---

* Valery Larbaud, *Oeuvres* (Paris: Gallimard, 1958), xxxiv.

The name, so much like Larbaud's, may have given him the idea of Barnabooth, the "rich amateur" of his poems. He may also have derived some ideas from his reading about Roman emperors of the Decadence.

His mother was dissatisfied with his progress at the Henry IV lycée and withdrew him before the end of the school year. She went traveling with him in France. In October he entered the de Moulins lycée as a boarder. His fellow students were preoccupied with "dandyism and literature," but he had an advantage—he was the author of a published work, a little book of verse inspired by the Parnassian poets. He titled it *Les Portiques (The Porches)*. His mother paid for the printing of a hundred copies.

In the Easter vacation of 1897 he traveled with his mother to Lyon, Nimes, Sète, Toulouse, Pau, Bordeaux, Saint-Sébastien, Santander, and Biarritz. This was his first glimpse of Spain—it made a great impression. On his return he worked with enthusiasm on his poetry. The next year his mother took him on a journey in Spain that included Burgos, Madrid, Toledo, and Seville. They crossed by way of Gibraltar to Tangiers, and returned by way of Grenada, Saragossa, and Barcelona.

When he passed the *baccalauréat* his mother rewarded him with a tour of Europe. He was accompanied by an old friend of the family, a Mr. Voldoire. They traveled to Paris, Liège. Cologne, and Berlin. They went to Russia . . . Saint Petersburg, Kronstadt, Moscow, and Kharkov. Then they traveled to Constantinople. Later journeys would take Larbaud to Italy, Greece, Algeria, Sweden . . .

In 1908 he published a limited edition of poems based on his travels. The author of *Poems by a Rich Amateur* is supposedly "Barnabooth." Marcel Arland remarks that Barnabooth is not Larbaud but "it is in their relations, through exaggeration and caricature, that Larbaud discovers and affirms himself."[*] In 1913 he published a much larger collection: *A. O. Barnabooth, his Complete Works, that is to say, a Tale, his Poems and his Intimate Journal.*

The poems are in free verse and clearly influenced by the poetry of Walt Whitman. In 1901 when Larbaud visited Berlin he was working on a study of Whitman, and thirteen years later he would write the introduction to a selection of Whitman's poetry. He had also read Laforgue and Rimbaud. Laforgue's sophisticated air and the casual forms of his monologues as he strolls may have contributed to the tone and form of Larbaud's poems. There are images in Larbaud that have the immediacy and vividness of Rimbaud's imagery.

But these influences do not detract from the originality of *A. O. Barna-*

---

[*] Valery Larbaud, xix-xx.

booth. "My friends recognise my voice, / Its familiar, after-dinner intonations," Barnabooth says in "Ma Muse," and the reader comes to know his voice, the rhythm of his thought. Barnabooth says, "I am moved by the invincible laws of rhythm, / I don't understand them myself."

> Lend me your great noise, your great smooth speed,
> Your nocturnal gliding across lighted Europe,
> O train de luxe! and the agonizing music
> That hums along your corridors of gilded leather . . .

Barnabooth gives us his impressions, and tells us what he feels, but he doesn't try to explain. This is modern.

Larbaud continued to travel. He obtained a bachelor's degree at the Sorbonne in philosophy and, later, "la licence." He kept up his studies in Greek and Latin.

He became a literary journalist and translator. Even in a nation that is famous for its "professionalization" of literature, Larbaud is an extraordinary example of the man of letters. He wrote monthly articles for *La Nouvelle Revue française*, contributed to *La Phalange* and, writing English, sent a "Letter from Paris" every week to London. He translated, among other works, Coleridge's "Rime of the Ancient Mariner," Shakespeare's sonnets, Thomas Browne's *Urn Burial*, Samuel Butler's *The Way of All Flesh*, and James Joyce's *Ulysses*.

He was appointed Commander of the Legion of Honor and Commander of the Order of Sainte-Agathe. He died at Vichy on February 2, 1957.

STÉPHANE MALLARMÉ
1842-1898

I have been unable to discover any event in Mallarmé's life that would appeal to the reader who thinks that poets have exciting lives. He was born in Paris on March 18, 1842, the son of an assistant director of Property Registration. He traveled to London. He married Marie Gerhard, obtained a certificate to teach English, and obtained a teaching position at Tournon. He admired the poems of Baudelaire—his own early poems are imitations of Baudelaire. He became acquainted with poets, among them Verlaine and Rimbaud. It would be interesting to know what Rimbaud thought of the village schoolmaster.

In 1865 *Le Parnasse contemporain* published ten poems by Mallarmé. In the years that followed he developed a theory, much of it taken from Poe whose poetry he translated. The language of poetry must be different from the language of speech, which he compared to a coin that was passed from hand to hand. Poetry must never state a thing explicitly . . . it must suggest: "Suggestion makes the dream." Poetry should be like music, and yes, poetry should be written with symbols . . . like constellations, the meaning flowering in the spaces between.

Michaud says that Mallarmé has a "message . . . an aesthetic that turns its back on the real but affirms essential connections between things and obstinately searches for the infallible word that will reproduce their structure." But what Mallarmé has left of most value to his admirers is not a metaphysical system, nor an aesthetic that is high and almost inaccessible, but poems . . . the early ones written in association with the Parnassian group, often under the influence of Baudelaire, with a mysterious music, and " 'Hériodiade' and the 'Faun,' which seem to open a new road, a new poetic itinerary, that of intellectual exploration, of density and pure poetry."*

In 1897, the year before his death, Mallarmé wrote "Un Coup de dés jamais n'abolira le hazard" ("A Throw of the Dice Will Never Abolish Chance"), in which he experiments with design and typography. The main clause, "Un coup de dés . . . ," is printed in large capitals over twenty pages, with subordinate clauses interspersed, some in smaller capitals and some in ordinary lettering. Chadwick says, "Mallarmé was clearly breaking away from the restraints of conventional forms of expression more than any of his fellow Symbolist poets. . . . he introduced a pictorial element into poetry. Much of the imagery of *Un Coup de Dés* is concerned with the sea and the sky and there is no doubt that the words sometimes set in isolation on the double page, like black stars in a white sky, and the lines of print trailing across the paper, like the negative of a photograph of the wake of a ship, are intended to reinforce this imagery . . ." **

In 1876 Manet painted Mallarmé's portrait, and "L'Après-midi d'un faune" was published in a de luxe edition. He continued to earn a living by teaching, moving from one lycée to another. He moved to Paris, and there on Tuesday evenings a circle would gather at his flat. Leaning against the mantel, smoking a cigarette, he would hold forth. One evening the English poet, Arthur Symons, brought the Irish poet, William Butler Yeats, to meet him.

Mallarmé was one of those who defended the music of Wagner. In 1888 he published his translations of Poe's poetry and two years later his own *Vers et*

---

* Guy Michaud, *Message poétique du Symbolisme* (Paris: Librairie Nizet, 1947), 197.
**Charles Chadwick, *Symbolism* (London: Methuen, 1971), 42.

prose. He was the head of a group of poets who were being called Symbolists. Claude Debussy wrote a prelude to "L'Après-midi," and at a banquet given in Mallarmé's honor he was hailed as an influence on the literature of the young.

It would be hard to overestimate the influence of Mallarmé on modern poetry . . . and prose. In spite of the narrowness of his idea of poetry—it excludes Homer, Dante, Chaucer, Villon, Shakespeare, Burns, Wordsworth, Goethe—what poetry, even his own, does it *not* exclude?—he did make a case for "pure poetry" so that others in the future would remember that there is, or almost could be, such a thing. The poems of Yeats, Rilke, Eliot, Dylan Thomas, and Wallace Stevens are indebted to Mallarmé. So are the works of many writers of prose. The most enduring legacy of Symbolism may be a novel by Marcel Proust.

Some years ago I was teaching a course and needed a translation of "L'Après-midi d'un faune" for the students. The available translations were by people who hadn't the slightest feeling for the movement and sound of verse. They couldn't rhyme, and Mallarmé rhymes continually. When the translator couldn't make out a meaning, he or she just reached for the dictionary and made a literal translation. Mallarmé said that poetry shouldn't be explicit—he didn't say that translation could be meaningless.

So I made my own translations of "L'Après-midi" and a few other poems by Mallarmé that appealed to me. If a meaning isn't clear it is not because I haven't tried to make it so. Mallarmé liked to place a little cigarette smoke between himself and us . . . sometimes more than a little.

See SYMBOLISTS

GÉRARD DE NERVAL
1808-1855

Gérard Labrunie, who would take the name Nerval, was born in Paris on May 22, 1808. His father was a doctor who served with Napoleon's Rhine army. His wife died and Gérard was raised by his maternal uncle at Mortefontaine in Valois. In 1820 he went to Paris and attended the Charlemagne school where Gautier was a fellow student.

At nineteen Nerval's translation of Goethe's *Faust* gained him entrance to the coterie of Romantic authors who were coming to the front. In 1834 he came into a legacy from his grandparents that enabled him to travel in Italy and to found a review, *Le Monde dramatique* (*The World of Drama*). He started the review in order to advance the career of an actress, Jenny Colon, with whom he was in love. Two years later she married someone else.

The review consumed Nerval's inheritance. He became a journalist, first in *Le Figaro*, then *La Presse*. He wrote articles, accounts of his travels (*Voyage en Orient*, 1843-51), essays (*Les Illuminés*, 1852), tales (*Sylvia*, 1853, *Aurélia*, 1853-54), and sonnets (*Les Chimères*, 1854). His poems are about the Valois country, the mother he hardly knew, his unhappy love for Jenny Colon, and esoteric literature. He makes connections between his personal life and his reading in mythology: his mother and Jenny Colon are identified with mythic figures.

Beginning in 1841 Nerval had episodes of "bizarre" behavior. On January 26, 1855, he hanged himself in rue de la Vieille-Lanterne.

He was considered by his contemporaries to be a likable fellow, a good companion and brilliant journalist— but only a minor poet, overshadowed among the Romantics by the towering figure of Victor Hugo. In the twentieth century Gérard de Nerval's reputation would rise greatly and Hugo's would sink.

Claude Bonnefoy speaks of Nerval's "influence on all modern literature." * Without going so far we may see the harmony of language and sound in a sonnet such as "El Desdichado" as the perfection and autonomy of art that Gautier, Baudelaire, Flaubert and those who followed in their steps would prize so highly.

Nerval's "Vers dorés" ("Lines in Gold") and Baudelaire's "Correspondances" are strikingly similar. Nerval writes, "Be careful! The blind wall is spying on us."—Baudelaire, "There are symbols in the forests where we walk/ That watch us . . ."

Nerval's sonnet was published in *L'Artiste* on March 16, 1845. Baudelaire wrote his either in 1845-1846 after he had been reading Hoffmann, Balzac and l'abbé Constant on the subject of "correspondences," or around 1855 after he had been translating Poe.** Scholars are happy to find "influences," but the ideas in "Vers dorés" and "Correspondances" cannot be attributed to a literary source. That there is a unifying life in nature, and that we share that life, is one of the oldest beliefs.

---

* Claude Bonnefoy, ed., *La Poésie française* (Paris: Éditions du Seuil, 1975), 245.
** Claude Pichois, ed., *Baudelaire, Oeuvres complètes I* (Paris: Gallimard, 1975), 839-847.

PARNASSIANS

See THÉOPHILE GAUTIER, JOSÉ-MARIA DE HEREDIA

BENJAMIN PÉRET
1899-1959

Benjamin Péret was born at Rézé, near Nantes (Loire-Atlantique) on July 4, 1899. In 1917 he and a friend were arrested for painting a town statue. He was given the choice of joining the army or going to prison. His mother insisted on the army, for which it is said he never forgave her. He enlisted and was sent to the Balkans.

After the war he got in touch with André Breton and came to Paris. He wanted to meet poets—he said that he was influenced by a poem by Apollinaire that he picked up on a bench. He met Breton, Eluard and Aragon at a reception given by *Littérature*. He participated in Dada manifestations and published poems in *Littérature*. In the mock trial of Barrès on May 13, 1921, organized by Breton and Aragon, Péret took the part of the unknown soldier, in a gas mask and marching with a goose step.

In 1921 Péret published *Le Passager du transatlantique* (*The Transatlantic Passenger*) with engravings by Hans Arp. Levi says that during this time Péret was at his most amusing, "known for his happy, relaxed attitude to life. He was, in fact, adept at playing the fool, an important part of his serious poetic repertoire."*

From December 1924 to July 1925 Péret and Pierre Naville edited *La Révolution surréaliste*. Maurice Nadeau remarks: "The Revolution is in ideas. . . . Yet let us not forget that this revolution they hailed was one they intended to create in their own existence first of all. Surrealism is not written or painted, it is lived. . . . Artistic work and work in general were in fact vilified and dismissed, life was to be consumed as it was given, not *earned*."**

Breton took over the editing of *La Révolution surréaliste* with the fourth issue. He saw its fundamental aim as the "creation of a collective myth." There was discussion of the need for social action. In 1926 Aragon, Breton,

---

* Anthony Levi, *Guide to French Literature: 1789 to the Present* (Chicago and London: St. James Press, 1992), 487.
** Maurice Nadeau, *The History of Surrealism* (New York: Collier Books, 1967), 101, 97.

Eluard, and Péret joined the Communist Party. Péret worked on *L'Humanité*, then he left the Party and joined the Troskyite opposition.

In 1927 he married the singer Elsie Houston whose brother, Mario Pedrosa, was a leading Brazilian Trotskyite. In 1928 Péret published his best known collection of poems, *Le Grand Jeu* (*The Big Game*). He resided in Brazil for two years, and was expelled for political activity.

At this time Breton had broken with the Communist Party and Aragon, a committed Stalinist, wanted Surrealism to be declared counter-revolutionary. Péret on his return to France refused to take this position: he "sought a non-communist, democratic form of left-wing political opposition."* He took up his work again as a proofreader and was an official of the printers' union. In 1935-36 he traveled with Breton to the Canaries in order to hold an international Surrealist exhibition.

Péret went to the Spanish Civil War, and it is said that he fought with the anarchists on the Aragon front. But he was disillusioned by the "counter-revolutionary" actions of the Stalinists in the Republican army. They killed anarchists and other Republicans who had their own ideas how the war should be fought and would not take orders from Moscow.

He traveled to Mexico and met Trotsky. He was called up in World War II. "His job," Levi says, "was to draw up lists of suspects, so he gleefully took off all the communists, substituting the names of parish priests." Levi says that "the most remarkable characteristic of Péret's verse is its absolute integrity . . . the poet fights against all oppression . . . poetry is never a political tool."** I wonder what the parish priests would have had to say about this.

In 1940 Péret was arrested for political subversion and imprisoned at Rennes. After the German invasion he was released from prison. He worked again as a proofreader in Paris, then he went to Marseille and from there to Mexico, accompanied by Remedios Varo, whom he married. He was refused entry to the United States on account of his political activity. A sale was organized in France to pay for his return fare.

In 1945 Péret published *Le Déshonneur des poètes*, attacking the use of poetry as propaganda by the Communist poets of the Resistance As a result, Levi says, Péret's reputation suffered. The Communists "marginalized" his contribution to Surrealism.

In Paris he again became a proofreader. He returned to Brazil in 1955 for six months to live with the Amazon Indians. He died of a thrombosis on September 18, 1959.

---

* Levi, 487.
** Levi, 487, 488.

In the opinion of Jean-Louis Bédouin, "Of all the Surrealist poets, Péret was certainly one of the most free, the most spontaneous, the most naturally poetic." *

Levi says that Péret thought of the poet as prophet and priest, and was fascinated by primitive societies in which the priest played this role. In his poetry he celebrated "the absurdities and marvels of everyday life. He had an acute eye for both, and specialized in the poetization of commonplace objects and in cascades of brilliant, sparkling images . . . " **

See DADAISTS AND SURREALISTS

CATHERINE POZZI
1882-1934

> *I, the Catherine of my Spirit, shall fly off to the light!!!*
> CATHERINE POZZI, *Journal de jeunesse*

Catherine Pozzi was born in Paris on July 13, 1882. Her father Samuel Pozzi was a celebrated surgeon. A Protestant, he married Thérèse Loth-Cazalis of a Lyonnais, Catholic family. The marriage was not happy—there was much quarreling between husband and wife, for Pozzi was also a celebrated womanizer.

The Pozzis, however, kept up appearances. They gave soirées at their apartment in Place Vendôme for rich people like themselves. They also knew artists and writers, among them the poets José-Maria de Heredia and Leconte de Lisle, the aesthete Robert de Montesquiou who was one of the models for Proust's Charlus, and the novelist Paul Bourget, a member of *l'Académie française*. Samuel Pozzi wrote sonnets himself, some of which were published in the *Revue de Paris*.

The Pozzis had three children: Catherine, the oldest, then a son Jacques, and another son Jean. Catherine was sent to a school for young ladies, then removed from school and tutored at home. She had an English governess and a German maid. We know from the journal she kept, beginning when she was eleven, that she read the poems of her father's friends, de Lisle and Heredia, and wrote some poetry of her own. She took music lessons.

She was strongly attached to her mother but felt neglected by her parents and her friends. In her journal she complains of her lack of beauty: she is tall

---

* Jean-Louis Bédouin, ed., *La Poésie surréaliste* (Paris: Seghers, 1964), 254.
** Levi, 488.

and awkward, her nose is long, her mouth too large. She deplores the behavior of young women in her generation—they flirt a great deal. If she were as pretty, would she behave as they do? She thinks that perhaps she would. She speaks of an *homme de rêve,* a dream man.

When she was sixteen she had a crisis of faith and refused communion. This does not seem to have concerned her parents unduly. Samuel Pozzi had his women—he was keeping a mistress—and he was a busy man. He had been elected Senator of the Dordogne. Thérèse Pozzi appears to have been at a loss, not knowing what to do about her failing marriage.

Like other young ladies from wealthy families, Catherine had an active social life. She played tennis, so well that in time she would play competitively, and she became an excellent rider. She traveled to Italy with her grandmother and her brother Jean. On a trip to Brittany she met her future husband Edouard Bourdet.

Samuel Pozzi was named to the chair of gynecology at the Faculty of Medicine. The quarrels between husband and wife became acute. Catherine took sides—she quarreled with her father, and from then on he treated her with cold indifference.

She became the close friend of a young woman, Audrey Deacon. The following year Audrey died in Rome. From the entries in Catherine's journal it is clear that this was more than friendship, it was love. Two years later an American woman named Georgie Raoul-Duval, who had been the lover of Willy Gauthier-Villars and Colette, tried to seduce her.

After another quarrel with her father Catherine obtained a measure of independence and traveled to England in order to study at Oxford. She had been reading philosophy and was also developing an interest in science. But she was not long at Oxford—her mother needed her at home and she returned.

In 1900 Catherine married Edouard Bourdet. That same year she gave birth to a son. Catherine and her husband soon realized that they were unsuited to each other, and separated.

She had a circle of friends, among them Albert Le Chaldier, an Islamic scholar and professor of the College of France, the writer Marcel Schwob, and a young writer, André Fernet. He was killed in the Great War, flying on the Western Front

She pursued her studies. In 1912 the signs of tuberculosis appeared. The disease too was a subject of study—and poetry.

Catherine Pozzi left six poems she wished to be remembered by. These were enough, she said—Sappho had left only fragments. There are also her journals, an essay in philosophy, *Peau d'âme (Soul Skin),* and an autobiographical tale,

Agnès. The poems allude to matters the reader may not know and call for an explanation.

In 1906 Pozzi read the American journalist Lafcadio Hearn's *Gleanings in Buddha-Field* and became interested in the Buddhist idea of the universe as being constantly in a state of dissolution and reconstitution. The individual goes through a series of reincarnations, and finally is rid of desire and individual consciousness and attains the blissful state of nirvana. Pozzi found a comparable cycle in the laws of physics and genetics.*

In the Greek mysteries of Eleusis she found another version of reincarnation. Divine thought descends from the solar regions of ether, passes through the atmosphere of lower skies and becomes soul, in proximity to the moon takes on the breath of life, descends further and enters an earthly body. The soul, having received desire and sensation, is bound both to the mortal body and divine thought. After death the soul separates from the body, and divine thought detaches from the soul and returns to the ether. But the elements, body, soul, and thought, retain the urge to be reunited one day and continue the personality.

In 1915 Pozzi wrote the thesis that would be published, unfinished, after her death with the title *Peau d'âme*. She argued that there was an inherited personality, "a complex of ideas, images and sensations that surrounded her body like an impalpable skin."* These elements were indestructible and after death would appear in other configurations.

How to reduce the grasp of matter that drew the human being toward moral and physical decadence, and strengthen the force toward spirituality and freedom? The answer was in the energy found in a lower form in matter, in a higher form as spirit. As matter and spirit were interchangeable, by practicing virtue—will power and courage—one could reverse the tendency to decay. Lawrence Joseph says that Pozzi developed a kind of "materialistic spiritualism." She discussed these ideas in *Agnès, Peau d'âme,* and the journals, and referred to them in her poems.

In 1924 Catherine met Paul Valéry and they became lovers. A year later she told Valéry's wife about it. The first of the poems on which Pozzi's reputation rests, "Vale," foresaw the end of the liaison years before it ended in fact.

She was suffering from tuberculosis and taking morphine and opium to relieve the pain. But she pursued her studies in earnest. She received the *baccalauréat* at Strasbourg and began the study of biology at the Faculté des

---

*Lawrence Joseph, ed., "Préface," *Catherine Pozzi, Oeuvre poétique* (n.p.: Ed. de La Différence, 1988), 10-11.

Sciences in Paris. She wrote articles popularizing science that were published in *Le Figaro*. She translated poems by Stefan George. And she had friends, among them Rainer Maria Rilke with whom she maintained a correspondence.

She had "mystical experiences" that were intensified by the use of drugs, and she believed that she was in contact with her dead friends. Her poems were written in visionary or hallucinatory states in which she relived her past and foresaw her future. At times she thought that the poems were dictated to her by "another" who expressed herself through her pen. The text would be obscure—she revised until it was a poem.

Toward the end of her life she said that suffering was her vocation and that she was a focal point of suffering on the planet. The last of the six poems, "Nyx," was written in November of 1934. She died in Paris in December at the age of fifty-two. The poems were published in the following year.

PIERRE REVERDY
1889-1960

> *The world withdraws.*
> REVERDY, "Verso"

Pierre Reverdy was born in Narbonne on September 13, 1889. His family is said to have traced their antecedents to the Roman conquest of Gaul. Among his ancestors were painters and sculptors who practiced religious art. He grew up in the country near Carcassone and attended lycées at Toulouse and Narbonne. He was considered a dull student.

He announced that he was going to Paris to be a writer. His father, a businessman who had once hoped to be a writer, promised to support him if he would be a journalist. Reverdy arrived in Paris in 1910. He made contact with avant-garde magazines, but his father died the next year and the promised support vanished.

He went to live in the "bateau-lavoir," the washboat, a rambling wooden building in Montmartre on the rue Ravignan. There he came to know Pablo Picasso, Juan Gris, Georges Braque, Max Jacob, and André Salmon . . . painters and poets, Lemaitre says, who for one reason or another had adopted a "violent, aggressive attitude toward all forms of reality."*

They led the movement known as Cubism. Several elements went into its

---

*Georges Lemaitre, *From Cubism to Surrealism in French Literature* (London: Geoffrey Cumberlege, Oxford University Press; Cambridge, Mass.: Harvard University Press, 1947), 71-76, passim.

making. For some time wooden statuettes from the Ivory Coast and the Congo had been appearing in Paris. Some of the artists in Montmartre were struck by the simple geometry of these imported carvings: "only the essential features were retained, and they were marked by bold planes, bulbous masses, sharp notches, or violent projecting angles."

The poet Max Jacob's brother had been an official in Senegal and the Sudan, and had a portrait of himself painted by a native artist in Dakar. The artist had been much impressed by the brass buttons shining on the official's uniform and painted them in a semicircle around the head of his model. He had taken the object apart and rearranged the elements to show the importance they had in his mind.

Some thought that by using mathematics and geometry they would approach the Absolute. Matisse, trying to explain the new technique of Braque to an art critic, said that the paintings seemed to be made of "little cubes." The word Cubist was used by those who wished to make fun of the new paintings, and the label was adopted by the painters.

Reverdy wrote about the Cubist painters. In 1912 he edited the *Bulletin* issue on the Cubists, and when, at his own expense, he published 100 copies of his *Poèmes en prose*, illustrated with drawings and etchings by Matisse, Picasso, Derain, and Gris, he was called a Cubist poet.

He rejected the description—he said it was ridiculous. But he too had "an aggressive attitude toward all forms of reality." He described the method of his art in sentences that would be quoted by André Breton in 1924 in his "Manifesto of Surrealism."

> The image is a pure creation of mind.
> It cannot be born from a comparison but from a juxta-
> position of two more or less distant realities.
> The more the relationship between the two juxtaposed
> realities is distant and true, the stronger the image will be
> —the greater its emotional power and poetic reality . . .

How can a relationship that is "a pure creation of mind" be known to be "true"? For it cannot be judged by any standard outside the mind. But it seems that analysis is beside the point: the truth and strength of the image are *felt*. Poets, Breton will say, are "modest *recording* instruments."

Reverdy was declared unfit for military service. In 1916 he began a literary review named *Nord-Sud* for the north-south underground line from Montmartre to Montparnasse south of the river where Picasso, Jacob, Apollinaire, and Salmon had moved.

Early in 1918 Breton, Louis Aragon, and Philippe Soupault called on

Reverdy in his sparsely furnished studio in Montmartre. As editor of *Nord-Sud* he interrogated Soupault and Breton and told them that they should not be writing for *Sic*—publishing in several magazines undermined their credibility. He was brusque and impatient.

"Reverdy was much more of a theoretician than Apollinaire," Breton recalls. "He would even have been an ideal master for us if he'd been less passionate in discussion, if he'd cared more genuinely about the objections that were raised. But it's true that his passion was a large part of his charm. No one was ever more thoughtful, or made you more thoughtful, about the deep wellsprings of poetry than he."*

Reverdy would retire to a farm in the country where he meditated. This added to his luster in the eyes of the younger generation who were busily promoting their works. He traveled and had business dealings but hardly anything is known about his life outside what he chooses to tell in his books. He published poems, tales, novels, books of aphorisms, and notes. In 1921 he was baptised a Catholic, and in 1922 he retired to Solesme where there was a Benedictine abbey. But he did not take part in the rituals—he said that he had looked for God but instead had found only religion.

All of his life, Lemaitre observes, Reverdy looked for an ideal. Objects and facts would gleam for a moment . . . stars, ocean, sky . . . fragments of a heavenly entity, *Epaves du ciel* (*Wreckage of the Sky*). He remained "astride two domains." He saw the poet in "a difficult and often dangerous position, at the intersection of two planes, having a cruelly sharp edge: the plane of dreams and the plane of reality." The poet aims to clear the obstacles of the world and reach the absolute and real." **

Marcel Raymond says:

> Like Rimbaud, Reverdy aspires to reach the unknown, that is, the real. He dives into a narrow zone between dream and wakening life, and then walks "with ease" like a somnambulist in the middle of the world. Miracles await him there: the sun roams round a house, the sound of a bell dies away, a word is said, there comes a bird, or the wind, or a hand, or another hand holding snow. And the things on which people ordinarily spend themselves relapse into nothingness.***

---

* Mark Polizzotti, *Revolution of the Mind: the Life of André Breton* (New York: Farrar, Straus and Giroux, 1995), 72.
** Lemaitre, 145-146.
*** Marcel Raymond, *From Baudelaire to Surrealism* (New York: Wittenborn, Schultz, 1950), 276.

Le monde s'efface . . . the world is wiped out.

See DADAISTS AND SURREALISTS

GEORGES RIBEMONT-DESSAIGNES
1884-1974

Georges Ribemont-Dessaignes was born at Montpellier on June 19, 1884. His father was a famous gynecologist. In 1887 the family moved to Neuilly-sur-Seine. Most of G. R-D's teachers were priests; he liked algebra and the natural sciences and played the flute. He left school without taking the *baccalauréat* and devoted himself to painting.

In 1911 he met Marcel Duchamp. They had a circle of friends who met frequently. Through Duchamp G.R-D met Francis Picabia. In 1915-16 he served in the office in Paris that provided information to soldiers' families. He began writing poetry. In 1919 he wrote to Tristan Tzara in Zurich and Tzara invited him to submit his writings to *Dada*. G. R-D's poems "Le Coq fou" and "Trombone à coulisse" appeared in *Dada, no 4-5*.

In January of 1920 Tzara arrived in Paris and Dada entered upon a period of intense activity, holding demonstrations and giving "matinées." G. R-D was "official polemicist" for the movement—he published poems and manifestos. *Littérature, no 13* published "13 manifestos of the Dada movement." G. R-D was one of the contributors, along with Aragon, Breton, Tzara, Arp, Eluard, Soupault, Serner, Dermée, Arnault, and Arensberg.

G. R-D wrote dramatic "anti-theater" pieces and held exhibitions of his paintings. He worked at his music and composed the prelude for a ballet. He published a novel, *L'Autruche aux yeux clos* (*The Ostrich With Closed Eyes*), and projected other prose works—novels and essays. He planned an edition of his poems with a design by Max Ernst, but the plan fell through.

In 1924 Surrealism was founded officially by André Breton. Tzara rejected the Surrealists' methodical approach to the unconscious— Dada had been against method of any kind. But G. R-D welcomed Surrealism. He said that his experiences with Surrealism had given him nothing from memory that he could put his hand on, but Surrealism had been very important to him, "like a magical object you knew was important but wasn't friendly." (*Déjà jadis,* 160).

In 1925 Surrealism became political, calling for revolution against a "dead

[Western] civilisation." In *La Révolution surréaliste, no 5* a group of Surrealists called for "Revolution First and Always." *G. R-D* participated in the disputes of the Surrealists, "happy and torn." He wrote novels, poems, plays, and essays. In 1929 he became literary editor of the magazine *Bifur*. At the end of 1934 he left Paris "for reasons of necessity," and lived in the Dauphiné region where he ran a family pension, La Maison du Villar.

See DADAISTS AND SURREALISTS

ARTHUR RIMBAUD
1854-1891

> *My two cents of reason are finished! The spirit is*
> *authority . . .*
>
> RIMBAUD, "Une Saison en enfer"

Jean Nicolas Arthur Rimbaud was born at Charleville in the Ardennes on October 20, 1854. His father was a captain in the infantry, his mother came of farming people. He attended the Collège de Charleville and advanced rapidly —at fifteen his Latin poem, "Jugurtha," won a first prize at the Concours Académique and he wrote his first poem in French, "Les Étrennes des orphelins" ("The Orphans' Gifts").

In 1870, his last year at the college, Rimbaud was befriended by a young teacher, Georges Izambard, who encouraged him to read Victor Hugo, Théodore de Banville, Leconte de Lisle, and the Parnassians. Rimbaud was especially taken with the poetry of the Parnassian Albert Glatigny. He found sympathetic Glatigny's "natural lack of respect and gravity, playfulness of expression, the boldness of his images."*

He was writing poems. Three would be published: "Les Étrennes des orphelins" in *La Revue pour tous* (January 2, 1870); "Trois Baisers" (Three Kisses") in *La Charge* (August 13, 1870), and "Les Corbeaux" ("The Crows") in *La Renaissance littéraire et artistique* (September 14, 1872).

At his graduation in August he was awarded many prizes. "I do not know what I have . . . that wants to come out," he wrote to Banville. In two years, perhaps in one, he would be in Paris. He would be a Parnassian!

---

* Antoine Adam, "Introduction," Arthur Rimbaud, *Oeuvres complètes,* ed. Antoine Adam (Paris: Gallimard, 1972), xvi.

France was at war with Prussia. Rimbaud wrote to Izambard, who was absent from Charleville, that instead of what he had been hoping for—baths of sunshine, endless walks, rest, voyages, adventures, a bohemian existence—he was stuck in stupid, provincial Charleville. He had Izambard's permission to use his room, and went through his books, reading furiously, everything from popular fiction to *Don Quichotte*. He advised Izambard to buy a small volume of verse by Paul Verlaine, *La Bonne Chanson*.

At the end of August he escaped and took a train to Paris. But he did not have the full price of the ticket, he was thirteen frances short, and the French take a dim view of people who ride trains without being able to pay. Rimbaud was arrested and placed in jail. Izambard obtained his release and returned him to his mother. But though he had promised to stay, he couldn't. "Let's go, hat, coat, two fists in your pockets, and let's go." This time he traveled on foot to Charleroi and Brussels.

Back in Charleville he studied in the library and wrote poems, among them "Le Dormeur du val" ("The Sleeper in the Valley") and "Le Mal" ("Evil"). The red and green battalions of "Le Mal" are Parnassian—he is using colors like a painter. But the description of a king who makes jokes as men march and die sounds a revolutionary note.

He traveled again to Paris and walked home. A friend encouraged him to write to Verlaine, and Verlaine answered warmly, inviting him to come to Paris. Verlaine and his young wife, Mathilde, were living in the apartment of her genteel parents, Monsieur and Madame Mauté. Rupert Christiansen has a vivid acccount of what followed: ". . . in September 1871 into the Mauté drawing-room, peremptory and unannounced, came a beautiful dirty boy with long blond hair, his wrists and ankles protruding awkwardly out of an ill-fitting jacket and trousers. He had no luggage, his socks were an alarming electric blue and he comported himself like a monosyllabic lout; in his pocket was the manuscript of 'Le Bateau ivre' . . ."*

He smoked a pipe, he stank of alcohol and sweat and crawled with lice. "The *farouche* Rimbaud thieved and sulked and showed no *politesse*, let alone gratitude. . . . By this time the highly susceptible Verlaine was infatuated with the boy—to the bafflement of his naïve and pregnant wife, who was quite at a loss to understand what was happening."

The Mautés couldn't put up with Rimbaud's behavior. He was asked to leave and went from garret to garret. "One friend of Verlaine's who kindly took him in was appalled to discover that he wiped his arse on pages torn out

---

* Rupert Christiansen, *Paris Babylon, The Story of the Paris Commune* (New York, London: Viking Penguin, 1995), 388-393.

of the expensive journal *L'Artiste;* at a dinner party, he lost his temper and attacked his host with a carving knife. He was drunk, he smoked hashish, he was foul-mouthed. . . . At the Café de Cluny, where the poets met to read, he would would lie across the seats, feigning sleep or snorting when the verse being declaimed met with his disapproval." Taken by Verlaine to look at the paintings in the Louvre, he said it was a pity that the Commune hadn't burned all this stuff.

Those who met Rimbaud had the impression of being in contact with a force of nature. It wasn't that he was rebellious and struggling like Verlaine to be free—he *was* free, treating conventions as though they didn't exist. As he would say, he was different from others. "Priests, professors, masters, you are making a mistake in bringing me to justice. I have never been one of those people; I have never been a Christian; I am of the race that sang under torture; I don't understand the laws; I don't have a moral sense; I am a brute; you are making a mistake" ("Une Saison en enfer").

Verlaine and Rimbaud began a homosexual relationship and paraded it in public. They traveled together to Brussels and London. Verlaine's wife and Rimbaud's mother tried to have them break it off. They would quarrel, separate, and come together again.

In July of 1873 they were together in Brussels. Verlaine was threatening to kill himself if his wife did not rejoin him, and his mother came to Brussels to prevent it. Rimbaud was preparing to go back to Charleville. Verlaine was desperate at the prospect of their separation. He fired two shots at Rimbaud and hit him in the wrist. For this Verlaine was tried by the Belgian court and given a two-year prison sentence.

Rimbaud had been writing the prose and verse of "Une saison en enfer" and "Les illuminations." And now, at nineteen, he stopped writing—he was through with it. How are we to understand this?

He said, "The Poet makes himself a *seer* [*voyant*] by a long, immense and reasoned *derangement* of *all the senses.*" He willed himself to see. "I cultivated the habit of pure hallucination: I saw clearly a mosque in the place of a factory, a school of drummers consisting of angels, carriages on the roads of the sky, a drawing room at the bottom of a lake; monsters, mysteries; a vaudeville sign conjured up horrors in front of me" ("Une Saison en enfer").

The poet is a creator. He invents language itself, the colors of vowels, "a poetic language that one day will be accessible to all the senses."

Michaud says that "the new secret of Rimbaud" is . . . that he is a poet! How can anyone have been so wrong as to take him for a mystic or metaphysician? The road Rimbaud follows does not go toward submission to reality nor a knowledge of reality. He isn't elaborating a philosophical system. He has only had an insight of what true poetry must be. The mission of the true poet is to give birth in himself, by a systematic culture of his imaginative senses, to visions of true reality.*

"He wants to be a demiurge, recreator of the world, an enterprise closer to magic than to mysticism. A New Prometheus, he nourishes unlimited ambition: once more to steal fire from the sky, to remake creation entirely. He thinks he has found again the secret of the gods, and soon he will throw himself into *living* the prodigious adventure."

As Rimbaud said, he was a visionary, a *seer*. Through a "long, immense and reasoned derangement of all the senses" he had made himself see clearly.

> I know waterspouts, skies that burst with light,
> And undertows and currents. I have been
> Where the dawn rises up like doves in flight,
> And at times I have seen what men think they have seen!

Why write out on paper what he saw? He had no wish to entertain the "reading public"—"*I have never been one of those people.*" He was really a very simple fellow . . . like a Red Indian. There had been something in him that wanted to come out, and now it was out and he was done with it.

"Une Saison en enfer" was printed in October, 1873, by a printer in Brussels, and Rimbaud gave a few copies to friends. He traveled to England with the poet Germain Nouveau and gave lessons in French. In 1875 he traveled to Germany, Switzerland, and Italy.

In the spring of 1876 he enlisted in the Dutch army and traveled to Batavia. He deserted and returned to Europe, reaching Charleville at the end of the year. He traveled to Austria, and was robbed and expelled from the country. He traveled to Sweden and Egypt.

In 1878 he went to Cyprus and worked as a foreman in a quarry. He returned to Charleville. After a period of illness he traveled again to Cyprus, from there to Egypt, and then to Aden where he worked for an export company. As buyer for the company he traveled in Somalia and Gala, and made reports to the Société de Géographie. In 1887 he was selling guns to King Menelik of Choa.

In February of 1891 he had a tumor in his right knee. The infection spread and he went to Marseille to have it treated. The leg was amputated. He returned to his mother and sister in Roche, but he needed further treatment and went back to Marseille. He died there on November 10, 1891.

In October, 1883, in *Lutèce,* Verlaine published a study of Rimbaud to-

---

* Guy Michaud, *Message poétique du Symbolisme* (Paris: Librairie Nizet, n.d.), 139.

gether with several of his poems. The next year he made Rimbaud the center-piece of his *Poètes maudits*. "This was the beginning of Rimbaud's glory."*

Some poems by Rimbaud were left by Izambard and Paul Demeny with the secretary of a review, *La Jeune France*, and he deposited them with a publisher named Genonceaux. Without any legal right to do so, Genonceaux rushed them into print. This edition, titled *Le Reliquaire*, was published in 1891.

Verlaine, with Léon Vanier as his editor, put together an edition of Rimbaud's poetry. They had considerable difficulty with Rimbaud's sister Isabelle who wanted Rimbaud's "impious" and "revolutionary" poems suppressed. But the *Poésies complètes d'Arthur Rimbaud* appeared in 1895. The edition was not complete as the title claims: some poems were missing and turned up later.

ROMANTICS

> I am commencing an undertaking hithero without precedent and which will never find an imitator. I desire to set before my fellows the likeness of a man in all the truth of nature, and that man myself.
>
> ROUSSEAU, *The Confessions*

The most famous writer in France at the beginning of the nineteenth century was François René de Chateaubriand. He believed with Rousseau in "the truth of nature" and that those who lived among natural surroundings were morally and spiritually superior.

Chateaubriand traveled in North America. During the Revolution he joined the Army of Emigrés and spent the years of the Terror in exile. In 1800 he returned to France. A year later he published *Atala*, a tale of the Natchez of North America, "children of nature." This was followed by the *Génie du Christianisme* in which he argued for the poetic and aesthetic values of Christianity.

Chateaubriand also invented a type, the "melancholy hero," that would appear frequently in the literature of the new century. The hero of Chateaubriand's *René* says, "Is it my fault if I find limits everywhere, if what is finite has no value for me?" He suffers from a "deep-seated feeling of boredom."

Napoleon Bonaparte had once been a melancholy hero. As a student at the Brienne military school he wrote: "Always alone among people, I escape human company to dream within myself and give myself to the fullness of my

---

* Antoine Adam, 839.

melancholy." * Napoleon also had something in common with Rousseau: he believed in nature, his own. His nature was to make war.

These were the days of "the career open to talent" when, it was said, every corporal carried a marshal's baton in his knapsack. But a military dictatorship could not tolerate the free expression of ideas. Under Napoleon's empire ten thousand copies of Germaine de Staël's *On Germany* were destroyed by the police. Chateaubriand was not allowed to republish his 1797 *Essay on Revolution*. "Classicism was the official culture of the Empire."

But Staël's and Chateaubriand's ideas prevailed, "a new literature born in the dark skies of the north." Staël "opened the way to an almost religious devotion to German Romantic poetry. Emancipated from the models of the ancients it substituted Christian and medieval evocations for Greek and Latin mythology, and stressed the role of human passions and poetic inspiration." **

Napoleon was defeated and sent into exile, and the monarchy and Church restored. In the 1820's there was a new wave of Romanticism: Shakespeare was performed, and a new generation of poets arrived: Alphonse de Lamartine, Alfred de Vigny, and Victor Hugo. In 1830 Hugo's play, *Hernani*, caused a tumult in the theater. In spite of the efforts of the defenders of Classicism to hoot it down, Romanticism triumphed.

Gustave Flaubert in his novel, *Madame Bovary*, would diagnose the Romantic temperament. It was marked by discontent and the "deep-seated boredom" of which Chateaubriand's René spoke. It suffered from a distaste for life as it is, banal and finite, and longed for an unattainable Beauty.

When Emma Bovary was a girl she dirtied her hands—Flaubert's phrase —with novels and poems that described exciting adventures and glorified passionate love. In order to escape from a tedious life on the farm she married a man who was completely ordinary. Disillusioned with marriage she turned to adultery. She ran up bills, and when they fell due she killed herself.

One could feel for passionate and foolish Emma Bovary. For the people in the provinces where she lived and died, a usurer, a chemist who mouthed platitudes about Progress, a priest who had no interest in souls, a seducer who was callous and unfeeling, one could only feel detestation. The novel exposed the banality and repression of life as many people knew it in France at mid-century. But Flaubert did not offer the consolations of an opposite way of life. To take "the truth of nature" and passion as a guide, to be Romantic like Emma Bovary, was to be deluded.

---

* Patrizia Lombardo, "Discipline and Melancholy," in Denis Hollier, ed. with R. Howard Bloch et al., *A New History of French Literature* (Cambridge, Massachusetts: Harvard University Press, 1989), 615-616.
** Lombardo, 615.

Flaubert, Gautier, and Baudelaire reacted against the Romantics. They were temperamentally different—they were not sentimental. But it was not just a matter of temperament. History made them different.

In the uprising of '48 radical reformers such as Blanqui failed to take over the government—power remained in the hands of the bourgeoisie. In 1851 Louis Napoleon overthrew the Republican government by a coup d'état. A year later he was elected Emperor by a plebiscite, that is, a vote of the nation.

Flaubert, Gautier, and Baudelaire supported the Republic. When it was replaced by a dictatorship—and this was what the people seemed to want—they turned their back on the hope, dear to Romantics like Lamartine and Hugo, that writers could play a decisive role in the life of the nation. Not until the end of the century when Emile Zola published "J'accuse" would writers again take an active part in politics.

At this time began the "alienation" of the artist about which so much has been said and written. To set oneself apart from the mainstream became a badge of honor, a sign of one's spiritual and intellectual integrity. Instead of trying to make a better world artists and writers would concentrate with an almost religious fervor on perfecting their art. Not all artists and writers of course—others would aim to please the many who wanted novels and plays and poems just to be entertaining, and art that would decorate a drawing room.

But there were writers and artists who stood apart. "What is beautiful to me," said Flaubert, " what I should like to write, is a book about nothing, a book dependent on nothing external, which would be held together by the strength of its style . . . a book which would have almost no subject, or at least in which the subject would be almost invisible, if such a thing is possible. The finest works are those that contain the least matter."

See VICTOR HUGO

PHILIPPE SOUPAULT
1897-1990

Philippe Soupault was born at Chaville (Seine-et-Oise) on August 2, 1897, into a suburban, middleclass family. His father was a doctor—he is said to have had a cheerful, open disposition. He died when Philippe was seven. Philippe's mother's sister married Louis Renault who became the famous automobile manfacturer. Renault was voted to be the worst employer in Paris, firing workers and hiring others at lower wages. In 1929 Soupault would publish a novel, *The Great Man,* satirizing Renault.*

Soupault went to school at the Collège Fénélon, which he described as a prison, then at the Lycée Condorcet, which he liked better. He admired the writings of Gide and Rimbaud. In 1913 he passed the summer holidays at Cabourg, the Balbec of Proust's novel. Proust was staying at the Grand Hôtel, and Soupault would recall that he occupied five rooms in order to have quiet around him. In 1914 Soupault went to London "where the sight of barges on the Thames filled his imagination with poetic images." He said that he became a poet in London.

After passing the *baccalauréat* he studied law, but was drafted and sent to the artillery. To the disappointment of his family he failed to make the grade as an officer. He was used in a trial of an anti-typhoid serum and had to be hospitalized.

He sent a poem, "Départ," to Apollinaire, who passed it on to the editor of *Sic,* and it was published in March, 1917. That October, Soupault published a booklet of poems, *Aquarium.* In May, 1918, he had five more poems in *Sic.* He was modernizing his style: in the poem "Escalade" ("Scaling" or "Climbing") he used the words "tramway" and "telephone." He met and became friends with André Breton—Breton thought him the most modern of the young poets. After Soupault's discharge from the army he also became friendly with Louis Aragon. He married "Mic" Verneuil and hung out with the avant-garde at Le Flore.

In March, 1919, Soupault, Breton and Aragon published the first number of *Littérature.* The October issue contained what has been said to be the first example of automatic writing, *Les Champs magnétiques* by Soupault and Breton. "Soupault was the one who rigorously insisted that nothing written 'automatically' should be retouched, Breton having been tempted to retouch the texts to enhance the impression of authenticity."**

Tristan Tzara, the founder of Dada, wrote to Soupault from Switzerland asking for a poem. Tzara moved to Paris, and Dadaists and Surrealists gave a joint "First Friday" at the Palais des Fêtes on January 23, 1920. They collaborated in other Dada "manifestations." Soupault was also writing poetry—in 1920 he published a collection of his poems, *Rose des vents* (*Wind Rose*).

Breton wanted to explore the unconscious along Freudian lines, recording the unconscious as it expressed itself in dreams and automatic writing. Tzara

* *Anthony Levi, Guide to French Literature: 1789 to the Present* (Chicago and London: St. James Press, 1992), passim.
** Levi, 618.

was for self-expression, rejecting all theories and systems. In 1922 Breton and Tzara quarreled and went their separate ways.

In 1926 Breton, Aragon, Eluard. Péret and Unik expelled Soupault, Desnos, Artaud and Naville from the Surrealist group. They were accused of pursuing "the stupid adventure of literature"—Soupault was writing novels and Desnos journalism. Surrealism was supposed to be a way of life, not literature.*

Breton attacked Soupault in the December 1929 issue of *La Révolution surréaliste,* and castigated him again, with other former members of the group, in the "Second Surrealist Manifesto" of 1930. He said that Soupault had slandered him and had accused him of theft.

Soupault traveled widely. He visited the United States and taught French literature for a summer at Pennsylvania State College. In 1930 he traveled to the USSR. On a return trip to the States he visited New York, Boston, Chicago, San Francisco, and New Orleans. He wrote novels, verse, journalism, and criticism of literature, painting, and music. He also wrote drama and for the cinema. The American poet William Carlos Williams translated Soupault's *Les derniers nuits de Paris* into English.

In 1938 Soupault was appointed director of Radio Tunis. He was dismissed by the Vichy government, and in March of 1942 arrested and imprisoned for spreading anti-fascist propaganda. He was tortured in prison, twice given electric-shock torture, but after six months released. He made his way to Algeria, and from there to New York, Canada, and the United States. He taught French literature at Swarthmore. In 1945 he returned to France where he directed overseas broadcasts.

He worked for UNESCO, traveling and consulting on radio, press, and cinema. He explored pre-Colombian civilization in Central America. "Even well into middle age," Levi remarks, "Soupault did not lose his immense enthusiasm for life and its marvels. There always remained in him something of the gleeful prankster of his surrealist days, the cultivated spontaneous fantasy which governed his love of life. . . ."

Soupault's poetry has been praised for its spontaneity, delicacy, and simplicity, its avoidance of rhetorical effects. In 1974 he was awarded the Grand Prix de Poésie by the Académie Française. He died in Paris on March 11, 1990.

See DADAISTS AND SURREALISTS

** Maurice Nadeau, *The History of Surrealism* (New York: Collier Books, 1967), 136-137.

The eighteenth-century Swedish philosopher Emanuel Swedenborg said, "All things which exist in nature are correspondences . . . the natural world with all that it contains exists and subsists from the spiritual world, and both worlds form the Divine being." He said, "The Word was written by pure correspondence as a means of union between heaven and man."

"The world," Emerson wrote, "is a temple whose walls are covered with emblems, pictures, and commandments of the Deity . . . there is no fact in nature which does not carry the whole sense of nature."

Poe received the idea of "correspondences" from Emerson, and Baudelaire may have taken it from Poe, whose tales he translated. In Baudelaire's poem, "Correspondances," "Perfumes, colors, sounds speak to each other." Like echoes in the distance they "merge and sound as one,/ Vast as night and shining like the dawn." The "one" he speaks of is an otherworldy realm of harmony and beauty.

The Symbolist poets looked back to Baudelaire as their progenitor. Mallarmé began by imitating poems by Baudelaire—the poem "Brise marine" ("Sea Breeze") for example is a frank imitation. But Mallarmé's later poetry is entirely original. He said that he was creating a new poetics that aimed "to paint not the thing but the effect that it produces"—in other words, render an "impression." Things were not to be named explicitly, for "suggestion makes the dream."

He seizes on Poe's saying that "It is in Music, perhaps, that the soul most nearly attains the great end for which, inspired by the Poetic Sentiment, it struggles—the creation of supernal Beauty." Poetry, Mallarmé declares, must "approach the condition of music." The evoking of a mood is prized above all other qualities. The language of poetry is different from the language of conversation, which he compares to a coin that is passed from hand to hand.

There was a musician to whom Mallarmé could turn as a model: the continuous flow and avoidance of definite cadences in Wagner's music were effects that he aimed at in his poetry. But of all the poets of the *fin de siècle* perhaps Verlaine came closest in "Chanson d'automne" and "Il pleure dans mon coeur" to writing poetry that was just music. "Pure poetry," however, was a mark to aim at rather than hit, for words do have meanings.

The Symbolist movement was a reaction to the Positivist philosophy of Auguste Comte and the twin idols of the bourgeoisie, Science and Progress. The Symbolists detested the materialism of life under the Second Empire of Louis Napoleon.

The novelist Emile Zola wrote about the materialism. He said, "When a society is putrefying, when the social machine is out of order, the role of the observer and thinker is to make note of each new sore, each unexpected shock." He said that the Romantics by their use of contrasts and antitheses for aesthetic effect had shown that the ugly, the wretched, the grotesque and repugnant were not in themselves inferior to the beautiful.

The Symbolists were as far removed as possible from the Naturalism of Zola and his school. They worshipped Beauty and were in flight from the ugly and repugnant.

The Second Empire came to an end in 1870. The army that Louis Napoleon led in person against the Prussians was crushed at Sedan. Paris was besieged and the population was reduced to eating rats.

After France accepted the Prussian terms of surrender there was the Commune—revolutionaries took over the government in Paris. Then troops were brought from Versailles and the Commune was put down in street fighting. The Communards were roped together and marched through the streets. "You have heard that I am cruel," General Galliffet told them. "I am more cruel than you can imagine." They were shot and thrown into mass graves.

"Nature has had her day," said Des Esseintes, the hero of J.-K. Huysmans's novel, *A Rebours* (*Against Nature*).

In 1885 Henry Beauclair and Gabriel Vicaire published a novel, *Les Déliquescences d'Adoré Floupette* (*The Liquefactions of Adoré Floupette*), a satire of certain *fin de siècle* poets who were called Decadent. The Decadent poet Floupette dismisses all previous kinds of poetry as being of no consequence. He is asked, "What then remains?" and he answers, "The symbol remains."

Mallarmé wrote about the use of symbols, and there was talk of a Symbolist school. But the sounds Symbolist poems made were as important as the ideas the symbols evoked—more important if the aim was to "approach the condition of music." And to call the poets a school was also misleading, for they were very different one from another.

Rimbaud, who is usually listed among the Symbolists, was a visionary poet rather than a maker of symbols—the scenes he envisions do not have hidden meanings, the images are to be received as what they appear to be. They are present realities, not keys to the "supernal."

Gustave Kahn, René Ghil, and Marcel Schwob experimented with free verse and argued as to which of them had invented it—they seem not to have heard of the American poet Walt Whitman.

Jules Laforgue translated poems by Whitman. His poems were different from Whitman's in idea and style, and unlike Whitman he would rhyme, but he learned from Whitman how to write "loose lines"—lines of irregular rhythm and length. Thirty years late T. S. Eliot brought "modern poetry" into the English language. The form and style of his "Portrait of a Lady" and "The Love Song of J. Alfred Prufrock" were pure Laforgue.

See CHARLES BAUDELAIRE, STÉPHANE MALLARMÉ

TRISTAN TZARA
1896-1963

> *There is a great, destructive, negative work to be done.*
>
> TZARA

The poet was born at Moinesti in Romania, in the province of Bacau. His parents, Philippe and Emilie Rosenstock, named him Samuel. He went to school at the Mihaiu Viteazul Lycée in Bucharest. While at school, with Ion Vinea and Marcel Janco he published a review, *Simbolul* (*The Symbol*). His first poems, in Romanian, were published in *Simbolul*. He was an outstanding and well balanced student, receiving high grades in languages—French, German, and English—and also in philosophy, mathematics, physics, chemistry, natural sciences, political economy, and music.

In the autumn of 1915 he left Bucharest for Zurich and enrolled at the university in Philosophy and Letters. Some of his poems in Romanian were published by Ion Vinea in reviews. The name Tristan Tzara first appears in *Chemarea* (*The Appeal*) in October, 1915.

On February 5, 1916, Hugo Ball and Emmy Hennings, together with Tzara and the painters Hans Arp and Marcel Janco, inaugurated the Cabaret Voltaire in Zurich. Tzara, Arp, and Richard Huelsenback are said to have found the word Dada by inserting a paper cutter at random in the pages of a dictionary. The first Dada evening was held on July 14 at the Zur Waag auditorium. Tzara gave his first manifesto and explained the new movement. The Dadaists began publication with Tzara's *La Première Aventure céleste de Monsieur Antipyrine*, with wood engravings by Janco.

Tzara corresponded with Max Jacob, Apollinaire, Reverdy, and a number of Italian artists and writers. He published poems in France and Italy, and met Maya Chrusecz, a student of dance, who would be his companion until 1922.

In 1916 Tzara began collecting texts of African songs and poems. They were an essential part of the Dada evenings in Zurich. The spontaneity of black art, the cadence and rhythm of African poems, the use of repetitions and ellipses, opened up new avenues for Dada experiment.

In 1917 Tzara organized a Dada Exposition and held conferences on ancient and modern art, that is, Cubism. A Dada Gallery opened and there was a conference on Expressionism and abstract art. Other "evenings" and exhibitions followed. July saw the publication of a review, *Dada*, edited by Tzara. There would be seven numbers, the first four coming out of Zurich.

Dada 1 (July 1917) carried a "Song of the Cacadou of the Aranda tribe" and announced a forthcoming collection of translations of "poèmes nègres." In *Dada 2* (December 1917) there were two poems of the Loritja tribe.

With Reverdy and Pierre Albert-Birot, Tzara began publishing in *Nord-Sud* and *Sic*. In 1918 he published *Vingt-cing Poèmes* (*Twenty-five Poems*) with engravings by Arp. In March there was a "Dada Manifesto 1918" in Zurich and a Dada exhibition.

The 1918 manifesto was published in *Dada 3*. On principle, Tzara says, he is against manifestos, and against principles. "I am neither for nor against and I do not explain for I hate good sense." The little bourgeois will look for the meaning of the word Dada, looking for reasons according to whatever method of psychoanalysis he may practice, but DADA NE SIGNIFIE RIEN (DADA SIGNIFIES NOTHING).

Dada was born of a need for independence, of distrust of the commonality. Those who are for us, Tzara says, guard their liberty. Dadaists recognize no theory. Does one make art, he asks, in order to get money or caress nice bourgeois people?

He rejects psychoanalysis, a "dangerous sickness" that reinforces the escapist *(anti-réels)* tendencies of mankind and systematizes the bourgeoisie. "There is no final Truth." He disposes of dialectic, logic, philosophy, experience, science. He is against systems: "the most acceptable system is on principle to have none . . . To fulfill oneself, to bring oneself to perfection in one's own littleness until the vase of one's me is full."

There is a great, destructive, negative work to be done: "To sweep, to clean." The cleanliness of the individual is affirming itself after the state of folly, the aggressive folly of a world left in the hands of bandits who are tearing apart and destroying the century. He calls for spontaneity and "Dadaist disgust," abolition of "every hierarchy and social system of values installed by our valets." He calls for abolition of memory, abolition of archaeology, prophets, the future . . . "DADA DADA DADA, howls of suffering, intermingling of opposites and all contradictions, grotesques, inconsequences."

It was the war that brought this on.

In mid-January, 1920, Tzara moved to Paris where he was welcomed by the *Littérature* group: Breton, Aragon, Soupault, Eluard, and Péret. Inspired by Dada they held "manifestations." On May 26 at the Salle Gaveau, Breton appeared with a revolver attached to each temple, Eluard as a ballerina, Fraenkel in an apron, all the Dadaists wearing tubes or funnels on their heads. The audience entered into the spirit of the proceedings, throwing eggs and tomatoes at the performers—some went out and purchased beef steaks and slabs of veal to throw. One of the best acts was Soupault's. He called it "The Famous Illusionist." He had multi-colored balloons, each bearing the name of a famous man, that he released.

On May 13, 1921, Dadaists and Surrealists held a mock trial of the writer Maurice Barrès in the Salle des Societés Savantes. Barrès denigrated "the cult of the self" and urged devotion to the soil and the dead, to nationalism. He was a member of the French Academy. The "trial" brought out the difference between Dada and Breton's kind of Surrealism. Breton wanted the event to bring together various avant-garde tendencies, finding principles on which they could agree. Tzara persisted in spreading confusion. He wasn't interested in Barrès—all that he knew of Barrès was the name. He sang a "Dada Song."

In 1922, at a "Congress of Paris" where Dadaists and Surrealists met to plan "the defense of the Modern Spirit," Tzara and Breton fell out along the line of difference indicated at the Barrès trial. Tzara wished to continue manifestations and publications according to the principle set forth in the 1918 manifesto—that is, to have no principles. Breton wished to explore the unconscious along Freudian lines, recording dreams and practicing free association and automatic writing. He saw Dada as only negation and a dead end. At a Dadaist theatrical evening in 1923, *Coeur à barbe* (*Bearded Heart*), Breton, Aragon, Eluard, and Péret violently disrupted the proceedings.

In 1925 Tzara married the Swedish painter and poet Greta Knutson. They had a house with very modern architecture built in Montmartre, and in 1927 Greta gave birth to a son. The quarrel with the Surrealists wasn't permanent—soon they were meeting at the Tzaras' new house.

Tzara and Breton collaborated in the last number of *La Révolution surréaliste*, Tzara publishing a fragment of *L'Homme approximatif (Approximate Man)* and Breton the "Second Manifesto of Surrealism." In 1931 Tzara published an "Essay on the Situation of Poetry" in Breton's *Le Surréalisme au service de la révolution*, placing Surrealism in the tradition of revolution. In the same year he published *L'Homme approximatif*, his most notable contribution to Surrealism.

In his Dada period Tzara had called for "a great, destructive, negative work to be done," the abolition of logic and social order. These were to be replaced by "an absolute belief in each god produced immediately by spontaneity." The Surrealist visions in *L'Homme approximatif*, years later, are the product of such belief.

The poem appears to be an updated *De Rerum natura*, an epic for a century of science. It ranges through the universe with a spate of images, many of which refer to science. But *L'Homme approximatif* is really about the nature of poetry.

Man is swept along by change and carries death within him. The "agony" of his senses, and the fear of death, impel him to create. The poet creates in language, by "allusion." (In the 1924 "Manifesto of Surrealism" this was described as "juxtaposition of more or less distant realities"). In the moment of allusion a god "placed between the cells" is revealed. The god takes the form of images.

In 1935 André Breton broke with the Communists. He had attempted to work with them but could no longer submit to their dictatorial methods. Tzara, however, supported the Party. He attended the "International Congress of Writers," supported the Republicans in Spain, and organized a second international writers' congress at Madrid and Valencia where he reaffirmed his revolutionary zeal.

During the Second World War he was in the Resistance and sought by Vichy and the Germans. He spent two years in hiding at Souillac, assisting with Resistance publications. He was placed in charge of propaganda and the Resistance radio at Toulouse. After the war he was naturalized a French citizen and joined the French Communist Party.

He had maintained his interest in African art and culture. In 1962 he traveled to black Africa for the first time, on the occasion of the Congress for African Culture, held at Salisbury in Rhodesia. His African sculptures and masks were solicited by organizers of exhibitions, and he wrote articles and held conferences.

He died in Paris on December 24, 1963.

See DADAISTS AND SURREALISTS, ANDRÉ BRETON

PAUL VERLAINE
1844-1896

> *The art, children, is to be absolutely oneself.*
>
> VERLAINE

Paul-Marie Verlaine was born at Metz on March 30, 1844. His father, a captain in the army engineers, was married to a woman forty years younger. The parents were bourgeois and respectable, everything their son was not to be. The family moved to Montpellier, back to Metz, and then to Paris where the future poet lived and went to school.

At the age of fourteen he had read, clandestinely, Baudelaire's *Les fleurs du mal* and the poetry of de Banville and Desbordes-Valmore.* He sent Victor Hugo a poem of his own, "La Mort" ("Death"). Three years later, by his own account, he had begun to drink and was chasing girls. His father, disturbed by these habits, obtained a job for him with an insurance company, then a position at the Hôtel de Ville, that is, City Hall. In 1863 Verlaine published a sonnet, "Monsieur Prudhomme," in the *Revue du progrès*. He published two more poems in the same periodical, also critical essays on Baudelaire and Barbey d'Aurevilly.

It is said that Verlaine nursed a "secret love" for his cousin, Elsa Moncombe, a married woman with children, and that when she died suddenly he was desolated. But he was launched on a literary career and he had influential friends. In 1868 he published eight poems in *Parnasse contemporain*. Among the poets in the same issue were Leconte de Lisle, François Coppée, Stéphane Mallarmé, and José-Maria de Heredia. He frequented the salon of Nina de Callas—belonging to a group or movement appears to be indispensable to French writers. He published poems. And he met his future wife, Mathilde Mauté. They were married on August 11, 1870.

Verlaine volunteered for military service in the war against the Prussians, but he was a reluctant soldier: in the hard winter of 1870-71 he was sent to prison for two days for being absent without leave. He lent his services to the Commune as a censor but took no part in the fighting.

In September of 1871 Arthur Rimbaud wrote to Verlaine expressing his admiration for his poems in *Fêtes galantes* and enclosing some of his own. Rimbaud was seventeen years old, a "big, awkard and cynical boy with blue forget-me-not eyes but the air of having escaped from a house of correc-

---

*Jean Richer, *Paul Verlaine* (Paris: Éditions Seghers, "Poètes d'aujourd'hui 38," 1960), 15.

tion."* Verlaine urged him to come to Paris and sent him a money order for the journey. They began a homosexual relationship that scandalized everyone. Jean Richer says, "without doubt it was Verlaine who first debauched Rimbaud by initiating him in the joys of absinthe. But . . . Rimbaud permitted himself audacities and eccentricities of which Verlaine by himself would have been incapable."*

To Verlaine, the birth of his daughter was merely an obstacle to his freedom. He began to abuse Mathilde physically. Verlaine and Rimbaud traveled to Belgium. Mathilde and her mother followed them. Verlaine and Rimbaud traveled to London. They separated, Rimbaud returning to his mother in Charleville, Verlaine remaining in England. Mathilde instituted proceedings to separate from her husband and obtain custody of their child.

Verlaine and Rimbaud would quarrel, separate, and come together again. In July of 1873 they were in Brussels. Rimbaud was planning to leave and Verlaine threatening to kill himself. Verlaine's mother traveled to Brussels to prevent it. Verlaine had obtained a pistol. He fired twice at Rimbaud and hit him in the wrist. Verlaine was arrested, tried, and found guilty of a premeditated criminal act. To his great surprise he was sentenced to two years in prison.

The incident colors much of the poetry Verlaine would write. He would say that he had suffered much. God chastised him terribly, but it had made him a better man than many of those who judged him harshly.

After his release from prison he attempted to reform. *Sagesse* was written during these years, poems that, as the title says, are "wise." Some poems express remorse for his sins and a love of God. At the same time, *Parallèlement*, he is writing verse that is highly erotic. There were times when he was sober and responsible, and times when he drank and consorted with drunkards and prostitutes. He was often in a hospital. In his later years he was famous. He died admired as a poet and deplored as an example.

*

In the poem titled "Art poétique," published in 1885 in *Jadis et naguère*, Verlaine says that, above all, poetry should be "music," and this should be "l'Impair," that is, uneven, which I take to mean unpredictable. The language should be vague, hovering between the exact and inexact. The poet should create nuances rather than "colors," that is, clear effects. He should avoid "la Pointe," explicit statement, and wit, "L'Esprit cruel," and laughter. "Take eloquence and twist its neck," he eloquently advises. Rhyme is often used clumsily. . . it should be used discreetly. He brings us back to his first principle,

---

*Richer, 32.

"Music again and always." Poetry should be a new thing, like the feeling of the morning air, scented with mint and thyme, "And everything else is literature."

There are poems by Verlaine—"Chanson d'automne" and the poem beginning "Il pleure dans mon coeur" are the best known—that depend on their "music," the sound of vowels and consonants and the cadence of the line. Writing such as this made him famous. But he did not hold by the principles he laid down in "Art poétique." The early poem, "Les ingénus," does not depend on the sound it makes but on vivid imagery, and the closing line is humorous as well as passionate, if such a combination is possible—and it is, for we have the line to prove it.

There is even laughter in Verlaine, for example in the late poem, "I've Had No Luck With Women." But as Verlaine himself says, he has two parallel and opposing lives. In the poetry of *Sagesse* where he is addressing his words to God there is no humor and there are few nuances.

Epilogue

La Jolie Rousse

Me voici devant tous un homme plein de sens
Connaissant la vie et de la mort ce qu'un vivant peut
    connaître
Ayant éprouvé les douleurs et les joies de l'amour
Ayant su quelquefois imposer ses idées
Connaissant plusieurs langages
Ayant pas mal voyagé
Ayant vu la guerre dans l'Artillerie et l'Infanterie
Blessé à la tête trépané sous le chloroforme
Ayant perdu ses meilleurs amis dans l'effroyable lutte
Je sais d'ancien et de nouveau autant qu'un homme
    seul pourrait des deux savoir
Et sans m'inquiéter aujourd'hui de cette guerre
Entre nous et pour nous mes amis
Je juge cette longue querelle de la tradition et de l'invention
         De l'Ordre et de l'Aventure

Vous dont la bouche est faite à l'image de celle de Dieu
Bouche qui est l'ordre même
Soyez indulgents quand vous nous comparez
A ceux qui furent la perfection de l'ordre
Nous qui quêtons partout l'aventure

Nous ne sommes pas vos ennemis
Nous voulons vous donner de vastes et d'étranges domaines
Où le mystère en fleurs s'offre à qui veut le cueillir
Il y a là des feux nouveaux des couleurs jamais vues
Mille phantasmes impondérables
Auxquels il faut donner de la réalité
Nous voulons explorer la bonté contrée énorme où tout
    se tait

The Pretty Redhead

Here I am before you all a man full of sense
Knowing life and of death what a living man may know
Having experienced the griefs and joys of love
Sometimes being able to impose his ideas
Knowing several languages
Having traveled quite a bit
Having seen war in the artillery and infantry
Wounded in the head trepanned under chloroform
Having lost his best friends in the frightful struggle
I know of the ancient and modern as much as a man
      by himself may know of them both
And without worrying today about this war
Between us and for us my friends
I am judging that long quarrel of tradition and invention
        Of Order and Adventure

You whose mouth is made in the image of God's
A mouth that is order itself
Be tolerant when you compare us
To those who were the perfection of order
We who are looking everywhere for adventure

We are not your enemies
We wish to give you vast and strange domains
Where the mystery in flowers offers itself to the one
      who wants to pick it
There are new fires with colors never seen before
A thousand imponderable fantasies
To which we must give reality
We want to explore kindness the huge country where
      everything is silent

Il y a aussi le temps qu'on peut chasser ou faire revenir
Pitié pour nous qui combattons toujours aux frontières
De l'illimité et de l'avenir
Pitié pour nos erreurs pitié pour nos péchés

Voici que vient l'été la saison violente
Et ma jeunesse est morte ainsi que le printemps
O Soleil c'est le temps de la Raison ardente
                    Et j'attends
Pour la suivre toujours la forme noble et douce
Qu'elle prend afin que je l'aime seulement
Elle vient et m'attire ainsi qu'un fer l'aimant
                    Elle a l'aspect charmant
                    D'une adorable rousse

Ses cheveux sont d'or on dirait
Un bel éclair qui durerait
Ou ces flammes qui se pavanent
Dans les roses-thé qui se fanent

Mais riez riez de moi
Hommes de partout surtout gens d'ici
Car il y a tant de choses que je n'ose vous dire
Tant de choses que vous ne me laisseriez pas dire
Ayez pitié de moi

Guillaume Apollinaire

There is also a time when one can drive away or
    bring back
Pity for us who are always fighting at the frontiers
Of the unlimited and the future
Pity for our errors pity for our sins

Now summer is coming the violent season
And my youth is as dead as the spring
O Sun it is the time of ardent Reason
            And I expect
Still to follow the kind and noble form
She takes so that I love only her
She draws me to her as the magnet iron
        She has the charming aspect
        Of an adorable redhead

Her hair is gold a glimmer
A beautiful light goes with her
Like the flames proudly displayed
In tea roses when they fade

But laugh laugh at me
Men everywhere especially here
For there are so many things I dare not say
So many things you would not let me say
Have pity on me

                    Guillaume Apollinaire

Table des titres et des incipit

Index of Titles and First Lines